THE NEW
MANNERS AND CUSTOMS
OF BIBLE TIMES

THE NEW
Manners and Customs
of Bible Times

Ralph Gower

MOODY PRESS

CHICAGO

Library of Congress Cataloging in Publication Data
Gower, Ralph, 1933–
    The new manners and customs of Bible times.

    Updated and rewritten version of Manners and customs of Bible lands, by Fred Wight.
    Bibliography: pp. 376-377.
    Includes index.
    1. Bible—Antiquities.
2. Jews—Civilization—To 70 A.D.   3. Palestine—Civilization.   I. Wight, Fred. Manners and customs of Bible lands.   II. Title.
BS620.G69   1987
220.9′5   86–31081

Designed and produced for Moody Press by Three's Company, 12 Flitcroft Street, London WC2H 8DJ, England
Design: Peter M. Wyart MSIAD
Editor: Tim Dowley BA PhD
Illustrations: Alan Parry
Diagrams: James Macdonald
Typesetting: Creative Editors and Writers Ltd, Watford, Hertfordshire
Worldwide co-edition organized and produced by Angus Hudson Ltd, London.

Moody Press, a ministry of the Moody Bible Institute, is designed for education, evangelization, and edification. If we may assist you in knowing more about Christ and the Christian life, please write us without obligation: Moody Press, c/o MLM, Chicago, Illinois 60610, U.S.A.

Preface

We live in an age of great change, and it is for this reason that books become dated. The knowledge explosion ensures that any book eventually has to be revised in order to keep its readers fully informed. There are also styles in writing and illustration that are characteristic of a particular time and place. These things have been true of *Manners and Customs of Bible Lands*, which was written by Fred Wight in 1953. Historians, archaeologists, social anthropologists, and theologians have worked hard on the Scripture text and at sites in the Holy Land to provide more information for the person who wants a deeper understanding of the Bible's setting. Much of their work is referred to in the bibliography of this book.

But there is another reason books become dated. They sometimes so stimulate the readers' appetites that those persons want more. This updated and re-written version of *Manners and Customs of Bible Lands* has attempted to provide additional information to meet such a need. In addition, travel to the Holy Land has shown many Christians that Bible background is a help in making Scriptures come alive. After travelers return home they want information of a more satisfying kind than they were able to glean from a short visit. Opportunity has been taken within this book to help people who still plan to visit the Holy Land.

Not only do many Christians owe Fred Wight a debt for opening their eyes and for creating an appetite for more, but they also ought to give him credit as they read this new book. Before I wrote it I read the older work several times until it became part of my own thinking. In the work of Christian ministry truly we enter into each others' labours.

I pray that the work we have both done, and the results of scholars' work made known during the past thirty years, will so stimulate readers to thirst for more.

Ralph Gower London 1986

Introduction

Christians are faced with problems of meaning when they come to the Bible. God's Word came in particular places, at particular times, to particular people. It is only as we stand in those people's shoes and understand what God was saying to them that the words can have full meaning for us. Part of standing in their shoes is to understand the language in which the revelation came. This has been made possible for most Christians through the work of Bible translations.

The other aspect of standing in the shoes of biblical people involves gaining a feel for what the terminology refers to. We can get such a feel by placing ourselves back into the context of the Bible era's homes, countrysides, and marketplaces. In this book I have sought to give the reader a feel for Bible times so that the whole Bible will come more alive.

We are fortunate that the life-style of the "people of the Book" has remained fairly stable for hundreds of years and that even in the twentieth century people can visit the lands of the Bible and see things that were happening centuries ago. The life-style of the people has also been recorded in words and artifacts, in pictures, and even in the rubbish of the past. It is through the study of such sources that it is possible to recapture something of how things were in Bible times.

The people of the Bible may have been conservative in attitude, but there was a richness and variation in their culture. Within the so-called Fertile Crescent between the Mediterranean Sea and the Persian Gulf there was great variety. Life for the poor was not the same as life for the wealthy; life in the hot valley of the river Jordan was different from life on the cool mountains surrounding Jerusalem; life in summer was different from life in winter; life for the nomadic herdsman differed from life for an urban tradesman; and in a land that was subject to continual warfare, life was different under the occupation of the Assyrians from life under the occupation of Greeks and Romans.

Contents

Part 2

National Institutions and Customs

Part 1

The Individual in Family Life

Opposite: Men's clothing. Left to right: a labourer with his tunic tucked into his girdle; a man wearing a thick woolen cloak over his tunic; and a wealthy man, with a colourful fringed cloak.

Clothing

The wardrobe of a person living in Bible times was fairly basic. A loincloth (maybe) was worn beneath a tunic, and there was some form of headwear. Footwear and coat were options. The slight variations in this pattern during Bible times were in colour, material, and style rather than in basic provision because clothes of this kind were best for a relatively hot climate. Paul uses the tunic, held in at the waist by a girdle, as a metaphor for the lifestyle of God's chosen people (Colossians 3:12), and everyone would have understood that he was talking about basics.

The undergarment, when worn, was either in the form of a loincloth or was a small waist slip. Peter was wearing the loincloth when he was "naked" or "stripped for work" in the family fishing boat (John 21:7). Jesus was crucified wearing only the loincloth, because the soldiers had already removed his tunic (John 19:23).

The tunic

The tunic was the essential garment. It was made from two pieces of material, seamed so that the seam came horizontally, at waist level. When stripes were woven into the material on the loom, they fell vertically in the finished article. In many respects the tunic was like a sack. A V-shaped opening was cut for the head, and slits were made in the two corners for the arms. A new tunic was normally sold without the V-opening so that it could be proved to be new. The material could be of wool, linen, or even cotton, according to the wealth of the wearer. Tunics made of sackcloth, or goat's hair, were very uncomfortable because they caused skin irritation. They were therefore worn in times of mourning and repentance.

Men's tunics were normally short and coloured;

women's tunics were ankle-length and blue, with embroidered edges to the V-neck, which in some cases identified the village or region of the wearer. The tunic that Jesus wore must have been one of the latest in fashion because it was without the centre seam. Looms able to accommodate the full length of the tunic were invented only in his lifetime (see John 19:23).

The tunic was held to the waist by a girdle made of leather or coarse cloth. Sometimes the girdle was slit to make a pocket for money or other personal possessions (Mark 6:8). The girdle was also handy for the insertion of weapons or tools (1 Samuel 25:13). When men needed freedom to work or for running, they lifted the hem of the tunic and tucked it into the girdle to gain greater freedom of movement. It was called "girding up the loins," and the phrase became a metaphor for preparedness. Peter, for example, commends clear thinking, by advising Christians to "gird up the loins" of their minds (1 Peter 1:13, KJV). The women lifted the hem of their tunics too — in their case to carry things from one place to another. At the end of the day there were no nightclothes to wear; the girdle was loosened and each person lay down in his or her tunic.

The cloak

When people were wealthy enough to afford it, or when cold weather made it a necessity, a cloak (or mantle) was worn on top of the tunic. Cloaks were made in two forms. In the country, where warmth was important, it was made by wrapping thick woolen material around the body, seaming it at the shoulders, and providing slits for the arms to go through. For many people the cloak was their only form of protection, so even if taken in pledge for a loan it had to be returned to the owner before nightfall for sleeping purposes (Exodus 22:26–27). For the same reason a Jewish court of law would never award a cloak.

The other form of cloak was like a loose dressing-gown with wide sleeves. When made of silk it was a luxury garment, and a wealthy person would never think of going out of doors without one. The Pharisees wore blue fringes at the bottom of their cloaks so that they could be seen to be keeping the

A leather sandal from the first century A.D., found at the stronghold of Masada.

law recorded in Numbers 15:38–39. Because this practice tended to be ostentatious it was condemned by Jesus (Matthew 23:5). It was probably this bottom part of Jesus' cloak that the woman who was healed of a hemorrhage wanted to touch (Matthew 9:20).

Footwear

The poor often walked barefoot, but others wore simple sandals. A sole was made from a piece of cowhide to match the shape of the foot. It was attached to the foot by a long thong that passed through the sole, between the large and second toe, and was tied around the ankle (Luke 3:16). Otherwise the thong linked together loops that had been made around the sole, crossing over and over the top of the foot. Slippers were also in use.

Hats

Most men seem to have worn a skull cap with a piece of material folded into a band around the turned-up edge, so that it gave the appearance of a turban. Women wore a square of material, folded to

The costume of a wealthy man and his wife. Notice his dressinggown-like cloak with its wide sleeves, and her bracelets, pendant, earrings and headband.

make a sunshield for the eyes and allowed to fall in folds over the neck and the shoulders to give full protection from the sun. It was held in place by a plaited cord. A light veil was sometimes worn over the head so that the woman did not show her face in a public place. Only the husband might look upon his wife's face. Hence Rebekah hid her face from Isaac before they were married (Genesis 24:65), and it was at the marriage ceremony that the veil was lifted from the bride's face and laid on the shoulder of the bridegroom, to the declaration, "the government will be upon his shoulders" (Isaiah 9:6).

Cleaning clothes
Clothes were cleaned by allowing the swift current of a stream to pass through the coarse-woven cloth, washing the dirt out and away, or else by placing the wet clothes on flat stones and pounding out the dirt. David used the picture of washing clothes as a symbol of the action needed to cleanse away his sin (Psalm 51:2). Soap was made either from olive oil or from a vegetable alkali.

Basic clothing
Clothes were not easy to come by for most people and were very costly. The poor had only the clothes they stood up in. It was therefore realistic to trade a person for a pair of shoes (Amos 2:6), and it was quite revolutionary for John the Baptist to tell people to give away spare coats (Luke 3:11). It is therefore interesting to see that in their codification of the law in the first century A.D., the Jews gave a list of clothes that might be rescued from a burning house on the Sabbath — interesting because the list indicates the value of clothes and mentions garments that were familiar at the time. The list is divided into two sections, for men and for women (children wore scaled-down versions of adult clothes), as on p. 18.

Many of the names are Greek names for the garments, but the basic patterns of clothing are exactly the same. So important were clothes that it was a sign of intense grief or mourning to tear them into pieces (Job 1:20).

Ornamentation
In addition to clothes there was heavy personal

Men

long garment	(haluk)
short undergarment	(nikli)
linen undergarment with short sleeves	(kolbur)
girdle	(hazor)
purse	(pundar)
breast scarf	(miktoran)
head scarf	(ma'aphoret)
cap	(pijlon)
hat	(koba)
scarf to go over the head	(sudarin)
breeches	(abrition)
pants	(subrikia)
stockings	(empiljjot)
sandals or shoes	

Women

long undergarment of linen	(klanidja)
short undergarment	(kolbur)
robe	(istomukhvia)
girdle	(pirzomath)
coloured girdle	(zonarim)

ornamentation by make-up, ornaments, and hair treatment. So important was this to the women of New Testament times that Christians were warned to ornament themselves with a meek and quiet spirit (1 Peter 3:3–4). Make-up was derived either from kohl (green copper carbonate) or from galena (black lead sulphide) (Ezekiel 23:40).

Isaiah describes in great detail the ornamentation

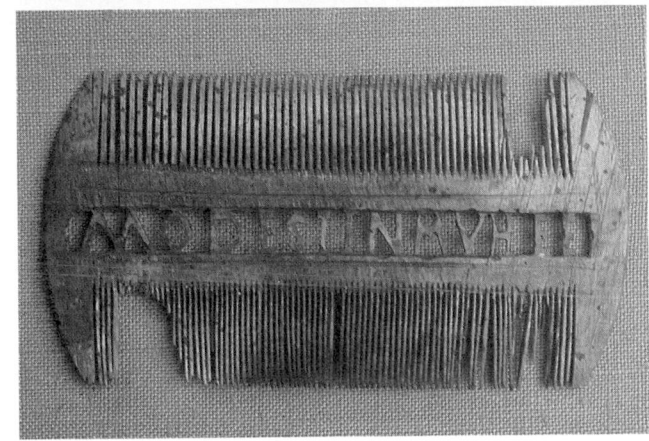

Above: Roman women's clothes and cosmetics are depicted on this panel dedicated by the female officials of a religious cult.

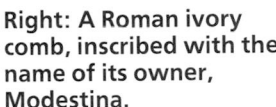

Right: A Roman ivory comb, inscribed with the name of its owner, Modestina.

used in his day (Isaiah 3:18–21). Many of the earrings, bracelets, and pendants were set with precious stones, but it is extremely difficult to identify the exact nature of the stone from the ancient languages. Oils were used as a base for pigments that coloured fingernails and toenails. Cosmetics were applied either with the finger or with a small wooden spatula. Men frequently wore a ring on the finger or on a chain around the neck, but the importance of such rings was more for sealing purposes than for decoration. In Old Testament times the hair was an important feature; it was seldom cut.

Now look at your Bible

Men's clothes/women's clothes
Deuteronomy 22:5. Because the tunic was so basic, it was identical for men and women, except that the man's tunic was often shorter (knee length) and the woman's was often longer (ankle length) and blue. The prohibition against exchanging clothes had its origin in the sexual stimulation that was part of Canaanite religion.

Joseph's "coat of many colours"
Genesis 37:3. Joseph received a tunic of many pieces. The additional pieces were probably long sleeves that were a nuisance and got in the way when work was to be done. (When women had long, wide sleeves, they tied them up behind their necks so that their arms would be free.) This indicated that Joseph was not expected to do heavy work; he was the chosen heir to rule over the family.

The cloak and the tunic
Matthew 5:40; Luke 6:29. Jesus hadn't got it wrong, and he was not contradicting himself. In the first case Jesus was talking about the law court that could take away a person's tunic but not his cloak. In the second case, a robber would grab the outer garment first; it was valuable.

Covering women's heads
1 Corinthians 11:10. Respectable women went out with their heads covered and wore veils. Only prostitutes displayed their faces and showed off their hair in order to attract men. Paul therefore tells the Christians that if a woman in the church will not wear a veil then she should be shorn; but it is best that her head be covered. Even when Christians have liberty in the practice of their faith they are not to shock propriety.

God's armour
Ephesians 6:10–11. Paul refers to the clothing worn by a soldier. He combines Isaiah's prophecy of the armour of God (Isaiah 59:16–17) with what he knows of the Roman soldier. Underneath the soldier's armour was a foundation garment to "hold him in" so that the armour (leather jacket and skirt, covered with metal plates) could fit on top. Roman soldiers had hob-nailed sandals that gripped the ground well. Paul uses the description to say that the devil will not be able to bring Christians down if they are strictly honest, utterly just in their dealings, and not easily upset. Add to this a salvation that enables them to live according to God's standard, with access to and trust in what God has said, and the Christian is well-protected.

The priests' clothing
Exodus 28. Priests wore a linen garment over the top of the tunic, perhaps to keep it clean. It was called an ephod (1 Samuel 2:18–19). The high priest wore special clothes, but they still followed the basic provision. The tunic was blue, the ephod was richly embroidered and carried a jewel-encrusted pouch containing two lots from which the will of God might be ascertained. The cloak was white. He wore a special turban on the head.

A peasant woman (foreground) – notice her simple leather sandals – and a wealthy woman. Both women have their heads covered.

The town of Hebron today. The houses and the haphazard street pattern are not dissimilar to those of biblical times.

Dwellings

There are two characteristics of dwellings in the Holy Land. First they have a typical shape and style of building. They tend to be squarish, with a flat roof and external staircase, and are often built of white limestone blocks. This has become the pattern because of climate, availability of building materials, and an original need to build so as to conserve space. The second characteristic is to preserve the very old with the relatively new, so that visitors to the area today can see alongside modern buildings dwellings of the type used by Abraham.

Dividing the land

The Israelites gained their land by conquest, and every tribe and family looked upon its inheritance or allotment as from God. The way the land was divided is described in the second half of the book of Joshua. The area was divided up by line and allocated by lot. A lot was literally a two-sided disc believed to be in God's control when thrown. The results of the throw were used to find his will. A proverb expresses it, "The lot is cast into the lap, but its every decision is from the Lord" (Proverbs 16:33). David was therefore able to thank God that the lines had fallen in very pleasant places for him — he had a good inheritance (Psalm 16:6).

The oasis town of Al Ula Hedjaz, Arabia (biblical Dedan). The courtyard houses are similar to those of Old Testament times.

Once allocated, inheritances were marked by landmarks — a heap of stones, a natural feature, or a double furrow of ploughed land — and the landmark could never be moved because to do so was to alter the gift of God (Deuteronomy 19:14). For the same reason, it was dishonouring to God to sell one's inheritance. Naboth refused to sell his vineyard to King Ahab for this reason (1 Kings 21:3).

Selling the land
There was need, on occasion, to realize the cash value of property when a particular family fell on

hard times, but all land sold for such a reason had to be returned to the original owner in the year of Jubilee, which came every fifty years (Leviticus 25:10). The sale value of the land was based upon the number of years left until Jubilee (Leviticus 25:13–17). Such transfers were very carefully arranged and monitored. Money was weighed, and deeds were drawn up describing every detail of the land in the presence of witnesses. The Jews seem to have taken over this practice of transfer from ancient times (compare Jeremiah 32:9–12 with Genesis 23:4–20).

If in the meantime a member of the family that had sold the land was able to raise the money to buy it back on behalf of the family, then the land had to be returned at once. Or if a childless widow remarried, her husband could purchase the land, but it would pass on to their firstborn child, who would carry the original family name, so that the land did not go out of the family (Deuteronomy 25:5–6). An example is recorded in the story of Ruth and Boaz (Ruth 4).

People of the land

The inseparable link between people and land caused the ordinary people to be known as the "people of the land," the *am-ha-aretz*. (It is this consciousness of land that lay behind the repurchase and repossession of land in modern Israel.)

Land passed from father to sons, the eldest son receiving twice as much as each of his brothers. Joseph, as Jacob's heir, received a double portion in the names of his two sons, Ephraim and Manasseh. Elisha asked for an eldest son's portion, a double portion, of the spirit of Elijah to fall upon him (2 Kings 2:9). The prodigal son was able to take his share of the inheritance with him, but when he returned, the whole property, a double portion, belonged to his elder brother (Luke 15:31). Case law established that the inheritance could pass to daughters if there were no sons. Numbers 27:1–11 describes the circumstances where this rule was given, along with other laws of inheritance.

Cave-dwellers

Although by Bible times people had moved out of the original cave dwellings that were abundant in

Finds in the caves on Mount Carmel show that they were inhabited from as early as the Old Stone Age.

the ancient Middle East, there were always people who lived in caves. Lot lived in a cave after his escape from Sodom (Genesis 19:30), and the Edomites made and enlarged caves in the rock face at Petra for living and for public affairs. Obadiah refers to the Edomites as those who dwell in the clefts of the rock, whose habitation is high (Obadiah 3). There were caves under the homes in Nazareth that were contemporary with Jesus, and traditionally (almost certainly) Jesus was born in a shepherd's cave. Caves were always in use for escape (Joshua 10:16; 1 Samuel 22:1; 1 Kings 18:4), and the Philistines taunted the Israelites for using holes in the ground to hide themselves (1 Samuel 14:11).

By Bible times people were either living in settlements in a good defensive position with a water supply, or else they had adopted a seminomadic form of life, living in tents and moving with their herds from oasis to oasis, where crops could be grown.

Sand-dwellers

Abraham left the settled community at Ur in Chaldea and became a "sand dweller" by faith, believing that God would eventually give his descendants another permanent land (Hebrews 11:9). The mode of life of the modern bedouin is similar to that

Opposite: The women's quarters of a tent. Notice the floor-coverings and the assortment of jars and pots for storage.

of Abraham; it has never been fully deserted. The Jewish festival of Succoth (Tabernacles) is a constant reminder of Israel's past, and Pesach (Passover) too became a camping festival, as thousands of people made their way to Jerusalem.

The tent life of Israel always seems to approach an ideal and became an important metaphor. When the prophets recalled a materialistically-minded people to God, they reminded them of the time spent in the desert and on the move — "Remember the former things, those of long ago; I am God, and there is no other; I am God, and there is none like me" (Isaiah 46:9). When John says of Jesus that the Word became flesh and *dwelt* among us (John 1:14), the word he uses is "tented" himself, or "camped" among us, to emphasize the temporary nature of his time on earth. Paul uses the same temporary nature of a tent to describe our own lives (2 Corinthians 5:1, 4).

The tent

The tent of the sand-dweller was made from a long piece of goatshair cloth about five or six feet wide. It was erected on a series of poles to provide a long awning, the two ends being pegged to the ground with tent nails (see Judges 4:21). The black colour of the tent is alluded to in Song of Songs 1:5. The strip was made on a loom pegged out on the ground; patches were inserted, like a huge darn, by the same method.

A bedouin family outside their simple tent near Hebron.

Below: Illustration showing the successive stages in the erection of a tent. The tent would be made of goatshair cloth.

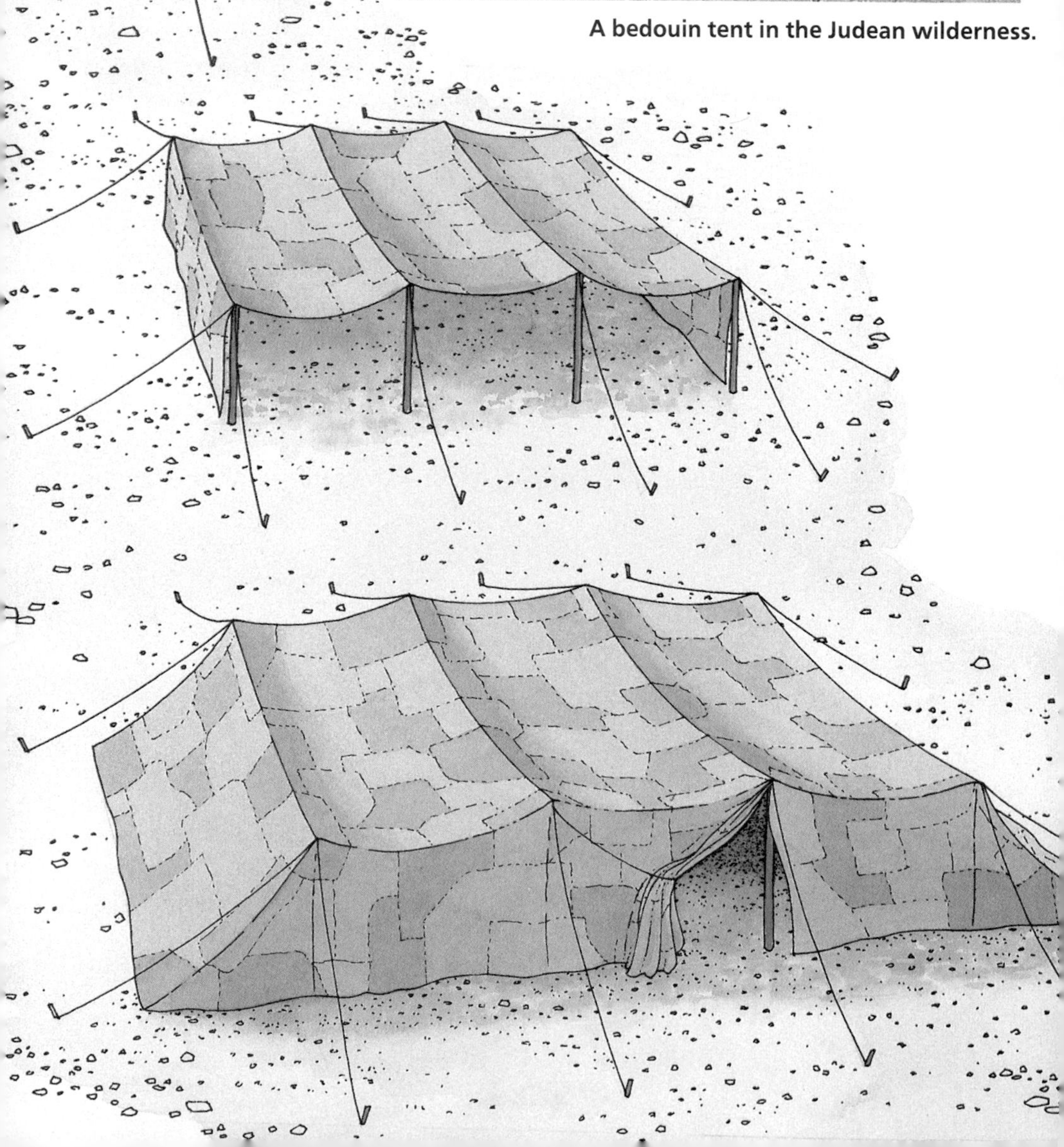

A bedouin tent in the Judean wilderness.

Vertical hangings were made either from worn roof-coverings or from other brightly-coloured materials. The hangings provided a "back" and "front" for the tent and divisions between. An area with a "back" and two dividing hangings therefore made an open porch where visitors could be received (Genesis 18:1–2) and where conversation could be heard by other people behind the hangings (see Genesis 18:9–15).

The tent could be extended simply by weaving an extra length onto the original awning and providing an additional hanging curtain (see Isaiah 54:2 where this is used as a metaphor for Jewish expansion). The awning was not waterproof until the first rains of the season had caused the cloth to shrink. Rugs were placed on the ground underneath the awning, and the families' possessions (food, cooking utensils, water carriers, and so forth) were kept beneath by the tent poles.

The only male allowed within the curtains of the tent was the husband/father; other men remained in the porch area. Entry of a male stranger within the women's quarters of the tent was punishable by death. Sisera paid with his life for going into Jael's tent, even though she had issued the invitation (Judges 4:18, 21).

Tents were not always primitive. When kings used their tents to travel with the army, they would have been luxurious, as was the tent David made to house the Ark of the Covenant at Jerusalem (1 Chronicles 16:1).

Tents were often informally grouped to accommodate all members of the extended family. The Ishmaelites had some kind of order among the tents (Genesis 25:16), and during the wanderings between Egypt and Canaan there was a strict order for the pitching of tents (Numbers 2). Some kind of ensign marked the leaders among the Jewish people; the Bedouin custom had been to put a spear upright by the tent door of the leader (*sheikh*) — see 1 Samuel 26:7.

Later, when the Israelites had abandoned tent dwellings and lived in houses, the annual festival of Tabernacles, when families spent the holiday in specially-constructed "booths" made of branches, reminded them of the time when they had lived in tents and wandered in the desert.

Brick houses

When the seminomadic Israelites under Joshua took over the Canaanite towns and villages, domestic architecture had developed a long way from the shelters used when the cave dwellers moved out into the open. Homes had developed from the mud brick, beehive-shaped dwelling, where the floor was at a lower level than the ground outside, to the single rectangular room that is still typical today.

Initially homes were made with sun-dried mud bricks, but technology advanced until it was possible to fire the bricks in a kiln, and until rough stone and rubble houses were being built. Not until the time of the settled kingdom under Solomon was squared stone used for domestic building. This was made possible because of the availability of iron tools to dress (or finish) the stone. In Galilee, the stone was normally black basalt, and on the coast, yellow sandstone; but for most of the country in the limestone area the stone was white.

House construction

Houses too were looked upon as the gift of God, and when a house was first built there was an act of dedication (Deuteronomy 20:5). The basic house for the poorest members of the community living in the country was a single room, about ten feet (three metres) square. The walls were thick, of mud brick or of rough stone and rubble, and contained niches for the storage of food and utensils. A single window was small and high and sometimes had a wooden lattice (Proverbs 7:6) to keep out intruders.

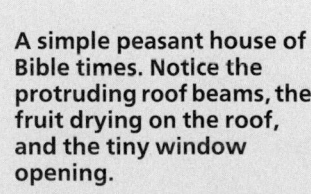

A simple peasant house of Bible times. Notice the protruding roof beams, the fruit drying on the roof, and the tiny window opening.

A small dwelling at Chorazin, north of the Sea of Galilee. It is constructed of black basalt, and has been partially reconstructed by archeologists.

In winter the lattice might be covered with a skin or some form of curtain. Because the walls were so poorly built, they harboured various kinds of animal life (Amos 5:19).

The main means of entry for light was through the single open door, which was shut with a wooden bar at night. Light was provided at night by an oil lamp standing on a projection from the wall, in an alcove, or on some form of utensil (Matthew 5:15). The floor was divided into two parts. The area nearest the door was levelled and stamped-down earth, but at the back of the room was a raised platform of stone that was used for family activities such as eating, sitting, and sleeping. Not until Roman times were tiles laid on the lower floor. The state of the floor and the lack of light would certainly make it difficult to find a lost coin (Luke 15:8). A fire for heating and for cooking was sometimes set up on the lower floor, with the smoke left to find its own way out. Animals, including a guard dog (Psalm 59:6), often used the lower floor overnight.

The roof
The roof was constructed by laying brushwood across rough sycamore beams and binding them together by using mud. It is hard to realize that in Bible times the country was heavily wooded and remained so until the depredations of the Romans and the Turks. A heavy roller was kept on the roof to compact the material after rain. Roofs were not watertight and therefore had two characteristics — leaks and a green colour. The period November to

March (the rainy season) was a cold and miserable time. Proverbs 19:13 refers to the continual drip of water (see also 27:15). The roofs were green because the seeds in the mud (natural and from drying out grain) sprouted. This is mentioned in 2 Kings 19:26; Psalm 129:6; and Isaiah 37:27.

The flat roof did have some advantages. It could be used as a vantage point (Isaiah 22:1; Matthew 10:27), as a place for cool and quietness that was conducive to worship (Zephaniah 1:5; Acts 10:9), for drying out of crops and storage (Joshua 2:6), and to sleep on a hot summer's night. So great was the use of the roofspace that the law required a parapet be built around it so that people would not fall off (Deuteronomy 22:8). When such houses were built in a city, they were literally joined house to house (Isaiah 5:8), the gaps in between forming the streets. It was therefore possible to run from roof to roof over the housetops — a way of escape to which Jesus alludes in Matthew 24:17.

Remains of a first century A.D. house in Jerusalem, burnt down when the Romans destroyed the city in A.D. 70. The rooms were identified by pieces of equipment they contained.

Right: The interior of a peasant house. Notice the oil lamp on the upturned bushel measure, the various pots and jars for storage, and the raised platform for family activities.

Left: A pottery oil lamp, decorated with an illustration of a seven-branched candlestick.

Lighting

Lighting for houses was provided by the oil lamp. Originally this consisted of an open earthenware saucer containing olive oil. Part of the saucer was "pinched" in manufacture, so as to provide a place for a flaxen wick. Such lamps obviously had problems arising from spillage, and closed containers were therefore developed with two holes — one for the wick and one to put oil in. When the oil began to run low, the flax would smoulder and the lamp would need to be refilled from a container (see Matthew 25:8).

Later, larger glazed and decorated lamps were made with handles and with multiple wicks to provide additional light. The higher the lamp, the better the light. Lamps were therefore put on a projection from the wall, hung from the ceiling, or placed on a simple lampstand (a thick tree branch pushed into the earthen floor). If nothing else was available, the lamp was put on an upturned measure or even on the floor.

Heating

Heating and cooking were done by fire, using natural combustible materials such as dried animal manure (Ezekiel 4:15), sticks, dried grass (Matthew 6:30), thorn bushes (2 Samuel 23:7; Isaiah 10:17) and charcoal (John 21:9). The fire could be made in the open (or in a depression in the earth floor) or contained in some kind of earthenware cooking box. Better homes were provided with a chimney (Hosea 13:3, KJV), but in most cases the smoke blackened the roof and choked the persons inside.

Fire was kindled by flint or by friction. One of the most important fuels was the wood of the white broom plant. Its embers stay hot for a long time and even the seemingly cold ashes can be easily fanned into a blaze. Heating is particularly important in the hill country; winters are cold and damp and there are falls of snow.

Women make dungcakes for use as fuel.

A bedouin girl draws water from a well in the desert. Notice the cistern next to the well.

Water

Water normally had to be collected from the local well, and because the collection was such a chore everyone dreamed of the time when he would have his own cistern (a hole cut out of rock and rendered with waterproof plaster so that water could be stored in and drawn from his own wellhead). Sennacherib promised that if the Israelites in Jerusalem would surrender to him, he would provide them with this status symbol (2 Kings 18:31).

When the cistern was dry, at the end of the summer, it made a good hiding place, as Jonathan and Ahimaaz found (2 Samuel 17:18–19). There was no means of sanitation in the simple peasant homes, although advanced drainage and sewerage systems did operate in later cities such as Caesarea and on the Temple site in Jerusalem. Health laws had been carefully laid down in the Torah (for example, it was stipulated that excrement should be buried during warfare, Deuteronomy 23:13), and supplementary laws were built up in Judaism that maintained basic health. No stables, for example, could be built under human dwellings.

Opposite: The interior of
the home of a wealthy
family influenced by
Roman tastes. Notice the
central area, or atrium,
with its pool open to the
sky.

Homes for the wealthy

The difference between the homes of the wealthy
and of the poor lay in the provision of a courtyard.
At the lowest level this was simply an enclosure
added onto the house. But the courtyard made immediate differences. Animals could be kept outside
the house, cooking could be done in a corner, there
would be no problems of security over access to the
roof because the stairway from the roof would come
into the courtyard, windows could open onto the
courtyard to let in more light, and the door of the enclosure could always be kept shut. A cistern now became a possibility.

People with greater wealth would build two or
three rooms round the courtyard, and rooms would
sometimes be built to provide an upper story
(2 Kings 4:10; Mark 14:12–16; Acts 9:36–41). It
was a home that was at once secluded and open to
the sky — a flashback to the seminomadic experience of Abraham's time.

Really wealthy people could add courtyards with
buildings around them by providing a porchway
through what was one of the original rooms of the
house. Pillars supported the roof beams so that the
size of the room could be extended. Pillars were
built parallel to the walls of the buildings so that colonnades or verandas could be made. Decorations
were added in the form of carved lintels, capitals,
and doorpost bases. Walls could be plastered and
decorated and floors covered with tiles, and, later,
mosaics of pebbles and of cut tiles. The courtyards
themselves could be made into gardens.

The porch

A wealthy house looked uninviting from the exterior because entry was through a single, locked
cedar door that was often guarded by a porter. The
lock was put on the inside of the gate, so that it was
necessary for the arm to be put through a hole in the
door before the key could be inserted (Nehemiah
3:3; Song of Songs 5:4). The key was a means of lifting up the pegs that held the wooden bar in place,
and the key was therefore rather large (see Isaiah
22:22). Roman locks of a later time were much
smaller and more complex.

The porter sat in a porch behind the gate and

A Roman couch.

waited until he recognized the voice of the person wanting to come in. Rhoda took the place of the porter and waited until she recognized the voice of Peter — but she still would not open the door until she had told the others who it was (Acts 12:13–14). When Jesus said that he stood outside the door of the church at Laodicea and knocked, it must mean it was a wealthy church (Revelation 3:20).

Furniture
Whereas the less wealthy managed a bed, table, and chairs (2 Kings 4:10), the wealthy had proper beds piled high with cushions (1 Samuel 19:15–16; Proverbs 7:16–17). Dining tables were to be found in the homes of the wealthy. Stools, together with backed chairs (1 Kings 10:18–19), were provided to rest the legs (Psalm 110:1). Lighting was provided by large candelabra. There was no real limit to the facilities provided in the palaces of the day, but there were fewer rich people than there are today.

Now look at your Bible

Property rights

Matthew 13:44. As part of the laws of property, everything buried on the land belonged to the person who purchased it. This lies behind Jesus' illustration of the truth that it is sometimes worthwhile giving everything you have for something supremely good. It was quite common to bury the family treasure in one's land in time of war or exile, which led to the common practice of digging for treasure (Job 3:20–21; Proverbs 2:3–5).

"Home"

To a nomad, a home is not a place of possession because it is moved from place to place; rather it is a place of welcome. When the British government drew up the Balfour Declaration and said that Palestine was to be a "homeland" for the Jews, the Arab people understood it to mean a place where they would welcome their guests. The Jews, on the other hand, look upon home and land as a possession, and they therefore understood homeland in the Balfour Declaration to mean a place for possession. Much of the original Arab/Israeli misunderstanding was based upon these different understandings of the word *homeland*. The nomadic idea of a home as a shelter is reflected in passages that describe God as a shelter (Psalm 61:3–4; Isaiah 4:6, "It will be a shelter and shade from the heat of the day, and a refuge and hiding-place from the storm and rain").

The open door

Revelation 3:8. "I have placed before you an open door." This refers to a house in the country. To have it shut would indicate that it was nighttime (compare Luke 11:7) or that people were not there. It therefore means that God is always available; it has nothing to do with opportunity.

Light in darkness

Isaiah 42:3. Light in the dark peasant home was a necessity. To sleep without a light was a sign of utter poverty. The light indicated to all outside that there were sleepers present. For anyone to be put outside into the darkness was therefore a disaster (Job 18:6). For God to light one's lamp was a supreme blessing (Psalm 18:28). Therefore when Isaiah says that the Messiah will not put out a lamp if the flax is smoking, but will trim the wick and replenish the oil, it is a comforting picture of God's care for wayward followers.

Charcoal fires

John 18:18; 21:9. Charcoal has a particularly pungent smell. It is referred to only on these two occasions in the New Testament. At the first, Peter was warming his hands at a charcoal fire when he denied Jesus three times. Jesus made the second charcoal fire on the shore of Galilee. It must have stirred up Peter's conscience!

Healing the paralytic

Mark 2:4; Luke 5:19. It has often been assumed that the four friends who brought their paralytic friend to Jesus broke through the mud and brushwood roof to let him down. This assumes that the roof was easily repaired. The tiles Luke refers to would then be sun-baked mud. But Luke was writing to a Roman who knew about Roman tiling. It is therefore more likely that Jesus was talking under a colonnade/veranda attached to the house, and that the friends, having gained access to the roof, stripped off some of the tiling of the colonnade.

Domestic Activities

Most people in Bible times got up early, before the sun was up, so that they could make the most of the hours of daylight and allow for the extreme heat at midday in the summer. Abraham got up early to obey God's command to sacrifice (Genesis 22:3); Moses got up early in the morning to meet God on Mount Sinai (Exodus 34:4); Job offered worship early in the morning (Job 1:5); Jesus prayed before sunrise (Mark 1:35).

Although it was possible for a person to stay in bed (Proverbs 26:14), it was very difficult to do so in a small house because everyone slept together on the platform. One person getting up would disturb the others — a point made when Jesus was telling the story of the friend who needed help with some extra food at midnight (Luke 11:7).

Breakfast

Breakfast was an informal meal taken some time after getting up — a cake of bread with something inside, such as olives, cheese, or dried fruit. While the men and older boys left for their work, eating as they went, mother and girls did the domestic chores for the day, together with any boys too young to work and unable (in early biblical years) to go to school. The youngest minded any animals possessed by the family (as David once did, for example, in 1 Samuel 16:11), while the others were busy in and about the house.

Milling

As soon as the men had disappeared the handmill was taken from its place on the platform and placed on a square of clean cloth. It was made of two disc-shaped stones about twelve to eighteen inches (thirty to fifty centimetres) across. The lower stone had an upright wooden stake that passed through

Opposite: Two women mill grain together. Notice the upright bread oven in the background.

An assortment of pots and jugs of Bible times. They were used for storage as well as at mealtimes.

an ample hole in the upper stone, which ideally was made of basalt, a lightweight rock. An upright handle fixed to the upper stone made it possible to rotate the stone about the wooden stake or pivot. Either barley grains (for the poor) or wheat grains were put into the pivot hole as the top stone was being turned. The grain was crushed between the two stones and came out onto the cloth as flour.

A woman could do the milling by herself, but it was easier working with a companion (see Matthew 24:41). If possible, slaves were used to do this work, as Samson found out in prison (Judges 16:21) and as the Jews found in captivity (Lamentations 5:13). It was, however, a basic, homely sound as the grain was milled. Jeremiah said that the absence of the sound would be a mark of the judgment of God (Jeremiah 25:10).

Fetching water

The two jobs outside the house — collecting water and going to the local market — were done by the older girls. Water was fetched from the local well or spring at the beginning or end of the day. Eliezer, Abraham's servant, utilized this fact to seek guidance from God in choosing a wife for Isaac (Genesis 24:11–13). He also knew that it was always the older, unmarried girls who came to fetch the water (see 1 Samuel 9:11). The water was carried in a large earthenware pitcher either on the shoulder (the method adopted by Rebekah, Genesis 24:15) or on the hip.

Shopping

If food was not available from one's own stores it was necessary to go to the local market to purchase provisions. This was a daily task because it was not possible to keep food for more than a day in the hot climate without recourse to drying or salting. This practice lies behind the words in the Lord's Prayer, "give us *today* our *daily* bread," where we pray for God's help to enable us to live one day at a time (Matthew 6:11, italics added).

As part of the visit to the tradesmen, some families would collect bread that had been baked in the community oven. Hosea tells us how loaves were put in the oven overnight and were cooked slowly, until taken out before the baker stirred up the fire in the morning again (Hosea 7:4–6), and while Jeremiah was imprisoned he received a daily loaf from the street of the bakers in Jerusalem (Jeremiah 37:21).

While the water and food was being collected the mother and the other girls had plenty to do. The floor of the house had to be swept carefully and the place made tidy (see Luke 11:25), particularly if animals had slept inside overnight, and washing had to be done (see p. 48). The fire had to be fanned into a flame so that cooking could proceed.

The foodmarket at Hebron. The markets of Bible times would have been rather similar.

Traditional type of oven.

Baking bread

Bread was the basic food. Flour from the handmill was mixed with water, and the dough was placed on flat stones that had been heated. If the bread was to be leavened, a piece of dough from the previous day (the leaven) was put into the new dough and the whole lump left by the fire until the yeast in the old dough had permeated the whole (Matthew 13:33; Galatians 5:9). It was then baked that way.

Other methods of baking bread were with the use of primitive ovens. One form was an earthenware dish that was inverted over the fire, the bread cakes being placed on the convex surface. Another was in the form of a truncated cone, with an opening at the bottom for the fire; the bread cakes were stuck onto the inside of the cone. Not until Roman times was an earthenware oven invented in which the firebox was separated from the cooking area and so made thicker loaves a possibility.

In fact, any earthenware receptacle or even an earth pit, where it was possible to get heat to the dough, could be utilized as an oven. Paper-thin loaves, biscuit-sized loaves, and heavier cakes of bread were all made in this way. (Compare the paper-thin bread used to scoop out the sauce in Matthew 26:23 with the lunch biscuits in John 6:9 and the much heavier loaf in Judges 7:13.) A metal tray was sometimes put on the fire so that grains could be placed over the fire. As the grains "popped" they formed popped corn or "parched corn" (1 Samuel 17:17; 25:18).

Siesta

As the heat of the day approached, it was time for a siesta out of the sun. Abraham sat in the door of his tent for siesta (Genesis 18:1), Saul went into a cave (1 Samuel 24:3), and Ish-Bosheth stayed in his house (2 Samuel 4:5).

Evening meal

Following the midday rest there were a number of important activities. The evening meal had to be prepared on the fire for the men when they returned from work. This normally consisted of vegetables or a lentil stew (Genesis 25:29, 34; Daniel 1:12), which was scooped out of the common pot with a piece of thin bread.

On special occasions, such as a festival or when a sacrifice had been made, meat was added to the stew; at Passover the meat was roasted. Blood had to be drained from the meat, and in later times meat could not be served with dairy products (Leviticus 7:26). There were also strict food laws about what meat might and might not be eaten (Leviticus 11). The meal would be finished with fresh or dried fruit.

A bedouin woman bakes bread on a large dish inverted over the fire.

**Shallow bowl for washing
the feet.**

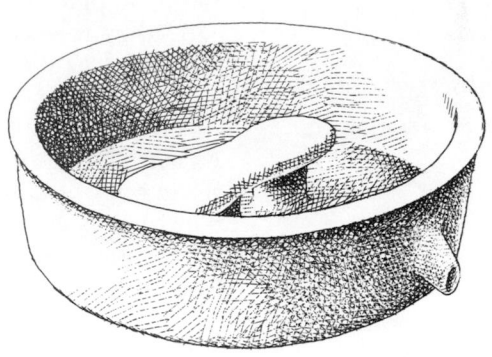

Crafts

Another important activity was spinning and weaving to make family clothing and craft work for sale. The ideal wife in Proverbs 31 is described as one who seeks for wool and flax and works willingly with her hands (v. 13). She spins, weaves, and makes clothes (vv. 19, 21), provides rugs and coverings for the home (v. 22) and sells the surplus at the market (v. 24). It was while she was busy at this kind of work that she would talk to other women and to the children.

Washing

At some time during the day, people needed to wash. If Bathsheba was typical, this too took place at the end of the day (2 Samuel 11:2). The normal small house seldom had bathing facilities; only in the homes of the wealthy could a room be provided with a bath tub. More common was a shallow earthenware bowl with a ridge in the middle for the feet. A full bath had to be taken in a spring or at the river. Even Pharaoh's daughter bathed in the river (Exodus 2:5). And Elisha seems to have referred to this practice when he told Naaman to go and take a bath in the river Jordan (2 Kings 5:10).

Once the meal was over and darkness came, people would go to bed early, so as to be up with the sun the following morning.

Now look at your Bible

The woman at the well
John 4:6. The Samaritan woman came at the sixth hour of the day (midday), despite the heat, because she knew there would be no other women at the well. Furthermore, because of the life-style she was following, she did not want to talk to them. She had brought her own leather bucket to the well to get the water out (v. 7).

A woman's job
Mark 14:13. Since it was always the woman's job to carry water, a man doing the job would be distinctive enough to be identified quickly. Jesus therefore used this means to help Peter and John locate the room where the Last Supper was to be prepared (see Luke 22:8–12).

Two basic meals
Luke 14:12. Jesus literally said, "When you make a *breakfast* or an *evening meal*, call not your friends." He was referring to the two basic meals of the day.

Food and Meals

We have already looked at the two meals of the day as part of the day's activities. Here we bring together additional information about food and meals.

Bread

For most people food was simple. Bread, olives, cheese, fruit, and vegetables formed the staple diet. Meat was eaten on rare occasions. Bread was so basic a food that it became synonymous with life itself. "Eating bread" was the equivalent phrase for "having a meal." The Egyptians could not "eat bread" with the Hebrews (Genesis 43:31–32, KJV). "Give us each day our daily bread" (Luke 11:3) was a prayer for daily provision of food itself. Bread was something so basic and so special that Jesus referred to himself as the "bread of life" (John 6:35).

Bread seems always to have been broken and never cut with a knife, which gave rise to the phrase "to break bread," used in Acts 20:7 to describe the Communion service. Bread made from barley was less favoured than wheat bread; it was also cheaper. In addition to being used for bread, grain was also parched (see p. 47) by heating the grains on a metal plate over the fire and was often eaten raw when people were walking through the grainfields. There is a well-known example of this when the disciples of Jesus were told that they should not eat raw grain on the Sabbath (Matthew 12:1). Such grain was known as "new grain" (Leviticus 23:14).

Vegetables

Vegetables were also in common use. Beans and lentils were common throughout the Old Testament period ("Take wheat and barley, beans and lentils, millet and spelt..." Ezekiel 4:9). It was a lentil-based stew that Jacob cooked and gave to Esau (Genesis 25:33–34) and beans that were given to David

A bedouin woman makes a sour milk drink outside her tent.

when he fled from Absalom (2 Samuel 17:28). Leeks, onions, garlic, cucumbers, and melons were familiar in Egypt (Numbers 11:5).

Milk

Milk was another basic food and was obtained from most of the animals that were herded. Some of it was fermented to produce yoghurt, and it is this that is sometimes referred to as milk (e.g., Genesis 18:8; Judges 4:19). Some of it was churned to provide butter (Proverbs 30:33). Milk was placed in a skin bag, and the bag was alternately shaken and squeezed until the butter was formed. Milk was also used to make cheese (2 Samuel 17:29). Presumably the buttermilk would have been used too, but it is never mentioned in the Bible.

Meat and fish

Meat and fish were luxury foods and were confined to the wealthy except at times of festival and sacrifice. King Solomon had meat in regular variety — beef, mutton, game, and fowl: "Solomon's daily provisions were thirty cors of fine flour and sixty cors of meal, ten head of stall-fed cattle, twenty of pasture-fed cattle and a hundred sheep and goats, as well as deer, gazelles, roebucks and choice fowl" (1 Kings 4:23). Abraham served veal to his guests (Genesis 18:7), and Gideon's guests ate goat meat (Judges 6:19). Meat was normally boiled as part of a stew because this naturally followed the draining of blood that was required by the law (Deuteronomy 12:15–25). However, meat could be roasted if care was used. The sons of Eli preferred roast meat to boiled meat (1 Samuel 2:15).

Meat from herded animals was supplemented by meat from hunting. The valley of the river Jordan was plentiful in wild animals during Bible times. Trapping of animals in a net (Job 18:8–10) or in a pit (Jeremiah 48:44) was common, and birds were trapped, too (Amos 3:5).

Fish were also available, but some varieties were forbidden for food (Leviticus 11:11–12). The work of the disciples of Jesus is evidence that much fishing was carried on at that time on the Sea of Galilee. Fish were familiar enough for Jesus to use in his parables (Matthew 13:47–48; Luke 11:11). Eggs do not seem to have been used for food until late Old Testament times, although they were familiar enough to Jesus (see Luke 11:12).

Fruit

Fruit was another necessary part of the diet. Olives were grown for eating and for use as cooking oil. Olive oil was mixed with flour and used for frying (Leviticus 2:5). Fresh figs and dried figs were available (1 Samuel 25:18; Jeremiah 24:2). Fresh grapes were eaten (Numbers 13:23), whereas others were dried as raisins (1 Chronicles 12:40). Pomegranates were popular (Deuteronomy 8:8), and melons had been eaten in Egypt (Numbers 11:5). Locust beans, sometimes called carobs, were a useful sweetmeat or candy, and almond and pistachio nuts were always around (Genesis 43:11). Dates are not mentioned in the Bible, but there are plenty of references to them in Jewish literature.

Honey

Honey was used for sweetening because there was no sugar. There are many examples in the Bible in which honey was obtained from wild bees. Samson

Endless supplies of salt were available near the Dead Sea.

found it in the carcass of a lion (Judges 14:8–9), Jonathan found it in a forest (1 Samuel 14:25–27), and Moses found honey in a rock hole (Deuteronomy 32:13).

Bees were colonized in hives in Egypt and Assyria, and this may have been taken up by the Jews by New Testament times (see Luke 24:41–43, KJV). When grape juice was boiled down it became a sweet, sticky syrup, and this too may have been referred to as honey in some Bible passages. It was spread on bread and sometimes diluted with water and drunk. Jacob sent this to Joseph in Egypt (Genesis 43:11), and it was exported to the Phoenicians (Ezekiel 27:17).

Salt

Seasoning was limited to salt, obtainable from the endless supplies in the salt hills near the Dead Sea. It was used to flavour and preserve food (Job 6:6). In New Testament times there was a thriving industry based at Magdala, where fish were salted and exported. Not until Greek and Roman times were other seasonings (spices) readily available, and this developed as trade grew.

Salt was believed to have healing properties (2 Kings 2:19–22) and was also used in sacrificial offerings (Leviticus 2:13). This may have led to the custom of using it in a meal held to celebrate the signing of an agreement (Numbers 18:19).

Hand-washing

Before meals were eaten the hands were always washed under running water because there were no utensils such as knives, forks, and spoons. In a wealthy home, this task would be performed by a servant. Elisha used to pour water over the hands of Elijah (2 Kings 3:11). By New Testament times this had become something of a ritual. Jesus reacted against the mere ritualization of the practice (Mark 7:1–8). He took on the role of a servant in washing the feet, but not the hands, of the disciples at the Last Supper (John 13:4–5). The hands were also washed at the end of the meal.

Thanksgiving was offered for the meal, traditionally "Blessed art Thou, Jehovah our God, King of the world, who causes to come forth bread from the earth." Jesus could have used such a blessing at the feeding of the five thousand (John 6:11), just as Samuel may have done centuries before (1 Samuel 9:13).

At table

In a simple home there was a common food pot, placed on a rug, and the family sat cross-legged around the pot. A piece of thin bread was used to scoop out the contents. When Ruth ate with the reapers, she was invited to eat in this way (Ruth 2:14). The "table" mentioned in the Old Testament is therefore nothing but a rug spread on the ground (Psalm 23:5).

Only the wealthy would own a table and chairs or couches as we know them. Joseph entertained at such a table (Genesis 43:33–34), David had a seat at King Saul's table (1 Samuel 20:5, 18), and Jesus reclined at table in the house of Simon the Pharisee (Luke 7:36). A description of the elaborate meals given as part of social life follows on p. 246.

Hygiene

The Jewish diet was generally good for health. (For instance, Daniel and his friends looked far healthier on a vegetarian diet than did their companions who ate meat, Daniel 1:5–16). The Jewish food laws gave a good degree of protection from food poisoning when cooking temperatures were low. The biggest health problem concerned the water, which was easily polluted through animal usage, washing,

A stone table and other furniture found in Jerusalem and dating from the time of Herod the Great.

sewerage, and plain dirt. When water was collected in a cistern, it had run off the mud and brushwood roof where all manner of things had been stored. For this reason, wine was a staple drink. Paul probably had water problems in mind when he recommended that Timothy should "use a little wine because of your stomach" (1 Timothy 5:23).

Illness

Sickness was not linked in thought with food and drink. It was normally attributed to the will (even the judgment) of God (Deuteronomy 28:60–61), and for this reason doctors were not approved. Prayer was believed to be more effective than medicine, and Hezekiah was a prime example (2 Kings 20).

Doctors could therefore cause loss of faith in God (2 Chronicles 6:29). But by New Testament times, Luke's skill as a doctor was appreciated by Paul (Colossians 4:14), although Peter's scepticism, recorded by Mark, concerning the woman with the hemorrhage is clear to see (Mark 5:26).

Now look at your Bible

Salt under foot

Matthew 5:13. When salt was collected from the Dead Sea area, some of it was good for salting and cooking, but other salt had lost its saltiness. This salt was not thrown away, however. It was stored in the Jerusalem Temple, and when the winter rains made the marble courtyards slippery, it was spread on them to reduce the slipperiness. Hence salt that has lost its saltiness is trodden under foot of men.

Locusts — or locust beans?

Matthew 3:4. It was perfectly all right under the food laws to eat locusts (Leviticus 11:22). It is much more likely, however, as locusts were not readily available all the time, and John the Baptist had to eat daily, that locust beans are being referred to. These beans (carob pods) are sweet and sticky. The prodigal son was also glad to eat the same food (Luke 15:16).

Meat without blood

Acts 15:29. The first-century Christians were encouraged to follow the Jewish food laws concerning the draining of the blood from the animal. It is difficult to know for sure why the Jews were forbidden to eat blood. It might have been purely ritual because life and blood are identified and the life belongs to God (Leviticus 17:14); the blood was therefore used as a means of atonement with God.

The prohibition against eating blood might have been based on an earlier practice that was intensely cruel. Because meat would not keep, some tribespeople cut parts from an animal and then kept the animal alive until more meat was required. The draining of blood prevented such practices. The prohibition might have been a health law to prevent blood-borne infections and diseases.

The Family

Family units in the West in the twentieth century are called *nuclear* because they are small — mother, father, and one or two children. Family units in Old Testament times were large and included every member of the family — aunts, uncles, cousins, and servants. We would call them *extended* families. The leader of the family was the *father*, and the head of a group of families was the *sheikh*.

Abraham and his heirs were sheikhs, and on one occasion Abraham was able to raise 318 fighting men "born in his household" (Genesis 14:14). Mary and Joseph seem to have travelled in such a family when they went with Jesus to Jerusalem, when he was twelve years old. They were travelling with "relatives and friends" (Luke 2:44). There were sufficient of them not to spot Jesus for a whole day, and Mary and Joseph were close enough in family ties to the extended family for them not to worry about it.

The father
The family was therefore a "little kingdom" that was ruled by the father. He ruled over wife, children, grandchildren, and servants — everyone in the household. Children were brought up to accept this authority (Exodus 20:12), and if they refused to accept it, thereby threatening the security of the family unit, they could be punished by death (Deuteronomy 21:18–21).

On the death of the father, succession normally passed to his eldest son. Isaac was a special case. According to family law practiced in Abraham's time, it was possible for a man to have a child by a secondary wife. Ishmael was born to Abraham and Hagar in this way (Genesis 16:1–2). But if any child was born subsequently to the first wife, then that child, in this case Isaac, became head of the family. The same law was followed in Jacob's case. Rachel was always intended to be his first wife. Therefore it was *her* elder son, Joseph, who became Jacob's heir and was given the distinctive coat to show it (Genesis 37:3–4), even though he was born long after his stepbrothers.

Women

The role of a woman always appeared to be subservient to men. She kept out of sight when visitors were present (Genesis 18:9), served the men in the family before eating herself, fetched the water, made the clothes, cooked the food, and walked while the men rode. Even when Lot and his wife were in full flight from Sodom, she walked behind him (Genesis 19:26, KJV). If Joseph had taken the position ascribed to him by many artists, of walking beside a donkey that was carrying Mary, he would have been the laughingstock of his contemporaries. This is clearly reflected in Paul's writings where "the head of the woman is man" (1 Corinthians 11:3). Paul gives theological reasons for this. He tells Timothy that man was first created, but that woman was first tempted into breaking God's law (1 Timothy 2:13–14).

The traditional role did not mean that a woman was unloved or subject to disrespect when she fulfilled her role (Proverbs 31). She was the only one who could have children, and so important was this aspect of the family that if she was unfaithful to her husband and family, she paid with the death penalty (Leviticus 20:10). But when a husband was unfaithful to his wife with an unmarried girl, the girl became a member of his family (Deuteronomy 22:13–30; compare v. 22 with vv. 28 and 29).

So important was motherhood that a woman's position was literally saved through childbirth (1 Timothy 2:15). With her husband the wife was looked upon as a representative of God to teach his laws (Exodus 20:12; Deuteronomy 6:7). This was to grow into a kind of equality.

In New Testament times wives were still to submit to their husbands, but the love that the husbands were to have for their wives (Ephesians 5:25) was itself to be a kind of submission (v. 21). (This is true because when you love someone you submit to what you know he or she wants, by positively putting the

Relief of Mary and Joseph fleeing Herod's slaughter of the infants. In Bible times no man would walk beside a donkey carrying a woman.

other first.) It was possible for a man to have more than one wife (Deuteronomy 22:28–29), but one wife seems to have been the ideal. The Jewish rabbis noted that God had produced only one wife for Adam, and Paul expected the church leaders of his day to conform to that pattern (1 Timothy 3:2). The family unit itself was the key thing.

Slaves

In settled times it was possible for the wealthier families to increase their size by the acquisition of slaves. Most had been captured in wartime (Numbers 31:26; Deuteronomy 21:10) or purchased from slave markets (Leviticus 25:44). Hosea bought his wife back again from a slave market. Although such slaves were regarded as property (Leviticus 25:45) they were carefully protected by the law. They could not be oppressed (Deuteronomy 23:15–16), and they had the right to Sabbath rest (Exodus 20:10) and to attend national festivals (Deuteronomy 16:10–11).

Slaves were often very well treated, as if members of the family. If they were circumcised they enjoyed most of the privileges of Jewish society except that they could not acquire property or marry foreign slaves. Good treatment was not solely a Jewish characteristic. Naaman's wife's slave was well treated (2 Kings 5:2–3), and so apparently was the Roman slave Onesimus, even at a time when Roman law made escape by a slave to be a capital offense (Philemon 17).

It was possible for a Jew to become a slave so as to repay money owed through debt or theft, or even because he found greater security in another man's house than in his own. Families and children could be sold in this way (Exodus 21:7; 2 Kings 4:1; Matthew 18:25). Such a person would normally sell his labour for seven years (Deuteronomy 15:12–18) unless he wanted to stay as one of the family (v. 16), in which case his ear was ceremonially pinned to the doorpost (v. 17).

Some slaves were entrusted with great authority by their masters. Eliezer was responsible for finding a wife for his master's son (Genesis 24). A master's daughter could marry a slave (1 Chronicles 2:34–35), but if the son-in-law decided that he wanted to leave the family after all, he had to leave his wife and children behind (Exodus 21:4). Normally slaves were set free in the year of Jubilee to return to their inheritance, which was freed at the same time (Leviticus 25:39–41). Slaves could be freed at any time if the debt they owed was paid by another member of their family, or even themselves (Leviticus 25:48–49); only girls sold as maidservants remained bound for life.

The generous Israelite rules toward slaves contrasted strongly with the harsh laws toward slaves in other areas of the Middle East. The economies of the Greek and Roman empires were largely built upon slavery. The New Testament accepted slavery as a fact of life (Ephesians 6:8; Colossians 3:22; Philemon 16) but it laid down the doctrinal foundations that would finally bring slavery to an end (Galatians 3:28).

A different form of slavery was known in Israel — "servitude" or "taxation by labour." Levies were taken by the authorities for so many months of the year for public works purposes. The original Canaanite population that survived the conquest was put to work in this way (1 Kings 9:21), but the Israelites had to work for three months of the year, too (1 Kings 5:13–14).

Rites of passage

Within the family there were four great occasions that marked the progress of life — birth, maturity, marriage, and death. Because of the importance of such occasions they were often marked with special social customs. However, when people believe that God is involved in the process of life, the important events take on a religious significance and religious rites are performed alongside the social ones. These are known as *rites of passage.*

Children

Because parents believed that they lived on in their children, children were looked upon as a great blessing (Deuteronomy 28:4; Psalm 128:3). The more children a person could have, the better it was. "Blessed is the man whose quiver is full of them" (Psalm 127:5a).

If a woman could not have children, that was therefore seen as a curse from God because it was as good as extinction. Rachel told Jacob that if she had no children she would die (Genesis 30:1). Hannah believed her childlessness was God's punishment (1 Samuel 1:16), and Elizabeth knew the reproachful looks she received from people because they believed she had done something to upset God. When John was born she knew that the Lord had "taken away my disgrace" (Luke 1:25).

A cause for joy though all babies were, boys were the real blessing. Men stayed with the family and so increased its size and wealth with wives and more children. Girls, on the other hand, were valuable only for the work they could do while they were young and for the bride-price that would be paid as a form of compensation when they moved to another family.

Birth

The expectant mother was not to take a hot bath in case it led to a miscarriage, and there were certain things she could not eat — green vegetables, salt food, and fat — in case they affected the unborn child. The local midwife assisted in the birth, which normally took place at home (Exodus 1:15–19; Jeremiah 20:14–15). The newborn baby was washed and then had salt rubbed over the skin in the belief that this hardened it. The Jewish mother believed that the limbs would grow straight and firm if they were bound tightly to the sides by what were called "swaddling clothes." These were bandages four or five inches (100–120 mm) wide and five or six yards (five or six metres) long (see Ezekiel 16:4; Luke 2:12).

Circumcision

Eight days after the birth the male baby was circumcised either by the head of the family or by a physician. The blessing was said, "Blessed be the Lord our God who has sanctified us by his precepts and has given us circumcision." There was normally some kind of family celebration during the eight days between birth and circumcision. It is difficult to know what circumcision first meant. Before it was taken on by the Jews it was probably some kind of initiation rite in which a young man's vigour and sexuality were dedicated to his god. God then took this celebration and gave it to the Jews as a sign that the whole nation was dedicated to him from the outset (Genesis 17:10).

Naming

The naming of the child frequently accompanied the act of circumcision. This happened in Jesus' case (Luke 2:21). Names normally had some kind of significance in the family, and it is interesting to follow through the meanings where they are given in the margin of a Bible. So important was the birth and the naming that parents' names were often changed. Father became "father of x," and mother became "mother of y."

After the birth the mother stayed at home — seven days for a boy and fourteen for a girl. Thirty-three days later (sixty-six in the case of a girl baby) she was ready to make the customary offerings.

Normally a lamb with a pigeon or dove were offered as a sin offering to restore a woman's fellowship with God (Leviticus 12). In case of poverty another pigeon or dove could be substituted for the lamb. The sin offering seems to have indicated that the woman had been ritually unclean, as she was during menstruation (Leviticus 15:19–24). The ritual uncleanness was not actual defilement through childbirth, but it was a means of protecting a woman from sexual relations in times of weakness and possible embarrassment. In the case of a firstborn child, redemption money of five shekels had to be paid because, since the preservation of the Jewish firstborn at the original Passover, all firstborn children belonged to God (Numbers 18:15–16).

Babies were normally breastfed by the mother (or, if necessary, by a wet nurse), and this often went on for several years (see 1 Samuel 1:24; Psalm 131:2; 2 Maccabees 7:27). The day the child was weaned called for a celebration (Genesis 21:8).

Entering manhood

The Jewish boy was recognized as entering manhood at thirteen years of age, but it is not certain when this practice began. By New Testament times a boy of thirteen became a "son of the law." The significance of the account of Jesus' being left behind at the Temple is that it showed he was leaving his childhood (Luke 2:41–49). It was the last time he would attend Passover as a child. Only after age thirteen did the child qualify to become one of the ten men who could constitute a synagogue.

Polygamy

Although marriage was allowed with more than one woman simultaneously, as when Jacob married Leah and Rachel, and had sexual relationships with their servants, polygamy was not common in Israel in biblical times. One reason was that a husband had to be quite wealthy to be able to afford more than one wife. Therefore it tended to be royalty who had many wives. David had many, including Michal, Abigail, and Bathsheba, and Solomon had still more during the wealthiest part of his kingship.

The high priest could have only one wife (Leviticus 21:13–14), and other leading figures of the Old Testament were monogamous — Noah, Isaac, Joseph, and Moses. It was often pointed out by the rabbis that more than one wife led to problems (Leah and Rachel, Genesis 30; Hannah and Peninnah, 1 Samuel 1).

Arranged marriage

Young people did not normally decide whom they would marry. It was marriage first and love afterwards. Although there was therefore a great deal more "will" than "romance," it tended to produce a stable pattern of marriages (Genesis 24:67). Esau was in trouble because he married contrary to the wishes of his parents (Genesis 26:34–35). The practice of arranging marriages did not mean that parents did not consider the feelings of their children (Genesis 24:58), or that love did not sometimes happen before marriage (Genesis 29:10–20).

A "friend who attends the bridegroom" (John 3:29) negotiated on behalf of the prospective bridegroom and his father with a representative of the bride's father. Arrangements had to be made for work compensation (the mohar) to be paid to the woman's family, and a dowry had to be paid to the bride's father. He could use the interest from the dowry but could not spend it (see Genesis 31:15) because it was to be kept in trust for the wife in case she was ever widowed or divorced. Where such sums of money could not be paid because of the poverty of the suitor, other means were found instead, such as service (Genesis 29:18) or elimination of enemies (1 Samuel 18:25).

It became a custom that part of the dowry should form a circlet of coins that were attached to the woman's head dress. They became a symbol like a wedding ring, and therefore the loss of such a coin (Luke 15:8–10) would be the cause of a great deal of anxiety. As part of the marriage agreement, the bride's father would make a marriage gift (dowry) to his daughter (Genesis 24:59–61; Judges 1:12–15).

Marriages were arranged, if possible, with members of one's own kin. Abraham sent a servant to find a bride for Isaac from his own people (Genesis 24:3–4), and Jacob was sent to the same place to find a wife (Genesis 28:2; 29:19). Samson's parents were upset because Samson had not chosen a wife from his own clan (Judges 14:3). Marriages sometimes took place outside the clan (Genesis 41:45; Ruth 1:4), and this usually happened for political reasons (1 Kings 11:1; 16:31). It was never approved, however, because people from other clans worshipped different deities and this affected the whole religious life of the people (1 Kings 11:4). Close marriages within the family were forbidden. The laws forbidding marriages between close relatives are set out in Leviticus 18:6–18.

Betrothal

Once the arrangement to marry was entered into, there was a betrothal that was more binding than the engagement in contemporary society. A man who was betrothed to a woman, even though not yet married, was exempted from military service (Deuteronomy 20:7). If a girl was already betrothed and was raped by another man she could not become that other man's wife, as would normally be the case (Deuteronomy 22:28–29), because she already belonged to her husband-to-be. Such violation involved the death penalty (Deuteronomy 22:23–27).

The formal words of the betrothal were probably those spoken by Saul when Michal and David were betrothed, "You shall be my son-in-law" (see 1 Samuel 18:22). The betrothal could be broken only by a legal transaction (in effect, a divorce), and the ground for such termination was adultery (see Deuteronomy 22:24). Betrothal lasted for about twelve months, during which the home was to be prepared by the groom, and the wedding clothes would be prepared by the bride. The bride's family would prepare for the wedding festivities.

Mary and Joseph were betrothed when it was found that she was pregnant. Joseph did not want to expose her publicly, because, as a supposed adulteress, Mary would have been stoned to death. It must have taken a great deal of love for Mary and a great deal of trust in God speaking through his dream that enabled Joseph to marry her. Maybe this is a reflection of the character God looked for in the man who was to bring up Jesus (Matthew 1:18–20). In New Testament times a man such as Joseph became formally betrothed when he gave a present to the girl and said, "By this, thou art set apart for me according to the laws of Moses and of Israel."

The wedding

There were several important parts to the wedding itself. The wedding was essentially nonreligious, apart from a blessing that was pronounced over the couple ("Our sister, may you increase to thousands upon thousands; may your offspring possess the gates of their enemies," Genesis 24:60). The marriage involved the drawing up of, and the acceptance of, a legal contract. This is still true of a Jewish wedding today. It may shock some Christians to realize that it was not until comparatively recent times that a rabbi or priest was required to be present at a wedding.

The wedding also involved dressing up. The bride was literally adorned like a queen (see Revelation 21:2). She was bathed, and her hair braided with as many precious stones as the family possessed or could borrow (Psalm 45:14–15; Isaiah 61:10; Ezekiel 16:11–12). The girls who had dressed her accompanied her as "companions." The bridegroom too was dressed in finery and jewelry (Isaiah 61:10) and was accompanied by the "friend of the bridegroom" (John 3:29). The dressing up for the wedding was so important that it was unforgettable (Jeremiah 2:32). The bride and groom looked like and acted like a king and queen.

Another important element of the wedding was the procession at the end of the day. The bridegroom set out from his home to fetch his bride from her parents' home. At this point the bride was wearing a veil. At some point the veil was taken off and laid on the shoulder of the bridegroom, and the declaration was made, "The government shall be upon his shoulder." A procession then set out from the bride's home to the couple's new home, and the dark roadway would be lit with oil lamps held by wedding guests. In the story told by Jesus, the bride and groom were later than expected so the oil in the lamps began to run low. Only those who had brought a reserve flask of oil were able to refill their lamps and welcome the bride and groom (see Matthew 25:1–13, esp. vv. 8–9). There was singing and music along the way (Jeremiah 16:9), and sometimes the bride herself would join in the dance (Song of Songs 6:13).

The procession sets out from the bride's house to the couple's new home. The guests hold oil lamps to light the way.

The bride and groom sit like king and queen under a decorated canopy at their wedding feast.

The wedding feast

Bride and groom entered under a canopy when they arrived at the house. There they presided over the wedding feast at which a great deal of time was spent in eating and drinking (Song of Songs 2:4 may allude to the canopy). At the wedding in Cana, Jesus provided one hundred twenty gallons of wine for the guests, but they had already drunk so much that the person in charge (the "ruler of the feast") thought it was a pity that the excellent new wine should have been left to the end when the people could not appreciate it (John 2:6–10).

Festivities often lasted for seven days (Judges 14:12), or perhaps even longer. The guests were there to witness that the marriage had been consummated (Genesis 29:22–23); the blood-stained bed-coverings were shown to demonstrate that the bride had been a virgin (Deuteronomy 22:13–21). (The veil does not seem to have been removed from Leah's face until after the marriage was consummated; Jacob did not know it was Leah until the light of day, Genesis 29:23.) During the festivities, God's blessing was asked upon the couple, and it may well have been for this reason that Jesus was invited to the wedding at Cana (John 2:2). In very wealthy families guests were actually provided with "wedding clothes" (Matthew 22:12).

Divorce

Marriages could and did break up, and it was possible for a man to divorce his wife if he could find "something indecent about her" (Deuteronomy 24:1). Jewish lawyers interpreted this phrase in different ways. In the time of Jesus the followers of Shammai believed it referred to adultery or sexual misconduct. The followers of Hill'el believed that the phrase could include even the spoiling of a dinner. In society of that time, it was possible for a man simply to tell a woman that she was divorced, but the Jews were required to give a written "bill of divorcement" that contradicted the original marriage contract.

Part of the bill (or writ) of divorcement allowed the woman to remarry (Deuteronomy 24:1–2), but a girl who had married a man because she had previously been raped by the man could not be divorced at all (Deuteronomy 22:28–29). A man who had falsely accused his wife of not being a virgin when they were married also could not divorce her (Deuteronomy 22:13–19). If a divorced wife remarried, and her new husband died or divorced her, the original husband could not remarry her (Deuteronomy 24:3–4), but if she had not remarried, her first husband could remarry her (Hosea 3). God's people were left in no doubt that divorce was unacceptable to God (Malachi 2:16), and Jesus reiterated that whom God had joined together, no one was to separate (Matthew 5:31–32; 19:6). Women were not allowed to initiate divorce.

Death

A man's life was complete when he was seventy (Psalm 90:10). Most people died before this, but there were some notable exceptions. Death was the final event for which there were rites of passage. There was no assurance of life after death in early Israelite history. Parents were believed to be able to live on in their children so that the writer to the Hebrews is able to say that when Abraham paid tithes to Melchizedek, Levi was already in Abraham; Levi therefore paid tithes to the Jerusalem king, and his priesthood was thereby judged to be inferior (Hebrews 7:9–10).

People believed that they were gathered to an underworld (Sheol), where people were shades (or

The remains of a synagogue at Capernaum dating from several centuries after the time of Christ. Relics of an earlier synagogue, possibly the one of which Jairus was ruler, have been discovered underneath.

shadows) of their past. Not until the time of Daniel was there revelation that a resurrection would occur — some to eternal life and some to eternal punishment (Daniel 12:2). Nothing became entirely clear until Jesus had opened the Kingdom of Heaven to all believers and become the "firstfruits of those who have fallen asleep" (1 Corinthians 15:20). Not only does the New Testament have to explain this to contemporary Christians, but those outside the Christian faith were "of all men most miserable" because their hopes were limited to this life alone.

Immediately when a person died, there was a time of wailing and lamentation. The wail was an announcement to the neighbourhood that a death had taken place. The Egyptians had so many dead on the occasion of the first Passover that the wail could be heard through the whole country. The family then gathered for lamentation — a time for a great show of weeping, almost as if those who were still alive wanted to impress the shade of the dead person that they were really sorry. Micah says that it sounded like jackals and owls (Micah 1:8), and Jesus was aware of it when he went to raise Jairus's daughter at the Capernaum synagogue (Mark 5:38). David's

The entrance to these rock-cut tombs could be sealed with a circular stone. These tombs in Jerusalem are known as the Tombs of the Kings.

expressions of grief for Absalom were typical. Wealthy families would hire groups of professional mourners who would add to the noise (Jeremiah 9:17–18; Amos 5:16). Goat's hair cloth garments (sackcloth) were worn so as to cause discomfort; the breast was beaten (Luke 23:48) and clothes were torn to demonstrate how grief-stricken people were (2 Samuel 3:31).

Burial

Burial had to take place quickly because the hot climate led to rapid decomposition. However, a burial never took place on a Sabbath or holy day (John 11:39; 19:31). The body was normally washed, wrapped loosely in a linen cloth, and carried to the burial place on a wooden stretcher (Luke 7:14, where the stretcher or coffin was used for a sick man). Burial could take place in a natural cave or in an artificially-made one (sepulchre) (Genesis 49:29–32; Judges 8:32). Natural caves were widened and provided with niches or shelves where the bodies could be laid to rest. Because there were limited numbers of caves, when the bodies had decomposed the bones were removed and put into stone jars called ossuaries. These jars were stored in a corner, and the niches made available for further burials. The mouth of the tomb was sealed either with a disc-shaped stone that ran in an inclined groove in front of the cave or with a boulder that fell

This ossuary, or bone-box, was found in Jerusalem. It has the inscription: "Bones of the family of Nicanor the Alexandrian who made the gates."

into the access hole beneath it. Either way, the stone was extremely difficult to move once it was in place. Burial caves and sepulchres were painted white as a warning to the living that the dead were there (Matthew 23:27). A living person could not always worship God after having had contact with the dead.

Alternatively, burial was effected by laying the stretcher on the ground and surrounding the body with boulders about eighteen inches (fifty centimetres) in diameter in a rough oblong. The body was then covered by earth, the boulders forming a boundary to the grave. (Burial as such was not common because of the hardness of the ground.) The simple graveyards were always kept outside a village or town (Luke 7:12); only royalty were buried within the city (1 Kings 2:10).

Exceptionally, a body was covered in spices and in paste, and these were tied to the body by layers of white "roller bandage." The paste hardened and impregnated the bandages until a hard preservative mould or cocoon was formed about the body. A cap was put on the head, and often the jaw was held in position by a bandage under the chin. This was done

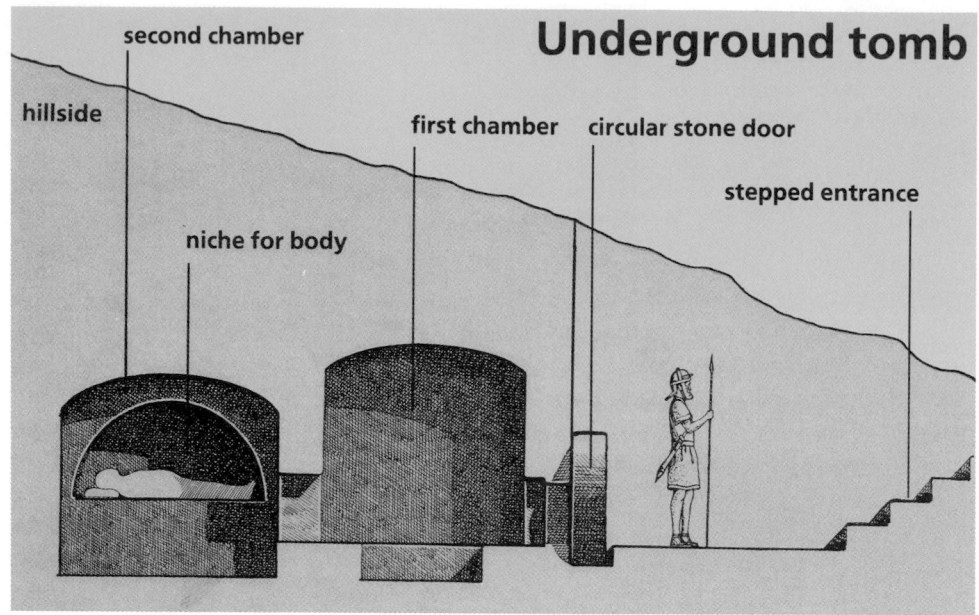

Underground tomb

second chamber

hillside

first chamber   circular stone door

stepped entrance

niche for body

Diagram showing an underground tomb cut into the hillside. Only the wealthy could afford such an elaborate burial.

for Jesus by two wealthy men, following the initial burial in the simple sheet (John 19:40). In Lazarus's case, his hands and feet seem to have been tied together before he was covered with a sheet. His jaw was tied by a bandage (John 11:44). Proper embalming was carried out in Egypt, where the removal of the internal organs took place. The body was filled with paste and the organs kept in a jar (see Genesis 50:2, 26). In Israel, following the burial there was a funeral meal to conclude the period of mourning (Jeremiah 16:7), often for a week or longer (Deuteronomy 34:8).

A woman who survived her husband was in a very difficult position. She could not inherit from her husband. She could remain in her husband's family if the next of kin would take her in marriage. More often the widow was without any financial support. The law therefore said that widows were to be protected (Deuteronomy 10:18; 24:17–21). In the early church, money was set aside to care for widows (Acts 6:1), because in the society of the day, prostitution was about the only way for women to obtain money to live. Paul expected widows to be supported by their families (1 Timothy 5:3–4, 8). The local church was to put the names of widows who had lived good lives and were over age sixty on a charity list (1 Timothy 5:9–11).

Now look at your Bible

Names

The name of God (*Yahweh* or *Jah*) was often incorporated into personal names. *Abijah* means "God is his father"; *Elijah* means "my God is Yahweh"; *Jonathan* means "gift of Yahweh." Other names remind people of birth. *Moses* means "drawn forth" because he was taken from the river Nile.

Jesus' childhood

Luke 2:21–39. Mary and Joseph had Jesus circumcised on the eighth day. At the end of forty days they went up to Jerusalem (about four miles from Bethlehem) to offer the required sacrifices and to pay the redemption money (vv. 22–24). It is clear that Mary and Joseph were extremely poor because they could afford only two birds. Immediately after this they returned to Nazareth with Jesus (v. 39). If the wise men arrived at the time when Jesus was approximately two years old (Matthew 2:16), then the wise men could have gone to Nazareth. The richness of the gifts (which had great symbolic value) must have been a fortune to Mary and Joseph. The gifts might have enabled them to set up a carpentry business and to look after Jesus and later a larger family.

Breaking the laws

Leviticus 18. The laws of Leviticus 18 were not always kept during Bible times. Sarah was Abraham's half sister (Genesis 20:12), and Amnon wanted to marry his half sister Tamar in 2 Samuel 13 (cf. Leviticus 18:11). Moses' parents were nephew and aunt (Exodus 6:20; cf. Leviticus 18:12–13). Jacob married two sisters (Genesis 29:16–30; cf. Leviticus 18:18).

Fidelity

Proverbs 5. A man was exhorted to be faithful, and he was put to death if he violated a married woman (Leviticus 20:10). He was not punished if he violated an unmarried girl: he had to marry her (Deuteronomy 22:28). The married woman on the other hand was put to death if she had sexual relations with any man other than her husband, unless her husband forgave her. This was called the "great sin." This was because the woman was the fundamental centre of the family, and for her to be unfaithful would be for her to destroy the family. This was not considered true of the man.

The burial of Jesus

John 20. Because Jesus was wrapped in a cocoon, one can understand why it was that the disciples saw and *then* believed in the resurrection, and why it was that the body had not been stolen. Jesus' body had passed through the cocoon of spice-impregnated bandages, just as it did through the door of the upper room. Looking quickly through the doorway of the tomb, John thought that the body was still there because he could see the cocoon, and therefore he would not enter. Only when John and Peter went in and saw that there was a gap where the face should have been (the cap was separated) did they realize what had happened.

Bereavement

Psalm 119:136; Jeremiah 9:1. These verses reflect an extreme kind of grief, which was much the same as that felt at time of death. The psalmist wept rivers of water because he knew what would follow the breaking of the law.

Education

Education is necessary so that the skills and understanding acquired by one generation can be passed on to the next. Such education always goes on in families, but as the skills and understanding become more developed, and as money becomes available in the economy to pay for it, a broader education can be given to more and more people. Reflections of this process can be seen in the Bible.

Sumerian education

When Abraham was called by God to leave the city of Ur in Sumer to "go to the land I will show you" (Genesis 11:31—12:5), his going was an act of faith. Ur was a highly civilized city, and Abraham was called to leave it for the unknown. Schools in Ur were used to train people for religious, commercial, and governmental work. The curriculum included mathematics, language, geography, botany, and drawing.

Writing was done by means of a wedge-shaped stylus that was impressed in soft clay tablets. Tablets from the city of Mari have been found with the children's exercises and the teachers' corrections in the clay. A "school father" ran the school with an assistant who prepared the exercises. There were also specialist subject teachers. One recovered tablet tells what a boy did in school: "I read my tablet, ate my lunch, prepared my tablet, wrote it, finished it." Trouble was corrected by the use of the cane. Education had to be paid for by parents.

There is no evidence that Abraham ever went to one of the "tablet houses," as the schools were called, but he certainly followed the laws of the Sumerians. The custom that a childless wife might have children by proxy through a servant girl (Genesis 16:1–2) was a Sumerian custom. But it was a law that, when the child was born, the girl should not be

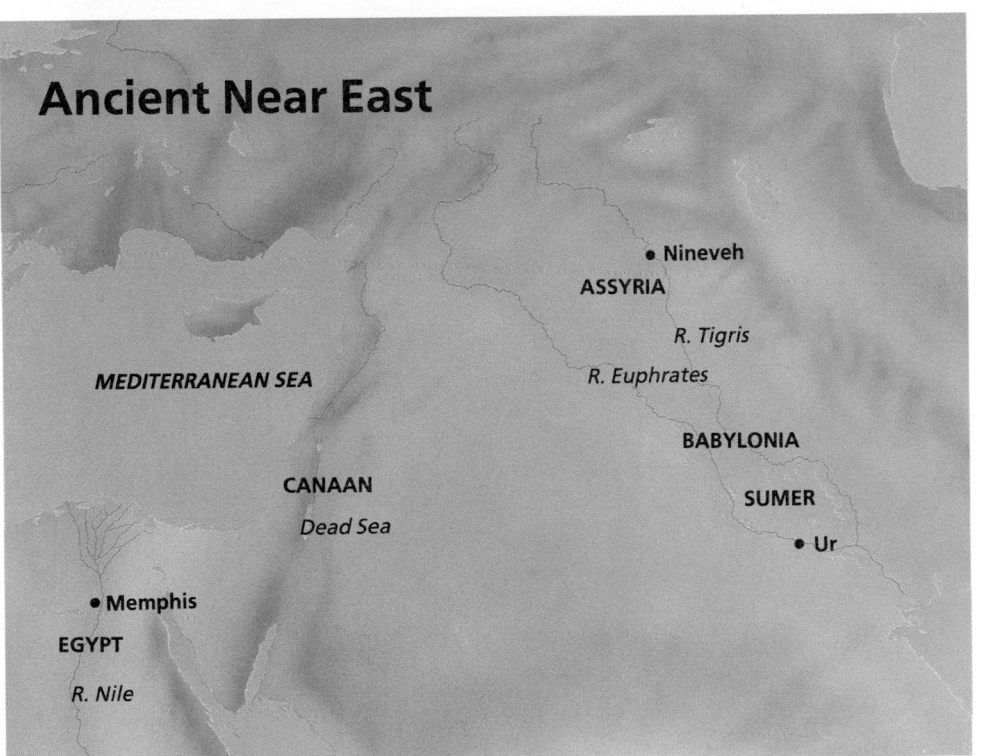

Ancient Near East

ill-treated by the wife (Genesis 16:6). When Sarah wanted Hagar and Ishmael to be sent away from the family home, Abraham was very uneasy, and he needed God's assurance that they were to go (Genesis 21:10–12).

Egyptian education

Because he was brought up by Pharaoh's daughter, "Moses was instructed in all the wisdom of the Egyptians" (Acts 7:22), and according to Jewish tradition this included arithmetic, geometry, poetry, music, astronomy, and many other subjects. Schools in Egypt were associated with the temples and were controlled by the priests. Medicine and religion were key subjects if the child was to become a priest.

Moses would have been brought up by the "teacher of the king's children" at the royal court and would have learned how to write Egyptian hieroglyphics with ink on papyrus. He most probably also learned the Canaanite script, because Canaan was linked with Egypt at the time. When Moses was told to teach the law to the people, it was

This clay tablet is typical of those used for writing in ancient times. It contains part of the Babylonian Chronicle, covering the fall of Nineveh.

effected by repetition and example (Deuteronomy 11:19), public reading (Deuteronomy 31:10–13), and the use of song writing (Deuteronomy 31:19). Since it was common in Egypt to sing lessons, this probably reflects the way that Moses was taught. It may be important to note that God called Moses to leadership from a strong educational background, just as Paul was called centuries later to lead the church.

Jewish education
When the Jewish people moved from the desert into Canaan, they did not have a sophisticated educational system. Such a system developed as their civilization developed, and it was influenced by the practices of the surrounding nations. Initially there-

fore, education was centred on the home. Education of both boys and girls was the mother's responsibility for the first three years (probably until weaning took place). She taught the girls their domestic duties throughout their childhood.

Boys were taught the law by their father from three years of age, and fathers were also responsible for teaching their sons a trade. A rabbi once said, "He who does not teach his son a useful trade is bringing him up to be a thief." Jesus was not just the carpenter's son (Matthew 13:55) but was also the carpenter (Mark 6:3). This explains why there were groups of linen workers and potters living in the same place (1 Chronicles 4:21–23). Girls were able to take on professional jobs such as midwifery (Exodus 1:15–21) and singing (Ecclesiastes 2:8).

Education was basically a religious education enabling children to understand the nature of God through what he had done and what he required in the law. Deuteronomy 6 is a key passage: the words of the shema (creed), "Hear O Israel: The Lord our God, the Lord is one. Love the Lord your God with all your heart and with all your soul and with all your strength," were to be taught, talked about, used in worship to declare symbolically that they were part of mind and action, and used as a reminder every time the house was entered or left (Deuteronomy 6:4–9; see Psalm 121:8). Children were stimulated to ask questions about festivals (Exodus 12:26; Deuteronomy 6:20–25) by facing them with unusual objects (Exodus 13:14–15; Joshua 4:6). In this way it became natural to teach them the acts of God.

As sacred shrines began to be a part of the lives of the Jewish people, the personnel who worked there probably began to provide some kind of formal education. Samuel was probably being taught by Eli the priest at Shiloh (1 Samuel 1:24). Samuel himself set up a school of the prophets at Ramah (1 Samuel 19:18–21), and some kind of theological schools developed from this (2 Kings 2:5–7; Isaiah 8:16). This is the origin of the practice of calling a priest "father." He exercised the role of the father in teaching the children (2 Kings 2:3, 12).

The writing of history was important at those centres. Although people still listened to the reading of the law (Deuteronomy 31:9–13) there were now

This inscription was found on the wall of Hezekiah's tunnel, at the point where the workmen tunneling from opposite directions met. It reads: "Behold the tunnel. This is the story of its cutting. While the miners swung their picks, one towards the other, and when there remained only three cubits to cut, the voice of one man calling was heard..."

a considerable number of people who could read and write. Judges 8:14 tells how a young man was able to write a list of names for Gideon. When Hezekiah had a water tunnel built under the city of Jerusalem, the workmen involved were able to write an inscription on the wall at the place where the tunnelers met. Writing was often done in ink on broken pieces of pottery (ostraca). Pens were made of hard cane, sharpened to a point (Jeremiah 17:1). The ink that was used was made from soot, resin, olive oil, and water.

Assyrian and Babylonian influences

It was the exile of the Jews into Assyria and Babylon that led to further developments in education. When they returned and their land became part of the Greek empire, there were still further developments. The Assyrian kings collected thousands of clay tablets into a library at Nineveh. They contain every kind of knowledge — botany, geometry, chemistry, astronomy, medicine, mathematics, law, religion — and give an indication of how far the Assyrian education system had developed. Daniel 1 tells how members of the Israelite hierarchy were educated in the Babylonian court. They were to learn the language for three years and then undertake an oral examination set by the king (Daniel 1:3–9, 19–20).

In order to preserve their identity as a nation it was necessary for the Jews in exile to become fully familiar with their own law. Therefore priestly and prophetic teachers seem to have taken this education in hand, and it continued when the Jews returned to their own land.

The scribes

When they returned, Ezra, a priest and a scribe (an interpreter of the law), had a commission from the Persian emperor to teach the Jewish people the law (Ezra 7:12–26). Everyone who returned stood to listen to the law all one morning (Nehemiah 8:1–8). The teachers then moved among the crowd explaining it to them. As a result the scribes became important in the community as teachers of the law. A scribe also wrote letters for people and could be recognized by the inkpot that was stuck into his belt (Ezekiel 9:2). These men were looked upon like the earlier prophets and were called "men of the great synagogue."

Entrance to the partially reconstructed synagogue at Chorazin, probably dating from the fourth century A.D.

The synagogue itself seems to have come into being during the Exile as people gathered together (literally, "synagogued") to learn the Torah and other sacred writings. When the Jews returned to their homeland they continued the practice of listening to the Scriptures being read and interpreted (see Luke 4:16–22). The buildings where this took place became centres of worship as well.

Some of the scribes differed in their interpretations of the law. The school of Hill'el tended to adopt a lenient interpretation of the law (a woman could be divorced for a minor fault, for example), but the school of Shammai took a stricter line. The teachings of the scribes were built up into large collections and were eventually written down in the Mishnah.

Greek culture

It was not long before the returned exiles came under the influence of Greek thought and culture under the alternate rule of their country by the Seleucids (in Syria) and the Egyptians. The wealthy and priestly families accepted the culture, using Greek language and literature and even allowing Greek games in Jerusalem. Like the Greeks they rejected traditional beliefs in angels, resurrection, and the providence of God, and they became known as Hellenists. There was a strong reaction against such views, particularly when the Greek games were introduced into the city. Some reacted so as to bring about a sense of national pride, but others, known as the Hasidim, were much more concerned to build a strong Jewish faith. Things climaxed when the Hellenists agreed to set up a Greek gymnasium (school) in Jerusalem in 175 BC, and many wealthy Jews sent their sons to receive a Greek form of education.

The Greek child went to school at the age of seven if his parents could afford to pay the fees. He studied basic skills (reading, writing, counting), music (poetry, dance, musical instrument), and physical skills (wrestling, boxing, running, throwing the javelin and discus; see 1 Corinthians 9:24–27). At sixteen, he went on to the gymnasium to study literature, philosophy, and politics.

Interested adults who lived locally were invited to the classes for discussion. Outstanding teachers set up their own schools in the city of Athens, and those who wished to do so went to the city to learn from them. This was under the general supervision of an education committee called the *Areopagus*. Paul used the Athenian system, setting up his own school in the city (Acts 17:16–34). He therefore had to give an account of himself to the Areopagus (Acts 17:22). In Ephesus he used the lecture hall of a teacher called Tyrannus as a preaching base (Acts 19:9–10).

The Pharisees

The Seleucid king responsible for the Greek school in Jerusalem was defeated in battle in 164 BC. The Hasidim, or Pharisees as they were beginning to be called, led by Simeon ben Shetah, insisted that from that time all Jewish boys should attend the "house of the book" for a Jewish education. It was to be led by a teacher who was paid for by the synagogue. Teachers had to be married men of good character. Higher education was available at a "house of study." Such a school was attached to the Jerusalem Temple, and it was here that Jesus was found when twelve years old (Luke 2:41–52).

Jesus would have gone to a house of the book at Nazareth when he was about six years old, sitting as part of a semicircle on the floor, facing the teacher. Much of the teaching was done by repetition, and the memorizing led to the common practice of reading aloud (see Acts 8:30). Writing was done in wax on a wooden tablet (Luke 1:63) or even on the ground (John 8:6). The only textbook was the Taanach: the Law, Prophets, and Writings that became the Christian Old Testament (2 Timothy 3:15).

The traditional law was taught from the age of ten to the age of fifteen, and Jewish law beyond that. The brightest of the boys, such as Paul, could go to Jerusalem to one of the law schools. They would sit at the feet of the great teachers (Acts 22:3) when they attended meetings of the Sanhedrin, the ruling council of the Jews. Not until A.D. 65 was school made compulsory for all boys. The high priest Gamala ordered that boys six years old and above in every town should attend school; too many boys had been engaging in truancy under the voluntary system. The early Christian community was too poor to provide schools for its children.

Young Jewish boys at the house of the book. Notice the scrolls on the low table in front of the teacher.

Now look at your Bible

Sweeter than honey

Psalm 19:9–10. When a boy first went to school in New Testament times, he went down to the synagogue while it was still dark to listen to the story of how Moses received the law. Then he was taken to the teacher's house for breakfast, where he received cakes with letters of the law written on them. In school, the boy received a slate with passages from the Scriptures written on it. The slate was smeared with honey. He had to trace the letters through the honey with his pen, and it was natural to lick the nib of the pen as he proceeded. The idea was that he would realize that the purpose of his going to school was to absorb the Scriptures. This learning practice seems to have been based on an old custom that David refers to in the psalm.

Teaching by rote

Isaiah 28:9–10. Here the people are complaining about the way the prophet is teaching them, for it is "do and do ... rule on rule ... a little here, a little there." It literally means, "s after s, q after q" and refers to the method of teaching by repetition. The master would say an *s*, and the scholars would have to repeat it.

"Schoolmaster"?

Galatians 3:24 (KJV). The "schoolmaster" of this passage is not the teacher, but the slave whose job it was to take his master's sons to school and to stop them from getting into mischief. Paul says that Jesus is the real teacher; the Jewish law was simply the slave that took the pupils safely to school.

Earning a Living:

Agriculture

When the Jewish people entered Canaan and took up agriculture after the seminomadic life of forty years in the wilderness, they were entering into work that went back in their own history for hundreds of years and into a country that was extremely rich in plants. Ur of the Chaldees, where Abraham had come from, was sustained by a healthy agricultural system based on irrigation ditches from the river bank, stone ploughshares, and flint sickles. With this technology the Chaldeans grew two crops each season.

Agriculture was also a feature of Egypt. Each year the river Nile overflowed its banks, and the land was

Even today farmers irrigate their lands by lifting water from the Nile by means of a shadoof or sweep device.

The Gezer Calendar – a schoolboy's exercise inscribed on a tablet and giving an account of the farmer's work throughout the year.

covered with fine river-borne silt that enriched the soil for the year. In the dry season, irrigation was used. Water was lifted from the Nile into ditches by a shadoof (sweep device) and directed by blocking off particular ditches with a system of mud walls that could be broken down again.

Canaanite agriculture

There was no such regularity or certainty in Canaan; there the success of agriculture depended not on the rise of great rivers but on the winter rains, which varied from year to year, and on the conservation of water. Moses warned the Jewish people that the climate was uncertain and that their security was in God, who would provide the annual rainfall (Deuteronomy 11:10–15). So uncertain was the rainfall that the Canaanite religion was based on a form of sympathetic magic that ensured fertility for the soil. Baal was a storm god (see Deuteronomy 11:16–17).

Capricious water supplies were not the only things that made Canaanite agriculture uncertain.

The hot desert winds from the southeast scorched everything that grew (Jonah 4:8; Luke 12:55). Another serious problem was the locust — a large variety of grasshopper that swarmed in millions (see Judges 6:5; 7:12) and ate everything green in its path. There is a terrible description of a plague of locusts in Joel 2. It was a plague of locusts that attacked Egypt as one stimulus to "let my people go" (Exodus 10:13–15). When the locusts arrived they seemed to be like an all-avenging army (Proverbs 30:27), although they stayed put on a cold day (Nahum 3:17). Erosion was another problem. The winter rains tended to wash the covering of soil down from the hills. Retaining walls had to be built.

Farming began when it dawned on early man that instead of gathering wild grains and vegetables, it was possible to collect the seeds and to sow them in one place. The first sites used to grow crops were the places where the wild varieties grew — in well-watered and drained spots with adequate warmth and suitable soil. It was only with the development of farm implements and irrigation techniques that agriculture began to advance.

The Gezer Calendar

By the time the Jewish people dispossessed the Canaanites there were a considerable number of crops. A boy from those days wrote an exercise of the "thirty days hath September" variety, and it has been discovered in Gezer. It tells what was being done through the year in agriculture:

The two months are olive harvest	(Sept./Oct.)
The two months are planting grain	(Nov./Dec.)
The two months are late planting	(Jan./Feb.)
The month is hoeing up of flax	(March)
The month is barley harvest	(April)
The month is harvest and festivity	(May)
The two months are vine tending	(June/July)
The month is summer fruit	(August)

(The planting in January and February was millet, peas, lentils, melons, and cucumbers.)

With the ownership of sheep, and perhaps some cattle, each on his own land, the farmer's system could be called self-sufficient mixed farming. This changed in the early days of the Hebrew monarchy, as land was accumulated by the nobles at the expense of the original farmers. A system of royal tenants developed, and stewards were appointed to be in charge of vineyards, olive groves, granaries, and cattle raising (1 Samuel 8:14). There were protests against this development from the prophets (Isaiah 5:8), and Nehemiah forced a return of property to the original owners (Nehemiah 5) — a situation that remained until the conquest of the country by the armies of Greece and Rome, when it was possible to amass land again (Luke 12:18–19).

Using the ancient schoolboy's calendar exercise we will now look at some of the things that were grown.

Grain crops

The two most important grains were wheat and barley, but millet was grown as well (Ezekiel 4:9). Wheat grew in the coastal Philistine plain, the Jordan valley, and the valley of Jezreel. Barley could be grown on poorer soil and needed a shorter growing season, and it was less valued as a crop than wheat (Psalm 81:16).

The cycle of grain production began when the former rains came in October/November and softened the soil sufficiently for it to be worked. The rains then continued intermittently and heavily throughout the winter. Joel calls them "the autumn rains" and the "spring rains" (Joel 2:23). Without rain the plough could not be used because the soil would be baked hard in the summer sun (Jeremiah 14:4). It was not pleasant work because the winter rains were heavy and cold, and it was always tempting to wait for warmer days (Proverbs 20:4).

Ploughing

Ploughing and sowing were often one operation. The grain was scattered from an open basket and replenished from a sack tied on the back of a donkey. It took about thirty pounds of seed to the half acre, although the Babylonians had invented a primitive seed drill that was in use in some places and was more economical with the seed. The seed was then

A bedouin farmer uses a donkey to pull his plough.

ploughed in so that it would not be taken by the birds (Matthew 13:4). This method of sowing underlies the parable of the sower in Matthew 13, where there was a hard path and thorns awaiting the plough.

The plough itself was made of two wooden beams, jointed T-fashion. The horizontal stroke of the T formed the handle for guidance, and the spiked end was to break the surface of the ground. The vertical section of the T was attached to the yoke that went over the necks of the animals. The yoke itself was simply a rough beam tied across the necks of a pair of animals and held in place by two vertical sticks that came down each side of the neck and tied beneath (see Jeremiah 28:13).

The animals used were oxen if possible, and if a bull was used it was castrated. The law forbade a mixture of animals such as ox and donkey (Deuteronomy 22:10), presumably because there would be an unequal pull that would cause suffering for the weaker animal. The regulation prohibiting partnership between believers and unbelievers in 2 Corinthians 6:14 ("Do not be yoked together with

A farmer of Bible times ploughs with a team of two oxen. Notice the blade of the plough, and the farmer's sharp goad.

unbelievers") was not simply exclusivist; it was made out of the knowledge of the suffering that could be caused.

The amount of land that a pair of oxen could plough in a day became a standard measurement (1 Samuel 14:14; Isaiah 5:10). In the early days of agriculture, the sharp end of the plough was little more than a heavy pointed stick. A great advance was made when copper was able to be smelted and a copper sheath or blade attached to the spike. An even greater advance was made when the Philistines brought iron to the land, even if this meant the Jews had to get their ploughshares sharpened by the Philistines (1 Samuel 13:20).

Ploughs

The early ploughs were light. Although they were portable and could be carried for some distance on the shoulder, they could scratch the surface of the ground to a depth of only three or four inches (70–100 millimetres). The reason the ploughman must not look back (Luke 9:62) was not because he would fail to plough in a straight line. Rather it was because he needed all his concentration so that he might push down hard and dig deep enough into the ground. He had to watch for stones and boulders, too, since they could wreck so light a tool, although the lightness did mean that he could lift the plough over the obstacle.

Ploughing was sometimes done in a team, each farmer contributing his own plough and oxen until the fields of the whole village were covered. Elisha was ploughing with eleven other people and twenty-four oxen when he was called to his prophetic ministry (1 Kings 19:19).

A mattock from the time of Christ. The hand-held mattock was used to break up the soil in places the plough could not reach. It would be fixed onto a long handle.

Ploughs could not be used on the hillside, near trees, or on exceptionally hard land. In such cases a mattock was used — a hand tool like a hoe, with a blade set at right angles to the shaft (Isaiah 7:25). There was an alternative method of sowing and ploughing where the ground would be ploughed first and sown afterwards. This would require a further ploughing at right angles to the first, or else a harrowing by pulling a large bush behind a team of oxen.

If the oxen were unwilling to move or were too slow for the farmer, he would encourage them to move by prodding them with a sharp pointed stick, or goad. It was heavy enough to be used as an effective weapon (Judges 3:31). Jesus used a symbolic goad to push Paul forward to the point of conversion. "It is hard for you to kick against the goads," he said (Acts 26:14).

The wheat (often called "corn" in the King James Version of the Bible) was sown first, then the barley, and the other crops followed — millet, lentils, peas, melons, and cucumbers. It was necessary to keep the ground free of weeds by hoeing from December until February. This was a time when, except in the hill country, movement from place to place was impossible because the rains turned the plains into a muddy morass. Then, as the temperature began to rise at the end of March and the beginning of April, the spring rains came (see Joel 2:23 again). These rains caused the grain to swell, and by the end of April the barley was ready for harvesting.

Harvest fields were divided by paths and it was permitted to pick the ears of the growing corn beside the path. This was particularly enjoyed in the spring before the grain had hardened. The twelve disciples who were with Jesus ate the ripening grain one Sabbath day (Luke 6:1–2). They were not criticized for taking the grain because this was allowed in the law (Deuteronomy 23:25). It was thought by some people, however, that even picking the grain could be considered "working" on the Sabbath.

Harvesting

The flax was harvested in March and April by cutting the stems with a hoe at ground level. As soon as that was completed the barley was ready for harvesting. The standing grain was cut by sickle — a hand-held crescent shaped tool with a sharp inner

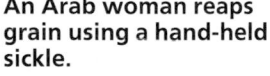

An Arab woman reaps grain using a hand-held sickle.

Threshing grain using a sledge drawn by two oxen.

cutting edge. In early times the implement would be made of wood or even the large jawbone of an animal, and flints would be set along the inner edge. Later in time, metal sickles were available (Jeremiah 50:16; Joel 3:13).

The stalks were cut near to the top and the remainder left in the ground for the grazing of the sheep (see p. 134). They were tied into bundles (Genesis 37:7 and Psalm 129:7) and loaded onto the backs of donkeys (Genesis 42:26–27) or put into a cart to be taken away for threshing. Occasionally the grain would be pulled out of the ground. The ground was normally cut by a group of people working together, but the corners of the fields had to be left for the poor (Leviticus 23:22). The poor were also allowed to walk behind the reapers to pick up or "glean" anything the reapers had missed (Deuteronomy 24:19–22). The story of Ruth is set against such a background. She was able to fill the large skirt of her robe with what she had collected (Ruth 2).

The grain was tinder dry at the time of reaping, and there was danger of fire (see Exodus 22:6). That danger was often exploited by enemies in war in the knowledge that such burning would seriously weaken the condition of the people who owned the crops (see Judges 6:1–6; 15:4–5).

Threshing

The separation of the grain from the straw was done on a threshing floor. This could be any hard, compacted surface. It may have been made of smoothed rock (as, presumably, was the threshing floor of Araunah the Jebusite, 1 Chronicles 21:18–26) or of compacted earth. The earthen threshing floors were often covered with grass and became an ideal place to pitch a tent. They were known as "summer threshing floors."

Threshing was sometimes done by beating the grain with a flail (a long, flexible stick) if small quantities were involved. Ruth used this method (Ruth 2:17), and Gideon did the same when he was using the stone bottom of a winepress (Judges 6:11). The psalmist imagines doing this to his enemies (Psalm 18:42).

Oxen were the other means of threshing grain. A pair was yoked together and the yoke attached to a vertical pole set in the middle of the threshing floor. They were driven round and round by a boy, and their sharp hooves did the rest. The law said that the oxen should not be muzzled when doing this kind of work so that they could eat (Deuteronomy 25:4), and the New Testament uses this to lay down the principle that ministers of the gospel should always be able to live from their ministry (1 Corinthians 9:7–9; 1 Timothy 5:18). The root meaning of the Hebrew word for "thresh" is "to trample," which comes from this second threshing practice (Job 39:15; Daniel 7:23).

At a later stage the threshing sledge was invented, which the oxen pulled behind them rather as they would have pulled a plough. Sledges were made of long planks of wood fixed side by side. Flints were sunk into the underside of the timber and fixed there by pitch. The sledge was driven over grain about eighteen inches (fifty centimetres) in depth and was a much quicker way of getting the job done. The grain fell through the straw to the hard surface beneath, but the straw was chopped up by this method. Chopped straw made excellent fodder for animals, for mixing with the grain. Later still a more sophisticated sledge was invented in which sets of toothed rollers replaced the flints.

Winnowing

In the evening, when the breeze developed, the separated grain and straw was gathered into a pile in the centre of the threshing floor for winnowing. For this the farmer used a five-pronged fork called a winnowing fan and a spade that was called a winnowing shovel. The fork was first used by putting it into the pile and throwing the mixture of grain and straw into the air. The heavier grain fell back, while the straw was blown away by the wind. When the remainder was too small to be picked up by the fork, the shovel was used for the same purpose. If there was no wind it was possible, while winnowing small quantities, to create wind by wafting a piece of matting. The chaff was gathered up and used to fire the domestic stoves; the straw was collected for the animals.

A wooden fork of this kind was used in Bible times for winnowing grain.

A peasant winnows grain. Notice that the laborer in the background has "girded up his loins."

A peasant sifts grain in a large sieve.

The grain then had to be purified by sifting. The wheat and barley grains were mixed with all kinds of loose frgaments from the threshing floor. Everything was put into large sieves that allowed the grain to pass through but left most of the rubbish behind. It was also necessary to remove any darnel grains at this stage. Darnel was called "tares" or "weeds" in the New Testament. It looks identical to wheat until the grain ripens, when it becomes black instead of yellow (see Matthew 13:24–30). The grains are bitter and cause dizziness and sickness if eaten.

The picture of the separation of good and bad was used as a picture of what God will do to judge people (Psalm 1:4; Jeremiah 15:7). The whole process was used by John the Baptist to illustrate the work of Jesus (Matthew 3:12). When Jesus said that Satan wanted to sift Peter like wheat (Luke 22:31), he was probably referring to the physical shaking of the sieve. When this part of the work was done, the farmer normally stayed with the grain at night, camping out on the threshing floor to ensure that the harvest was not stolen (Ruth 3).

Storage
The following day the grain would be measured into standard earthenware receptacles that took their names from their capacity. As much as possible was put into a receptacle, until it overflowed (Luke 6:38). The grain was then stored — small quantities in earthenware jars and larger quantities in a dry pit or cistern, in a room attached to the house, or even in a barn (Deuteronomy 28:8; Proverbs 3:10; Matthew 13:30; Luke 12:18). There were also public storage granaries (Genesis 41:48), and public grain silos.

There were a number of ways of keeping pests away. The storehouses were built of brick with thick walls, and the only way in was through a hole on the top of the building. The insides of the walls were

Grain was stored in earthenware receptacles to keep it dry.

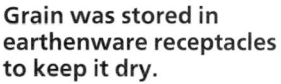

plastered. Such storehouses were used to provide a central place to receive the offerings that supported the ministry. One tenth of the produce of the land (fruit and crops) had to be offered (Leviticus 27:30–32; Deuteronomy 14:22–29).

We are not aware of fertilizer's being used for grain crops, although animal manure was sometimes used in other places. The land was instead given a rest every seventh or sabbath year (Leviticus 25:1–7). God promised a bumper harvest in the sixth year to enable people to live through the seventh (Leviticus 25:18–22). Whatever grew in the seventh year was the property of the poor (Exodus 23:10–11). This law was not kept in the early days of the kingdom and the Chronicler saw the Exile as the means of giving the land its stolen sabbath rests (2 Chronicles 36:21). After the Exile Nehemiah attempted to restore the practice of resting the land (Nehemiah 10:31), and it was in operation during the Greek period. In 163/162 BC, the Jews lacked provisions "for it was a sabbath year granted to the land" (1 Maccabees 6:49, 53).

Terraced vineyards near Hebron, Israel.

Pods of the carob tree. The carob beans were eaten by cattle and by the poorest people. (See also p. 56.)

Vegetables and other crops

Flax was grown to provide linen thread. The spies who visited Jericho in Joshua's time hid under flax stalks that were laid out to dry on the roof of a house (Joshua 2:6). Linen thread was used for spinning (Proverbs 31:13), but Isaiah disliked the "linen garments" that were often produced because their transparency led to sexual stimulation (see Isaiah 3:16–24, esp. v. 23). Cucumbers, melons, leeks, onions, and garlic were probably brought from Egypt (Numbers 11:5), and many crops were grown so that their green leaves could be eaten (mallow, sorrel, and artichokes). Beans and lentils were used to thicken stews (Genesis 25:34).

Vines

According to Genesis 9:20, Noah was the first person to cultivate the vine after the Flood. At the personal level, every Jew wanted to have his own vine. It would be grown on a trellis alongside his house and would provide shade during the hot summer (1 Kings 4:25). Having a vine was part of a settled life and therefore rejected by the Rechabites who wanted to bear witness to the nomadic way of life (Jeremiah 35).

It was most economical for a village to invest in its

A makeshift shelter built of branches, leaves and sacking, used by a farmer to keep watch over his land.

own vineyard. In good vine-growing country, however, the small vineyards were bought up by absentee landlords, and the small-time farmers became tenant farmers, receiving a percentage of their produce as payment (1 Kings 21:6; Matthew 20:1; Luke 20:9–10). The development of the vineyard therefore became a major capital undertaking. It was already well developed when Moses sent spies into Canaan (Numbers 13:23).

Building a vineyard

Isaiah 5:1–2 outlines the process of building a vineyard:

> My loved one had a vineyard on
> a fertile hillside.
> He dug it up and cleared it of stones
> and planted it with the choicest vines.
> He built a watchtower in it
> and cut out a winepress as well.

(See also Matthew 21:33.) The vineyard was placed on the hillside where there was good drainage and where the grapes could catch the sun. The land was first terraced so as to use up the stones that littered the soil, at the same time providing a means of soil conservation during the heavy rains. The plot was then surrounded by a wall and a ditch, the excavated soil from the ditch forming the foundation for the wall. A fence of thorns was placed on top of the wall to keep out any damaging wild animals (Proverbs 24:30–31; Song of Songs 2:15). Psalm 80:12–13 mentions human beings who might raid the vineyard to steal the fruit, although the law allowed grapes to be picked so long as they were not carried away in a container (Leviticus 19:10; Deuteronomy 23:24). The soil was prepared by turning it over with a mattock (Isaiah 5:2).

Finally, a watchtower was constructed that served as a summer cottage, a place for the family to stay during the summer while the grapes were being picked. It was not a cheap thing to build. Jesus once told a story of a man whose money ran out during the building of a tower (Luke 14:28–30). The upper story of the tower was used as a look-out post (Isaiah 5:2). If the owner could not afford a tower, the workers set up a tent.

The slips were planted up to about twelve feet apart to give the branches room to run. If the vineyard was on flat ground there was sufficient space to get a plough between the rows. Some varieties were left to run on the ground, but others were supported

Crumbling watchtower in fields near Samaria.

An Arab woman picks grapes.

on rough trellises of forked sticks. Once the vines were established, pruning was done with a small pruning hook (Joel 3:10) during the winter months to get rid of weak, broken, or diseased branches so that the vine would produce the best possible grapes. This process was referred to as "cleaning the vine." We are being pruned, or made clean, by the teaching that Jesus has given to us (John 15:3). Good branches that are not doing very well are taken away (John 15:2) from the ground and put into a better position more favourable for producing good fruit.

The vintage

The vintage begins in July but lasts until September. The whole village may move to the vineyards (as in Judges 9:27) because the work has to be completed quickly. Harvesting grapes was hard work during Bible times, but there was singing, dancing, and celebration. The celebrations were so much a part of the vintage that if they were absent, it would be seen as a mark of God's judgment (Isaiah 16:10). Everyone brought huge baskets (Jeremiah 6:9) in which

Overhead vines near Hebron.

the grapes were placed. Some grapes were eaten fresh or pressed to provide fresh grape juice. The butler in Joseph's dream-interpretation pressed a bunch of grapes into Pharaoh's cup (Genesis 40:11). Fresh grape juice was used for laxative purposes. Some of the juice was also made into wine, known as "sweet wine" (Hosea 4:11).

Other grapes were dried so as to provide raisins. They were laid out in a corner of the vineyard, turned daily, and sprinked with olive oil. David received large quantities of raisins on a number of occasions (1 Samuel 25:18; 2 Samuel 16:1; 1 Chronicles 12:40) because they were a staple food. There were far too many grapes to all be utilized in raisin making. Most were pressed for their juice.

The winepress

The winepress was a cistern cut out of rock with an exit hole in the bottom. The juice ran out of the hole into a vat or other collecting vessels. Several people at once would get into the cistern and tread the grapes with their feet to great laughter and enjoyment. The first part of Isaiah 65:8: "As when juice is still found in a cluster of grapes and men say, 'Don't destroy it, there is yet some good in it'" may be part of one of the songs that were sung during the process. Like Isaiah, Jeremiah sees judgment in the time when there is no joy or singing as the grapes are pressed (Jeremiah 48:33). Isaiah presents a sad picture of a man who was treading grapes alone because all of his companions had gone (Isaiah 63:3). An even more violent picture of judgment is given when people are placed in God's winepress and trodden upon. God's robes are covered with blood instead of the red grape juice (Isaiah 63:3–6; Revelation 19:13, 15).

Some grape juice was boiled down to make a thick syrup called *dibs*. This may well be what is called *honey* in most places in the Bible. That is because bees were not kept in hives until Roman times.

The top of this Roman lamp shows two men treading grapes.

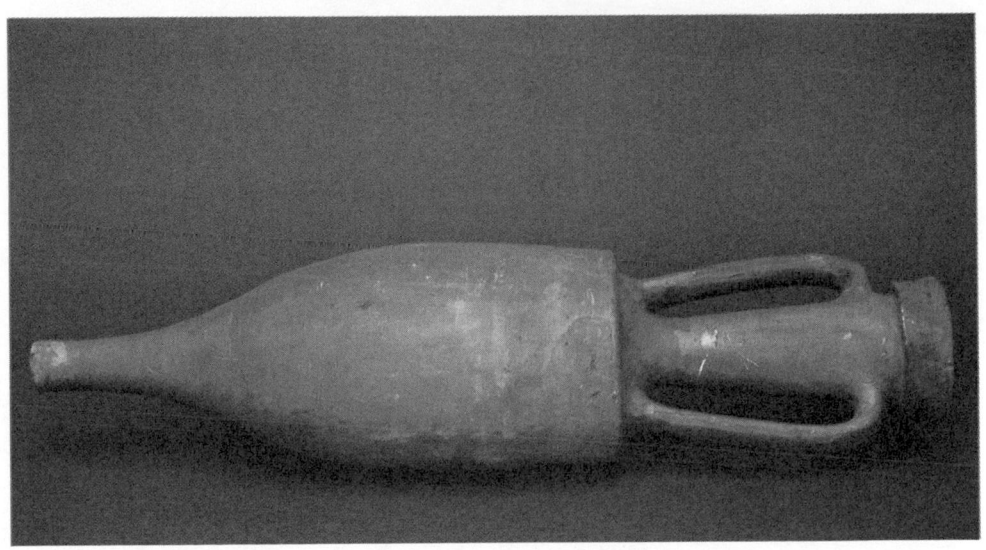

Roman jar, or *amphora*, used for storing wine.

Regular honey was taken from wild bees (see p. 52). The honey that "flowed" in the land is therefore more likely to be related to the grape. It is sometimes spread on bread and sometimes diluted with water to make a drink.

Most of the grape juice was made into wine. This was done not simply for pleasure; it was a necessity. The water was unsafe for drinking unless it came from a fresh spring, and the milk supply was limited. When Paul told Timothy that he should drink a little wine for his stomach's sake, it was not necessarily because the wine would do his stomach good, but because the water might do it harm (1 Timothy 5:23, KJV).

Wine-making

The grape juice was allowed to stand and ferment in the collecting vessels for about six weeks. A sludge known as *lees* formed at the bottom of the vessel. The wine was then tipped up gently into jars without disturbing the sediment (see Jeremiah 48:11). The jars were sealed with clay, but there was a small hole by the handle that allowed the gases released during the remaining fermentation to escape. When the process was complete, the hole was sealed with a blob of wet clay and the owner's name or seal was put on the clay. It was possible to put the wine in wineskins (goatskin bottles), but if the aged skin did not expand to take the gases, then it would burst

**Egyptain woman washing
out a wineskin in the river.**

and the wine would be lost. This is the point of Jesus' illustration in Matthew 9:17.

In New Testament times, wines were imported into Judaea from all over the Mediterranean world. The rich had cellars in their houses and stored the wine in narrow jars with pointed ends called *amphorae*. The pointed ends were buried in the earth to help keep the wine cool. Wine was also made from dates, pomegranates, apples, and grain. The wine made from the grain is probably referred to as "fermented drink" in the Bible (Leviticus 10:9; Isaiah 56:12).

There were a number of uses for wine beside the obvious. It was used as a disinfectant to clean wounds before inserting the healing olive oil (Luke 10:34). The cheap wine (the soldiers' wine), produced before the fermentation was completed in the clay storage jars, was mixed with myrrh or gall so as to relieve pain (Matthew 27:34).

Vine symbolism

The vine was of great importance in the religion of Israel. It was used as a symbol of the religious life of Israel itself, and a carving of a bunch of grapes often adorned the front exterior of the synagogue. The symbolism was based upon passages such as Psalm 80 and Isaiah 5:1–5 where Israel is God's vine. The importance of the vine is why the Pharisees took the point so angrily when Jesus told the story of the wicked tenants in the vineyard (Matthew 21:33–41, 45–46). As the fulfilment of all that Israel should be to God, Jesus was the true vine (John 15:5–7).

The vine was also important because it brought out teaching about right and wrong usage. Wine was one of the good things that God gave (Genesis 27:28; Judges 9:13) and as such was to be offered back to him in thanksgiving (Exodus 29:40). If a farmer lived too far from the central sanctuary to

Carving of a bunch of grapes from the masonry of the synagogue at Capernaum.

deliver the wine tithe, it was to be sold and used to buy something to thank God for (Deuteronomy 14:22–26).

Wine was however to be abstained from for disciplinary purposes. A Nazirite took no fruit of the vine at all (Numbers 6:3). John the Baptist took no wine (Luke 1:15), and it was forbidden for priests (Leviticus 10:5–9) when they went into the presence of God. Wine could be used for good (Genesis 14:18; Psalm 104:15; Ecclesiastes 10:19) or for evil (Genesis 9:21; Isaiah 5:11; 28:7). It was merely the behavioural excesses associated with wine drinking that were condemned in the Bible and not the drinking of wine itself (Romans 13:13; 1 Corinthians 11:21; 1 Timothy 3:8; Titus 2:3).

Olive growing
Olive trees were associated with vines; they too were a vital element of the food supply. Psalm 128:3

Gnarled olive tree in the Garden of Gethsemane, Jerusalem.

speaks of God's blessing on families that trust him: "Your wife will be like a fruitful vine within your house; your sons will be like olive shoots around your table." The family olive tree could be grown beside the family home on the inheritance, but with the passage of time olive groves were planted alongside the vineyards and the grainfields, when the oil was used to pay taxes. Olives grew so well that the land was sometimes called "a land of olive...oil" (Deuteronomy 8:8).

Olive trees were grown by inserting a graft from a cultivated tree into a wild stock. The wild stock was then cut down to the ground. The roots of the tree go down very deeply into the rocky soil, and this fact may lie behind Deuteronomy 32:13 that refers to oil being sucked from the flinty rock. The tree takes about fifteen years to grow to maturity, and then it bears fruit for centuries. The old roots often throw up new stems, which gave the prophet the picture of the stump of Jesse that throws up the Messiah (Isaiah 11:1). The new shoots were grafted into stocks. Paul says that when Christianity followed the Judaism of the Old Testament, then it was as if, contrary to normal practice, a wild olive were being grafted onto a cultivated stock (Romans 11:24).

The olive tree

The olive tree is not attractive in itself. It is about eighteen feet (six metres) high when fully grown. The bark is gnarled, and the leaves have a dull green coloration. But they take on a silvery sheen in the sunshine, which probably made the tree appear beautiful to people of Bible times (Psalm 52:8; Jeremiah 11:16; Hosea 14:6). The tree is covered with white blossoms in the spring, and the falling blossoms look like a shower of snowflakes (Job 15:33).

The fruit is ready for picking by women and boys in September/October. A large cloth is laid under the tree, and the branches are beaten to shake the olives onto the cloth. In Old Testament times those that did not fall had to be left on the tree for the poor to gather (Deuteronomy 24:20; Isaiah 17:6). The beating of the branches almost certainly destroyed the tender young shoots, so that there was a poor crop the following year. This resulted in alternate good and bad years for the crop.

A farmer pushes round the stone wheel on his olive press. Sometimes this work would be done by a donkey.

The olive press

Many olives were eaten with barley bread and constituted the normal breakfast for the working man. Preservation was made possible by immersing the olives in salt water. The main importance of the crop, however, was its oil. The olive press consisted of a flat, cylindrical stone that was hollowed out on the top to provide a large, shallow saucer to contain

the olives. Another stone wheel was set up on edge, and, aided by a donkey, it was rotated round the saucer, crushing the olives beneath it. The resultant pulp was then treated to extract the oil.

One method of obtaining oil was by putting the pulp in baskets, one on top of the other, and squeezing them together in a press, either by operation of a screw thread or by a wooden beam that was levered down while thrusting against a wooden frame. Another method was to put the pulped olives into cloth bags that were then trodden underfoot. The oil came through the cloth. The oil released was drained into jars and allowed to stand until the sediment had settled. Then it was drawn off and stored in a cool place. The crop from just one tree would produce about twenty gallons of oil. Gethsemane on the Mount of Olives means "the oil press" because there must have been a press there. It was possible to tread the olives like grapes in the press, but because olives were so much harder than grapes, little oil was produced this way (Micah 6:15).

This type of olive press used a screwthread to lower a beam onto the basket of olives to crush them.

Olive oil

Olive oil took the place of butter and cooking fat and so was crucial for diet (Ezekiel 16:13). It therefore formed part of the meal offering (Leviticus 2:1). It was used as fuel for lamps (Matthew 25:3, 4), and when boiled with soda it formed soap. Oil was used for rubbing into the skin to give it a shine and for anointing the head to make the hair shine, too.

The beauty brought about by the oil may underlie the use of it in religious life, because those objects consecrated to God's service were anointed with oil. Prophet (1 Kings 19:16), priest (Leviticus 8:12) and king (1 Samuel 16:13; 1 Kings 1:34) were all anointed with oil because they were separated, or consecrated, for the service of God. Ritual use was so important that it was an offense leading to excommunication to use holy anointing oil for a common purpose (Exodus 30:32–33), and a person who had received such an anointing was to be obeyed (1 Samuel 24:6). The prophet spoke to the people from God, the priest represented the people before God, and the king established God's law.

The word for "anoint" is *Maseiah*, and the Messiah is therefore "the anointed one." Jesus gathered up into himself the triple function of prophet, priest, and king. Much symbolism is involved in this. Oil seems to have been recognized as the gift of God; an olive tree growing in a rocky place will yield an abundance of oil. Oil is therefore associated with God's gift and with God's outpouring of the Spirit. Jesus said that the Spirit of God was upon him because the Lord had anointed him (Isaiah 61:1; Luke 4:16–21).

A person was consecrated to God by anointing because it was believed that the oil itself was from God and because oil on the skin and on the hair made persons look their best. Christians too receive an anointing (1 John 2:27), which must also be the Holy Spirit because it results in learning God's truth (John 14:26).

Oil was also used for healing. When the Good Samaritan helped the man who had been mugged on the road from Jerusalem to Jericho, he poured in oil and wine. This medicinal property might lie behind the use of oil in divine healing. Early Christians were told to anoint the sick person with oil and to pray (James 5:13–16). Other people believe that the anointing was a means of consecrating, or giving, the sick person into God's care. Mark 6:13 tells us that when the Twelve went out on a two-by-two ministry, they took oil for healing.

The wood of the olive tree is used for small pieces of cabinet work and for woodcarving. The gnarled state of the trunk makes it impossible to get beams. The wood is attractive, with dark grain against a yellowish background. The cherubim of the Temple were made of olive wood together with the inner and outer doors.

Shields were oiled (2 Samuel 1:21) to keep the leather from cracking. This had the same function as leather preservative or shoe polish.

Fig trees

Fig trees were valued for their fruit and for their shade. Like the vine, fig trees became a symbol of security and of prosperity (1 Kings 4:25; Micah 4:4; Zechariah 3:10). When Jesus first met Nathanael, he was sitting under his fig tree (John 1:48). They grew wild, and in the wild state the female fig blossoms had to be pollinated by a wasp that developed inside the inedible caprifigs, which grew several times a year. When the fig tree was cultivated over a period of time (see Luke 13:6–9), it did not need the insect pollination. The cultivated tree was often planted in a vineyard (Luke 13). If the tree was allowed to grow to its full height it could reach thirty feet (ten metres), but if it was on rocky soil or was cut

A fig tree at Banias, northern Israel.

back regularly it could be limited to a bush.

The leaves of the fig tree were large enough to serve as coverings for Adam and Eve (Genesis 3:7). The leaves developed at the end of spring, at the end of April, and were therefore a sign that summer was approaching (Matthew 24:32). Fruit could be found on the tree for about ten months of the year. The first-ripe figs (Hosea 9:10) were ready in June, but the main crop matured in August. There was then a small crop of winter figs that often remained until the spring. The figs could be eaten fresh or pressed into a cake and preserved by drying (1 Samuel 25:18; 1 Chronicles 12:40). It was in this form that Hezekiah used the figs as a poultice (2 Kings 20:7).

The sycamore tree

Another form of fruit tree, similar to the fig, was called the sycamore tree. In David's time sycamores were numerous enough for him to appoint an overseer to look after them (1 Chronicles 27:28). It was from such a tree that Zacchaeus heard Jesus tell him to come down so that they could have a meal together (Luke 19:1–4). Again, the tree was about thirty feet (ten metres) in height and was grown for its timber, which was light and long-lasting, as well as for its fruit. Young trees were cut back to stimulate the growth of timber in multiple stands, and they were cut back after seven years.

The Mishna allowed a man who rented a field with a sycamore tree in it to cut the limbs only in the first year of a seven-year lease. The economic importance of the tree was so great that when the Egyptians lost their trees through frost, it was a disaster (Psalm 78:47). Amos was a dresser of sycamore fruit as well as a herdsman (shepherd; Amos 7:14–15). Sycamore fruit needed to be pierced and wiped with oil if it was to become ripe and juicy. The owner of a sycamore plantation would allow a shepherd to graze his sheep under the trees in return for the shepherd's undertaking this monotonous job.

Now look at your Bible

A perfect sacrifice
Numbers 19:2. The law said that oxen could be sacrificed only if they had not been yoked. This is because a bull that had been ploughing had been castrated and would therefore be imperfect for sacrifice.

Swords into ploughshares
Joel 3:10. Joel speaks of people preparing for war who beat their ploughs into swords and their pruninghooks into spears. Isaiah 2:4 and Micah 4:3 speak of peace where people beat their swords into ploughshares and their spears into pruninghooks. Metal was so scarce at the time that there was a need for change of use.

Life-cycle of fig trees
Song of Songs 2:13; Jeremiah 24:2; 29:17; Matthew 21:18. It is not easy to relate the biblical references to the life cycle of the fig tree. The reference in the Song of Songs is probably to the first-ripe figs because they are ready at the time that the vines are in blossom. The bad figs seen by Jeremiah may be the inedible male caprifigs, which house the fig wasps while they develop. Jesus may have been looking either for remaining winter figs or for the first-ripe figs. Whichever was missing indicated that the tree was infertile and would not give a main crop at "the time of figs." Jesus confirmed its uselessness by causing its death.

Earning a Living:
Collecting Food

Early man, who lived in caves, hunted or caught his food. It was only at the first agricultural revolution, when it was realized that grain seeds could be sown in one place and the crop harvested, that settlement began. It was necessary to live by the fields, and the best fields were not always beside cave dwellings. Later there was relatively little hunting, although Nimrod (Genesis 10:9) and Esau (Genesis 27:5) were both hunters. Isaac told Esau to take his weapons, his quiver, and his bow and go out into the fields to take venison (Genesis 27:3).

When the Jewish people occupied Canaan, hunting seems to have been a necessity because there were so few of them that there was a chance the wild

Papyrus swamp at Lake Huleh, biblical Waters of Merom, an area well known for its lions in Bible times.

animals would multiply against them (Exodus 23:29). The mountains of Lebanon and Syria were full of wildlife; so was the gorge of the Jordan. The Rift Valley of the Jordan has a stepped gorge at two levels. At the lowest level, the river overflowed its banks in the spring, and this combined with the intense heat of the summer led to dense tropical jungle that was the home of other wild animals. The waters of Merom (Lake Huleh) were well known for lions (Jeremiah 49:19), and even the desert seems to have been a place for wild creatures (Mark 1:13).

In Egypt and in Assyria, hunting seems to have been a sport. The Assyrian kings kept large game reserves, and there was much hunting in the Nile valley. In Roman times, animals were hunted for use in warfare and in circuses.

Hunting

Hunting was no easy occupation. Pits were dug to trap large animals. They were covered over with brushwood, and often approaches were built so that animals could be driven toward the pit. Ezekiel tells how a man-eating lion was caught in such a pit. He uses it as a picture of what will happen to the princes of Israel (Jeremiah 48:44; Ezekiel 19:1–4). At other

Assyrian relief of a lion hunt.

times a net was used. Sometimes it was suspended over a pit and at other times pegged out on the ground. In some cases the net probably covered the animal.

Job 18:8–10 refers to some of the methods of trapping — in this case with respect to a wicked man:

His feet thrust him into the net
   and he wanders into its mesh.
A trap seizes him by the heel;
   a snare holds him fast.
A noose is hidden for him on the ground;
   a trap lies in his path.

Once the animal was trapped, it was killed with bow and arrow, spear, or knife (see also Ecclesiastes 9:12; Isaiah 51:20; Ezekiel 12:13; Amos 3:5.)

The dietary laws of the Old Testament prevented many animals from being eaten (Leviticus 11), and other laws laid down the way in which the animals were to be killed before being eaten (Leviticus 17:13; Deuteronomy 12:15). The blood had to be drained from the animal. If the hunter took something he had not killed, because it had died naturally or had been killed by another animal, he became ritually unclean (Leviticus 17:15–16).

Opposite: Fishing is still an important activity on the Sea of Galilee.

Fishing

The early Jewish people do not seem to have been very good in boats although they liked fish (Numbers 11:5). The only navy they had was sunk in port in a storm at Ezion Geber (1 Kings 22:48). The Philistines came by sea from Cyprus, and the Phoenicians were a seafaring nation, but little is heard about fishing.

It was not until New Testament times that fishing developed, and then on the Sea of Galilee. Magdala was one of the centres of the fishing industry; the name *Magdala* actually means "fish salting." There was a large market around Galilee itself.

It is hard to realize when one sees pictures of rural Galilee today that the lake was surrounded with large cities with ribbon development between, and that it was not at all easy for Jesus to find a deserted place round the lake where he could have a rest away from the crowds. Peter, Andrew, James, and John, partners in a fishing business, were not poor men but were sharing in a viable industry. Fishing never developed in the Dead Sea. At thirteen hundred feet (four hundred metres) below sea level, the evaporation of water kept pace with the inflow, and the water became more and more impregnated with chemical salts. Only in the very limited area where the fresh water streams enter the Dead Sea can any fish be found.

There were a number of ways of catching the fish, as follows.

Rod and line fishing

Isaiah tells how the river Nile will dry up as part of the judgment of God (Isaiah 19:5–8) and refers to "all who cast hooks into the Nile." When Jesus told Peter to use a hook to catch a fish with a shekel coin in its mouth to pay the Temple tax, we have a New Testament example (Matthew 17:24–27): "go to the lake and throw out your line. Take the first fish you catch..."

Spear fishing

Job was asked by God which means he would use to catch Leviathan, the great sea creature. "Can you fill his hide with harpoons or his head with fishing spears?" he asks (Job 41:7). Men would go out in a boat at night with a lantern held over the prow of

Net fishing on Galilee.

the boat. As the fish rose, attracted by the light, they would be speared from the boat.

Cast net fishing

The cast net was a circular net about fifteen feet (five metres) in diameter, weighted at the edges. A long rope was attached to the centre. When a shoal or school of fishes was seen in the shallows, the net was dropped over them. The weights carried the net down, and the fish were trapped underneath. The net was then pulled into the shore. Peter and Andrew were using their cast net when they were called by Jesus (Mark 1:16–17). Cast nets were also used from boats and were then pulled to the shore through the shallow water.

When a person stands above the shoreline it is often easy to see shoals of fish that at shore-level are difficult to see. It is therefore possible for someone higher up the shore to tell a fisherman where to cast his net. This may be what happened when Jesus told the disciples from which side of the boat to cast their net (John 21:4–6). They were fishing in the shallows, because Peter was able to wade ashore to meet Jesus, and they were within calling distance.

The cast net brought in everything from the bed of the lake, so that when it was hauled ashore it was necessary to separate the good fish from the rubbish, which was then thrown back into the water (Matthew 13:47–48).

A fisherman throws a cast net to trap a shoal of fishes in the shallows.

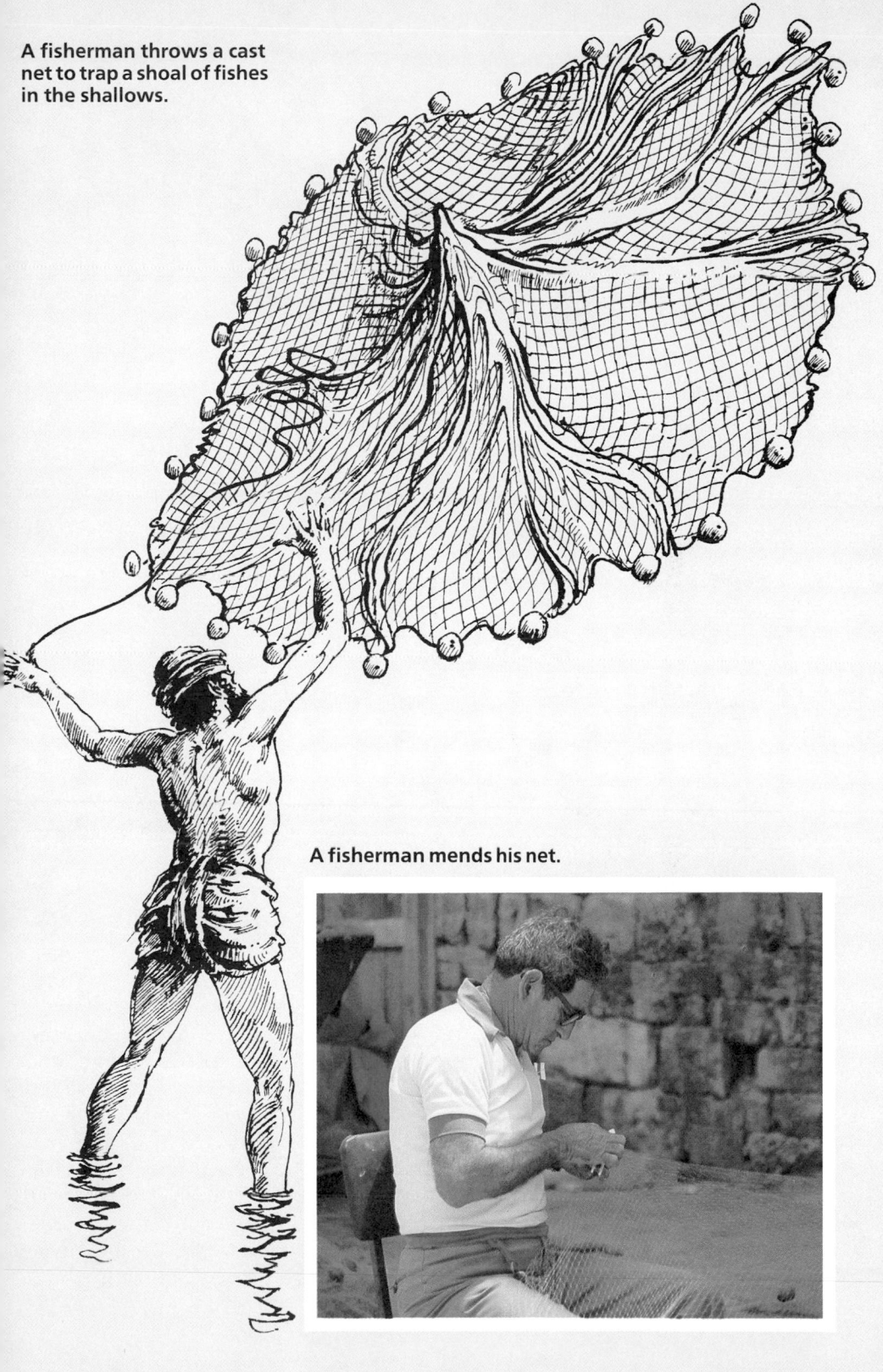

A fisherman mends his net.

Seine net fishing

(Ezekiel 26:5; Habbakuk 1:15; Luke 5:4). The seine net was about eight feet (three metres) broad and hundreds of feet long. It was suspended in the water like a net fence, kept afloat by corks, and weighted down with stone weights to keep it vertical. Either a single boat would make a huge circle with the net, or two boats would suspend the net between them and make a sweep toward the shore. When the net was in a tight circle, it was possible to pull in the lower rope so that the net formed a huge bag from which the fish could not escape.

Fishermen from two boats combine forces to haul in a seine net suspended between their vessels. Notice that most of the fishermen are stripped to the waist.

The boats used for fishing were not normally very large, taking about four men comfortably. A large triangular sail was attached to a wooden support and suspended on a central mast so that it could be moved to catch the wind. Steering was from the rear, with a large oar that acted as a rudder. Two men could operate a boat, and they often worked in partnership with another boat. The boat that Jesus used with the twelve disciples would have been of the same basic design but larger. When the disciples are listed in pairs in the Bible (Simon and his brother

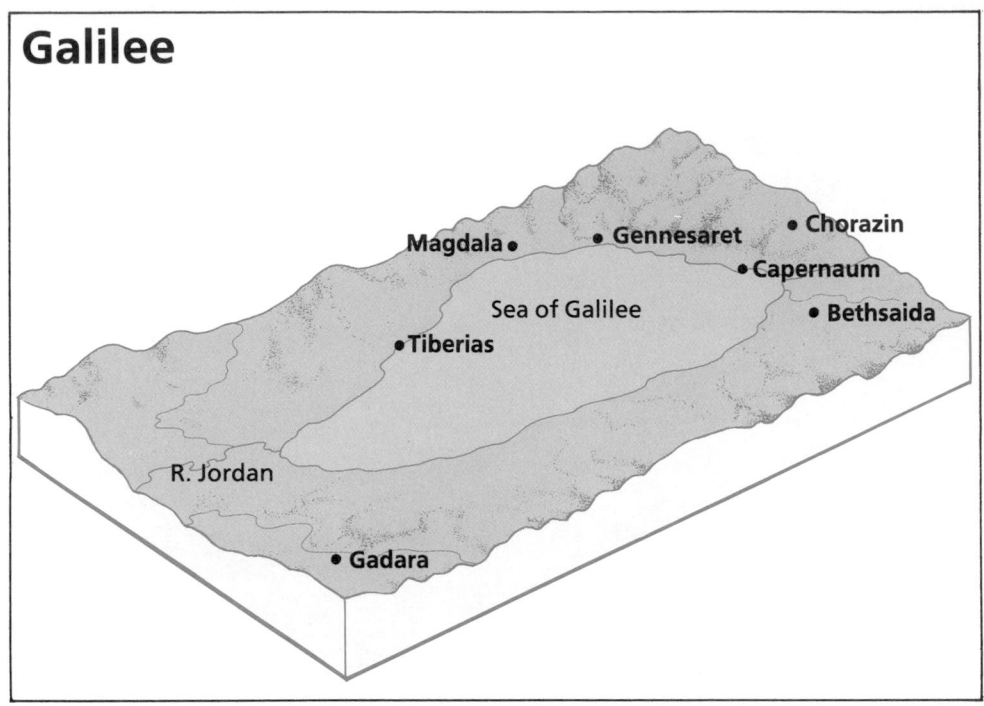

Galilee

- Chorazin
- Magdala
- Gennesaret
- Capernaum
- Sea of Galilee
- Bethsaida
- Tiberias
- R. Jordan
- Gadara

The fishing towns of Galilee in Bible times. Storms can sweep down suddenly onto the lake from the surrounding hills.

Andrew; James son of Zebedee and his brother John; Philip and Bartholomew; Thomas, and Matthew the tax collector; James the son of Alphaeus, and Thaddeus; Simon the Zealot and Judas Iscariot, who betrayed him — Matthew 10:2–4), the pairs may represent the way they sat in the boat and rowed together, as seen from the position of Jesus who sat in the stern (Mark 4:38).

Because the boats were quite small, they were very vulnerable in a storm. The Sea of Galilee is about six hundred feet (two hundred metres) below sea level and is surrounded by hills. In the hot summer sun, the water evaporates. If the vertical air stream is met by cooler air from the Mediterranean, there is great turbulence and an unexpected storm arises. This may be what happened when the disciples were caught in a sudden storm on the lake (Mark 4:35–41). When the wind stops, the lake calms quite quickly because it is not a large stretch of water (about twelve miles [twenty kilometres] long and six miles [ten kilometres] across at its widest).

When fishing was over, the nets were spread out on the shore for drying (Ezekiel 26:5), and any broken pieces were repaired.

Honey

Although the Egyptians kept colonies of bees in hives, this was not developed by the Jews until Roman times. One reason may be that the land was full of honey from wild bees (Exodus 3:8; 13:5), although *honey* may also refer to grape syrup (see p. 108). Swarms of bees might settle in a hollow tree (1 Samuel 14:25–27), a hole in the rock (Psalm 81:16; Deuteronomy 32:13), or even in an animal carcass (Judges 14:8–9). John the Baptist was able to find honey in the desert (Matthew 3:4).

Honey was used as a natural sweetener in the absence of sugar. God's words are therefore sweet like honey (Psalm 19:10), pleasant words are like it (Proverbs 16:24), and so is wisdom to the soul (Proverbs 24:13–14). It was used for food as well as for sweetening. Jesus was given some of the honeycomb that was part of the meal shortly after his resurrection (Luke 24:41–43, KJV).

Now look at your Bible

St. Peter's fish

Matthew 17:24–27. The fish concerned was the *tilapa* (nowadays called "St. Peter's fish"). Tilapa carry their eggs and later the young fish within their mouths. Even when they go in search of food for themselves, the young still return to the protection of the mother's mouth. When the mother fish wishes to keep them out she will pick up an object (a bright one, preferably) and will keep it in her mouth to prevent their return. In this case the fish has picked up a shekel piece.

"Quiet! Be still!"

Mark 4:39. When Jesus said, "Quiet! Be still!" he used the word *phimothete*, which would normally be used to exorcise evil spirits. Jesus recognized the devil's attempt on his life in the storm and spoke accordingly.

Earning a Living:

Shepherding

When Abraham left Ur and took on a nomadic form of life, he would have turned his wealth into flocks and herds so that his wealth could travel with him (Genesis 13:2). The bedouin followed his flocks from pasture to pasture, water to water, and the lifestyle was so different from that of the farmer in a settlement that there was often misunderstanding, tension, and conflict between the two. This conflict may be reflected in the story of Cain and Abel (Genesis 4:2), and it becomes explicit in Genesis 43:32, where Joseph (as an Egyptian) cannot eat at the same table as nomadic shepherds.

When the bulk of the population had left the nomadic life and was living in towns and villages, there was still need for shepherds. The nomadic stage of life was never forgotten; in their statement of belief, the Jewish people began, "My father was a wandering Aramean" (Deuteronomy 26:1–5).

Sheep were needed to provide wool, meat, and horn containers. The fleece itself was sometimes used for clothing. The writer to the Hebrews remembered people persecuted in the past who wandered about in sheepskins and goatskins (Hebrews 11:37). The meat was eaten on special and sacrificial occasions and was normally boiled, occasionally roasted; the Passover lamb was always roasted whole (Exodus 12:9). Sheep also provided milk, and even their horns were used as containers for oil (1 Samuel 16:1; 1 Kings 1:39) or as a trumpet, or shofar (Leviticus 25:9; Numbers 29:1; Joshua 6:4).

Sheep and goats

A *sheep* in the Bible can be either a sheep or a goat; the same word is used for both on many occasions. Goat's milk was not only important because of the quantity (some six pints per goat, per day) but also because it was used to make a type of yoghurt

A bedouin woman sorts goatshair outside the tent.

(leben) and cheese (Proverbs 27:27). One goat was therefore kept with the family even though others went with the shepherd, and it often became a family pet. The meat may not have been as good as lamb or veal (see Luke 15:29), but it was substantial and often used for a meal (Judges 6:19) and was therefore used for sacrificial purposes (Leviticus 1:10).

Goat hair was woven into sackcloth that was used for tent covering as well as for coarse clothing. The hangings in the Tabernacle were made of goat hair (Exodus 26:7; 35:23, 26). It was used for stuffing articles such as pillows (1 Samuel 19:13), and the skin itself was a source of excellent leather. When a goat was killed, its skin was often impregnated with fat and sewn up to become a water carrier (a goatskin bottle).

The problem with settlement was that people could not take their sheep out to pasture. A shepherd was therefore employed to look after the sheep for the whole village. It was not worthwhile to sell off one's sheep, because there was more security in them than at first appeared. Proverbs 27:23–27 sets out the wisdom of the bedouin — real wealth

A bedouin with his sheep in the Judean wilderness.

does not lie in jewelry but in herds; sheep provide clothing and goats provide food and ready money.

There were probably several ancient breeds of sheep in the village flock. Abraham brought the Asiatic moufflon from Sumeria, and the long-legged Egyptian sheep was involved in the Exodus. One of the most important breeds had a large, fat tail that was fried and eaten (Exodus 29:22; Leviticus 3:9).

The shepherd's task

In the springtime, after the winter rains, there was plenty of pasturage near the village. When the grain was reaped the sheep were allowed to feed on anything that was left. When that was gone they had to leave the area and seek the dried grasses that remained under the hot sun (1 Chronicles 4:39–40). Sources of fresh grass where a water supply (still water, if available) made such movement possible (Psalm 23:2). When surface water had disappeared, it was necessary to use well water for the sheep. It was customary to cover the wellhead with a large heavy stone that required several men to lift, thus protecting water rights. (The story of Jacob gives an example of this happening. Genesis 29:10 indicates the incredible strength that Jacob had, which also comes across in other parts of his story.)

The sheep needed constant protection because in Bible times there were plenty of dangers to the flock from the wild animals that came up from the jungle surrounding the Jordan river gorge. Lions and bears were common (Judges 14:8; 2 Kings 2:25), and David's adventures in protecting his own flock were commonplace (1 Samuel 17:34–36). Amos tells of a shepherd who actually tried to take a sheep from a lion's mouth (Amos 3:12). Hyenas and jackals were also common. Not accidentally Jesus said that the Good Shepherd had to give his life for the sheep (John 10:11). The shepherd had to fight back, because he had to make good any losses to the owners (Genesis 31:39; Exodus 22:10–13). Any hired help the shepherd might have used did not have the same kind of commitment (John 10:12–13).

The sling

For weapons the shepherd used a heavy club and a sling. The club is referred to as a "rod" in Psalm 23:4, but it was a heavy weapon, and flints (later

Sheep and goats were often herded together.

nails) were often embedded into its heavy "working end" to make it more effective. The sling was made from a small pouch of leather that could securely hold a stone about one and one-half inches (forty millimetres) in diameter. The pouch was attached to two cords of sinew, rope, or leather about two feet (sixty centimetres) long. The stone was placed into the pouch and the sling whirled about so that the stone was held in place by centrifugal force. When one of the strings was released, the stone would leave the pouch with tremendous force. In the hands of a shepherd who had time to practise, the sling could be used with great accuracy. The sling was also used to control the sheep. A well-placed stone dropped in front of the sheep that was wandering from the main flock would bring it back again. When the sheep was tired or sick, the shepherd carried it on his shoulders (Luke 15:5), and when it was lost, the shepherd went to search for it (Psalm 119:176; Isaiah 53:6; Luke 15:3–6).

A shepherd leads his flock
through barren lands.
Notice the shepherd's rod
and staff. His herd includes
sheep and goats.

The staff

The shepherd was also equipped with a staff, but it was not a weapon, although it was used as such on occasions. The staff was about six feet (two metres) long and sometimes had a crook at the end of it. It was normally used to help the shepherd get around easily in hilly or rough country. It was often used to help control the sheep. When the sheep were passing through a narrow entry, as for example when they entered the sheepfold at night, they were counted in under the rod or staff. Ezekiel uses this term to say that God will prevent rebels from returning to their homes after the Exile. Only those who had been loyal to him would "pass under my rod" (Ezekiel 20:37–38). It was also used to mark the sheep. The end was dipped into dye, and as the sheep passed under the rod, every tenth one was marked and given to God as the tithe (Leviticus 27:31–33).

The scrip

The shepherd carried a second leather pouch, considerably larger than the one used in the sling, known as a scrip. It was to hold food while the shepherd was away from civilization. David must

A shepherd boy plays his pipes at Palmyra, biblical Tadmor, Syria.

A stone sheepfold near Mount Nebo, Jordan.

have already eaten his food when he filled his scrip with stones, one of which was used to fell Goliath (1 Samuel 17:40).

A musical reed pipe was also part of the shepherd's possessions. It was made from two hollowed-out pieces of cane. The sound was made by blowing across a sharp edge and the notes were controlled by blocking off holes with the fingers in each tube. They could provide bright music on holy day parades (1 Kings 1:40) and sad music as well (Jeremiah 48:36). They were easily made and easily broken, so when damaged the shepherd would normally discard the old and make a new. When it was said of Jesus that "a bruised reed he will not break" (Matthew 12:20) the prophet was saying that contrary to practice, Jesus' way was and is to repair the broken rather than discard them.

The sheepfold

At night the shepherd gathered his sheep to a safe place and kept watch (Luke 2:8). A shallow cave was a good place of safety, and a wall was often built partly across the cave mouth to form an enclosure in front of it. The wall was made of local stones and was topped with thorns. It was in such a cave the King Saul went to sleep (1 Samuel 24:3). If there was no cave, a pallisade of stones was made out in the open, thorns being substituted for stones if necessary (Ezekiel 34:14). The shepherd lay down across the one opening, effectively becoming a door for the sheep (John 10:7). It was a tough life. Jacob spelled out the thirst, the frost, and the lack of sleep (Genesis 31:40). Although the shepherd carried a tent with him (Song of Songs 1:8), it was no camping trip.

Sheepfolds were often set up in the home village at a sunny spot, so that when the flock returned it could be kept in safety. The sheepfold was a low, arched building with a drystone wall enclosure attached. The flock could be kept indoors or out of doors according to the weather. A watchman was set to guard the flock. Jesus referred to this kind of setting when he said that thieves and robbers do not use the door but climb over the wall (John 10:1–3, 10). The current criminal practice was to climb over the wall, slaughter as many sheep as possible before detection, and throw them to accomplices outside.

The good shepherd

Living and working with sheep in isolation leads to a close relationship between shepherd and sheep. The shepherds know their own sheep so well that they respond to them instantly. The shepherd has a name for each sheep, the significance being that the name says something about the individual sheep's character or mannerisms. Jesus said that he *knows* his sheep (John 10:14a). His sheep also know him (John 10:14b), so that when they are called they respond to his voice (John 10:4–5).

Detailed knowledge enabled the shepherd to separate the sheep into different flocks, if he was responsible for more than one village, and to be able to return them to individual families. In John 10:16, Jesus refers to the fact that he has sheep that are not of this fold (which may refer to the Jewish nation). Jacob found there were three flocks lying by a well awaiting the removal of the stone at the well-head (Genesis 29:1–3). By calling, and by the use of stones in a sling, the shepherd was able to keep the sheep together (Ezekiel 34:1–3), although dogs were used by some men (Job 30:1). When a shepherd led the flock (Psalm 23:3) the dogs always brought up the rear, ensuring that the sheep were not attacked by wild animals and that they kept up with the shepherd. (Isaiah 52:12 sees God in a double relationship to his people. He leads them from the front and at the same time guards them from behind.)

Jacob lived at a time when his knowledge of breeding techniques was put to use. He knew that strong sheep produced strong lambs (Genesis 30:41), but he did not realize that whether sheep were pure white (providing the most valuable wool) or speckled also depended upon inheritance. He believed that the environment at the time of conception was responsible for the colouring of the sheep (Genesis 30:42). Fortunately for Jacob, God overruled his ignorance by ensuring that justice was done and that Jacob got the best sheep out of a bad bargain (Genesis 31:5b–9).

Goats

Goats were normally driven by the shepherd ahead of the sheep. Therefore a goat was up in front and gave Isaiah the picture of the kings leading the

Bedouin bargain at the sheep market at Beer Sheba.

people (see Isaiah 14:9; Daniel 8:5; Zechariah 10:12). The sheep and goat relationship might lie behind Jesus' words that he would separate people as a shepherd separates the sheep from the goats (Matthew 25:32), although the staff was used to separate them, the goats being made to go one way and the sheep another — "under the rod." Sheep and goats were kept nearby because they both needed grazing and because they ate more or less the same thing.

There are a number of differences between the two animals. Goats are generally dark and sheep, white. Goats are able to cope with mountains and rocks, but sheep prefer the flatter valleys. Goats eat the leaves of trees (often helped by the shepherd who

Remains of the Pool of Bethesda, used in Bible times to bathe sheep.

knocks off small branches with his club), whereas sheep prefer grass. Goats graze all day, but sheep lie down in the shade when the sun is at its hottest (Song of Songs 1:7).

The goat was always less popular than the sheep to most people. It was a goat that became the "scapegoat," taking the sins of the people to the desert (Leviticus 16:22). The "goats" were reserved for destruction by Jesus in his description of the coming of the Son of Man (Matthew 25:33, 41). This unpopularity may be because the goat is destructive; goats grazed closer to the ground than the sheep and destroyed the pasture. The Greeks believed in mythical creatures, half goat and half man, called satyrs. Bacchus was half goat and half man. Isaiah's prophecy of judgment upon Babylon mentions goats (Isaiah 13:21; 34:14).

Sheep shearing

There were two very important times of the year for the shepherd: lambing time and sheep shearing. Lambing time was in January/February. Sheep shearing was after the summer grazing when the profits were distributed and several days of celebration followed. 1 Samuel 25 tells the story of a sheep-shearing when all those who had been involved in the care of the sheep (in this case, those belonging to a huge estate) were invited to the celebrations. Such was the drinking and rejoicing that it was an effective time for a murder (2 Samuel 13:23).

Shepherding was not always on a small scale. Large sheep farmers employed shepherds to care for their huge flocks. Mesha, king of Moab, had to pay the king of Israel a hundred thousand lambs and the wool from a hundred thousand sheep in protection money (2 Kings 3:4). Job had fourteen thousand sheep at the end of his story (Job 42:12), and Solomon sacrificed one hundred and twenty thousand sheep at the dedication of the Temple (1 Kings 8:63). A special gate was built in the northwest corner of Jerusalem to get the sheep into the Temple site for sacrifice. It was called the Sheep Gate (Nehemiah 3:1), and nearby the pool known as the Pool of Bethesda in New Testament times was used to bathe them (John 5:2). Nabal, with three thousand sheep, was a relatively small sheep farmer (1 Samuel 25:2, 7).

Sometimes caring for sheep was not even on a shepherd scale. The poorest families used the youngest children to look after the sheep. David was in this position when Samuel came to Jesse's home to look for the future king of Israel (1 Samuel 16:1). The poorest families of all would try to buy two lambs at Passover. One would be eaten according to the law, but the other would be kept to be fattened up throughout the summer. It became a family pet in a way that the goat never did. Often it would sleep with the children and even share the same drinking vessels. It was a tragic day for the children when the sheep was killed and preserved in the fat of its own tail. It is this practice that lies behind Nathan's parable in 2 Samuel 12:1–7.

Now look at your Bible

Shepherd-kings

Micah 7:14. Micah looked forward to the time when kings would shepherd their people as a shepherd looked after the flock, "Shepherd your people with your staff, the flock of your inheritance." The rod symbolized the protection of the people and was eventually stylized into a sceptre.

Two pouches

1 Samuel 25:29. Abigail made an interesting contrast between the two pouches used by the shepherd. "Even though someone is pursuing you to take your life, the life of my Master will be bound securely in the bundle of the living by the Lord your God. But the lives of your enemies he will hurl away as from the pocket of a sling." The bundle of the living is the pouch that held food; the hollow of a sling is the pouch that held the stone.

Care of the sheep

"When you pass through the waters, I will be with you, and when you pass through the rivers, they will not sweep over you" probably refers to the care the shepherd has to take when he takes the flock through running water (Isaiah 43:2). Isaiah 40:11 utilizes the action of the shepherd's carrying the lambs and not pushing the ewes too hard when it is lambing time to demonstrate God's care for his people: "He gathers the lambs in his arms and carries them close to his heart; he gently leads those that have young." Any flesh wounds incurred by the sheep were anointed with olive oil (Psalm 23:5) — the same method as was used for dealing with human wounds (Luke 10:34).

The scapegoat

John 1:29. It is normally assumed that when John refers to the "lamb of God who takes away the sin of the world" that he was referring to Isaiah 53:7, "a lamb to the slaughter." However, because sheep and goats are the same so far as language is concerned, he may be referring to the scapegoat — Jesus taking away the world's sin when he died and left the world.

Jesus' birthday

Luke 2:8. Nobody knows the exact birthday of Jesus. December 25 was chosen as the "official" birthday because it coincided with the Jewish festival of Hannukah (25th Chislev), which was a festival of light, and with many of the festivities that were invented to counteract the dark winters of the northern hemisphere. The fact that there were sheep on the Bethlehem hills indicates that Jesus was actually born about Passover time, because sheep were kept on the hillsides of Bethlehem to provide for the Passover lambs at Jerusalem. The fact that there was no room for Jesus to be born at a *kataluma*, a rough marquee for shelter (see p. 240) that was also put up for pilgrims unable to find a bed in the city at Passover time, is additional evidence. Because God sent his son "when the time had fully come" (Galatians 4:4), and his whole life was bound up with the imagery of sheep, some people believe Passover would have been the most appropriate time for the birth.

The pastor

Ephesians 4:11. This verse describes one of the leaders in the church as a "pastor." The actual word is *shepherd*. The pastor is in relationship to the Chief Shepherd (1 Peter 5:4) as shepherds would have been to the king's stockmaster in the days of the kingdom of Israel.

Earning a Living:

Craftsmen and Traders

When the Jews settled in Canaan after their semi-nomadic life, which was interrupted only by their settlement and slavery in Egypt, they had to develop many skills that had already been developed by the Canaanites whom they dispossessed. Some skills came hard. They never did achieve the same expertise in the making of pottery as that exercised by other nations, and therefore many pots were imported. Jewish pots were made soundly enough, but they never reached the same high standards of decoration as others. The first time pottery is actually mentioned in the Bible is when David was on the run from Absalom and crossed the Jordan to the eastern side. There the Gileadites and Ammonites brought bedding, bowls, and articles of pottery that he needed (2 Samuel 17:27–28).

After individuals developed skills, the skills were transmitted to their own families and groups until it became customary for groups of craftsmen to be found together. There was a Potsherd Gate in Jerusalem opening onto the Hinnom valley in Jeremiah's time, presumably because the potters were in the vicinity (Jeremiah 19:2). When the wall of Jerusalem was repaired in Nehemiah's time there was a tower of the ovens (Nehemiah 3:11; 12:38), presumably because kilns or bakers' ovens were situated there. As technology and materials developed, and as the population grew, there was a bigger market for goods. Craftsmen therefore joined together to provide mass production methods, protected by trade guilds. Centres of crafts placed their own trademarks on the articles they produced. In New Testament Ephesus, the guild of silversmiths was strong enough to promote a public demonstraton against Paul, whose preaching was affecting the sale of obscene models of goddesses made in silver (Acts 19:23–29).

Earthenware pots of Bible times.

Workers with clay

Clay was dug out from the locality and left exposed to the weather until it was ready for use. It was then mixed with water and trampled into a plastic mud. After this it was brought to a bench where with carefully added water it was brought into the right consistency for work. Additives such as ground limestone were sometimes added to the clay to enable the completed article to withstand heat better and be used for cooking. Isaiah describes the treading out of the clay in Isaiah 41:25.

When the Jews learned to make pottery, they entered into a craft with a long history. Fifteen hundred years earlier, the first pottery had been made by laying a long "worm" of clay, coil upon coil, until a bowl or pitcher was complete. The ridges on the outside were then smoothed down and decorated. It was extremely difficult to get an even shape on the outside of the vessel. Then it was discovered that such pots could be made in a circular hole in the ground and rotated against the hole.

The Potter's Wheel

The process of rotation was developed further by someone who had the idea of putting the clay on a horizontal wheel. In Old Testament times a flat wood, clay, or limestone wheel was rotated horizontally on a workbench by hand about an axle that pierced the bench. One person pushed the wheel while the other shaped the clay upon it. When Jeremiah went down to the potter's house and saw a pot being made and then remade as a fault developed in it, he was watching a wheel of this type. Not until about 200 BC did it occur to those in the trade that a second wheel could be added to the axle under the bench at foot level, and could be pushed by the same person as was making the pot. It is therefore in the book of Ecclesiasticus in the Apocrypha, which was written in that same period, that we have a description of this kind of second wheel: "So is the potter sitting at his work and turning the wheel about with his foot... he will fashion the clay with his arm and find its strength with his feet" (Ecclesiasticus 38:29).

A potter turns his wheel with his feet. Notice the different types of pots, bowls and lamps in his workshop.

Decorated pots from Hazor.

Decorating pots

Bowls and pitchers were made on the wheel and were set on one side to harden off. When the vessel was dry, any desired decoration could be added. There were several methods of decoration. Some pots were decorated by making scratches in the surface. In some cases this was done by pressing such articles as woven rope into the surface before the vessel left the workbench. Other pots were decorated by having coloured clay added to the outside, either in bands or in a pattern. Normally red or black clay was used for this purpose. Another method of decoration was by "burnishing." The vessel was returned to the wheel and while it was being rotated, a piece of bone, metal, or pottery was held against the surface to give it a shine that stood out when the pot was fired. (In other lands glazes were developed made of liquid glass. Soda, lead, tin, copper, and silver were needed, but this was not developed by the Jews.)

Any of the methods of decoration could be combined. There were many possible variations in shape and in decoration to such a degree that it is now possible to date the period when a pot was made from its shape and decoration. This has been used by archaeologists to date the destruction of certain buildings, because no pottery beyond a certain style was found in the ruins. The Canaanite pottery that preceded the Jewish occupation was rounded and had painted decorations, but after the settlement had taken place, shapes were much more angular and burnishing replaced the painted designs. After the destruction of the Jerusalem Temple by Nebuchadnezzar, pottery became very poor (which is explained by Jeremiah 52:15–16 "Nebu Zaradan the commander of the guard ... carried into exile ... the rest of the craftsmen... But Nebu Zaradan left behind the rest of the poorest people of the land to work the vineyards and fields") with little variety of shape and no decoration, although the potters did begin to produce jars with pointed bases, which were different. When Alexander the Great conquered the country, pottery adopted Greek patterns; jars were made with high necks and vessels were built with rims so that lids and stoppers could be fitted.

In addition to the use of the wheel, potters also used wooden moulds into which the clay was pressed. Seals (Job 38:14) were made in this way, and the two halves of oil lamps were made in moulds before being cemented together. It was also possible for the clay to be modeled freehand. Toys,

An oil lamp from Judea.

figurines, and ornaments were produced in this way, as were the larger clay ovens produced for domestic use. Potters also made repairs to broken pieces of pottery, using wire and rivets to hold a joint that was then sealed with wet clay.

Firing clay

When the objects had been dried and, if required, decorated, they were fired in one of several forms of kiln. In one, a dome-shaped clay oven was placed at the bottom of a shallow well, which was about four feet (122 centimetres) deep and ten feet (305 centimetres) in diameter. Pots were placed under the dome, and the dome was covered with brushwood that was then set on fire. Other ovens were made where the pots were placed on shelves and fires lit beneath. The writer in Ecclesiasticus describes this part of the process, too: "He will apply his hand to finish the glazing and will be wakeful to make clear the furnace" (38:30). Pottery produced in this way tended to be very brittle. A pitcher put down heavily at the wellhead could easily be broken (Ecclesiastes 12:6), and the finality of breakage was often used as a picture of the finality of coming judgment (Psalm 2:9; Jeremiah 19:10–11; Revelation 2:27).

Broken pieces were not altogether useless. They were used as scrapers, and they were used for writing messages. In this form they were known as *ostraca*. The larger pieces could be used for carrying things. Isaiah says that judgment will be so severe that no big pieces are found — they cannot be used for scooping water from a cistern or taking coals from a hearth (Isaiah 30:14).

As pottery developed, methods of mass production were operated. Apprentices would make rough pots to be finished by master craftsmen. Large lumps of clay were put on wheels, and items were made from the top of the lump. Specialists developed in the preparation of the clay and the maintenance of its consistency, in its design, and in its drying and firing. David seemed to be organizing things in this direction even in the time of his kingdom (1 Chronicles 4:23).

Workers with wood

Jesus was a carpenter (Mark 6:3), and as a result the work of a carpenter in Bible times has been some-

A carpenter's tools.
1. Axe
2. Chisel
3. Hone for sharpening tools
4. Adz
5. Bradawl
6. Bowdrill
7. Adz
8. Small handsaw
9. Mallet
10. Saw

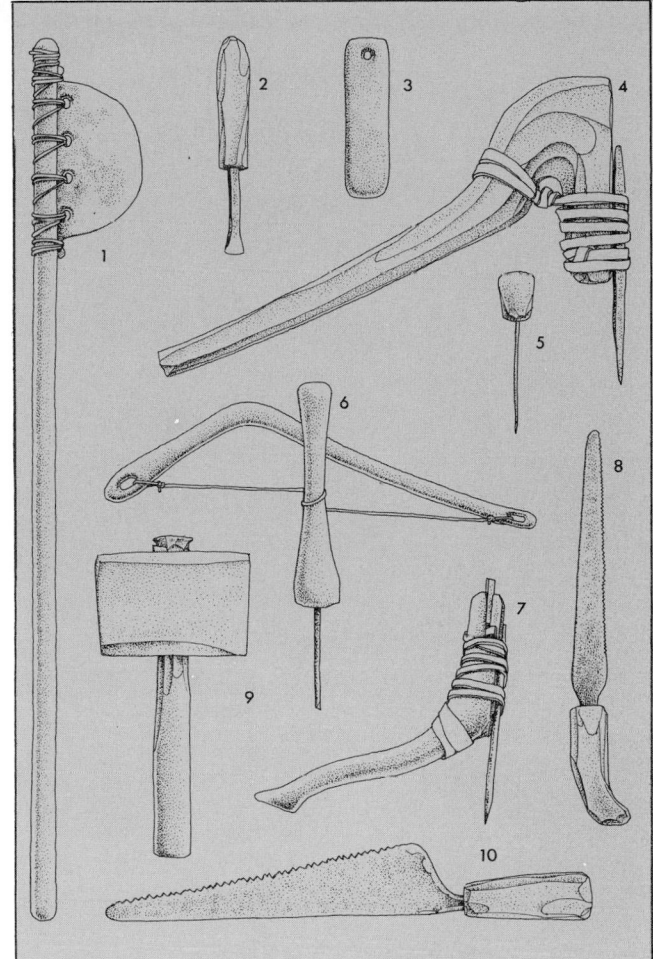

what idealized. Carpentry was a rough, tough job that demanded a great deal of physical strength and endurance as well as great skill. There were two aspects to the carpenter's work: firstly building and secondly the making of smaller objects that included furniture.

Until the Romans invented the arched roof, roofs were constructed by laying timber beams from wall to wall and filling in the gaps with matting that was plastered down with mud. The carpenter had to cut down trees and square up the logs so that they could be used as beams. This was done either with a hand adz (axe-like tool used primarily for shaping wood) or by sawing the length with a primitive saw. Either way was hard physical work.

Axe heads were made of bronze (later of iron) and

were lashed to a shaft. The bluntness of the edge and relatively insecure fastening ensured that the head fairly regularly came off the shaft. This happening was given as an example of manslaughter in Deuteronomy 19:5. If the head was lost it was a disaster because of the cost of replacement (2 Kings 6:5). Saw blades were initially made from ribbon flints set in a wooden frame, and it took two men working either side to saw through a tree trunk. Later, metal blades were used, and the teeth arranged so that they cut on the "pull" stroke. The saw is mentioned in Isaiah 41:15 alongside the axe.

Because the Jews had been a seminomadic people, carpentry had not been one of their developed skills. The standard of carpentry in Canaan in general therefore went down noticeably after the Israelite occupation, until the Phoenicians were called in to help (1 Chronicles 14:1). They were expert carpenters and built their trading fleet on this basis. In loaning their skills for the building of Solomon's Temple and other public buildings, they taught the Jews many of their skills, which included paneling, cladding, and carving (1 Kings 5:18). Although the Jews adopted carpentry so that their work is described by Isaiah as involving the use of measuring line, marker, chisels (possibly plane), and compass (Isaiah 44:13), and they were skilled enough to be taken into exile at the destruction of the Temple, by Nebuchadnezzar, their work still deteriorated when their alliance with Phoenicia was concluded.

The carpenter also undertook many smaller jobs, working on the ground outside his dwelling; benches were not used until Roman times. Doors, doorframes, window lattices, and locks were made for buildings, and stools, low tables, and chests for inside the home. Agricultural implements such as yokes, ploughs, and shovels were also part of the carpenter's work. The fact that tools were relatively crude meant that a good finish was an extremely skilled task. The hammer (Judges 5:26) was normally a piece of stone. The nails used to fasten to-

Opposite: Carpenter's workshop. Notice many of the tools shown on p. 153. The carpenter is making a cartwheel, while his young son is making part of a winnowing fork.

Coppersmith at work outside his workshop.

gether pieces of wood (Jeremiah 10:4) were made first of bronze and later of iron. Holes were bored with an awl, although its use in the Bible is confined to making holes in ear lobes (Exodus 21:6; Deuteronomy 15:17).

Workers with metal

The metalsmith has a very old pedigree. Cain means "smith," and it was one of his descendants, Tubal-Cain, who was described as "the forger of all instruments of bronze and iron" (Genesis 4:17, 22). Cain was the father of the Midianite tribe of Kenites who seem to have been involved in many aspects of Israel's history (see, for example, Genesis 15:19; 1 Samuel 15:6.) They appear to have exploited the copper of the Sinai with the Egyptians. Artifacts of

Kenite metalworking have yielded much of the archaeological information we know concerning ancient metal-working.

Gold was one of the first metals to be extracted and used because it is found in a relatively pure state and can be melted at low temperatures and poured into moulds. It was refined (like silver) by heating it in a clay crucible and skimming the top of the liquid to remove impurities (Zechariah 13:9). It was also beaten into thin sheets for overlay work (Jeremiah 10:3–4), and the thin sheets were cut into strips fine enough to be woven into gold thread (Exodus 39:3). Israelite art and craft was at its best in many small objects such as jewelry, and the goldsmiths were therefore important as a group (Nehemiah 3:8).

Copper was extracted from its ore by heating. It could be beaten and shaped by cold hammering. It was mined from shafts as much as one hundred and fifty feet (fifty metres) deep, and the description of mining given in Job 28:2–11, seems to have been written from some experience. The ore was broken down to small pieces in stone mortars and smelted in a simple furnace fired by acacia wood. The furnace consisted basically of a depression in the ground where the copper ingot would ultimately be collected, surrounded by three low walls of stone and clay. The third side gave access to a bellows and to the prevailing wind. Remains of mortars, furnaces,

Silver jewelry found at biblical Shiloh.

Israelite pitcher and oil lamp, both made of metal.

and slag heaps are to be found in plenty along the Gulf of Aqaba.

By 2000 BC metal workers had discovered that by adding up to four percent of tin to the copper, they obtained a harder metal with a lower melting-point which could be poured into moulds. This was bronze. In the Hebrew language there is no distinction between bronze and copper. Because bronze was attractive and cheaper than gold it was sometimes used as a decorative substitute (see 1 Kings 14:27). The copper industry died out in the south because of the lack of fuel; the acacia trees were all burned up. There was no revival of the industry in the country until Roman times.

Iron was originally removed as an impurity from copper. It was not until certain technological advances had been made that iron could be extracted from its ore. It required more heat both for extraction and for shaping (Isaiah 44:12; Jeremiah 6:28–29). The Hittites developed iron first and exported it and the related skills to the Canaanites and the Philistines. Since iron was much stronger than bronze, and the Canaanites had iron fittings to their chariots (Judges 1:19), the Jews had problems in battle. At a later period the Philistines, who were not great in numerical strength, were able to dominate the Jews because of their monopoly of iron (1 Samuel 13:19–22). In 1500 BC iron was so new that it was being used to make jewelry, but by 1000 BC it was being used in weapons. David had plenty of iron to provide construction materials for the Temple (1 Chronicles 22:3).

Bronze age weapons from Israel.

Workers with leather and cloth

Tents were originally made from skins; only later were the skins replaced with goat's hair. A tentmaker was therefore a leatherworker, and the name stuck (Acts 18:3), even though leather was used to make bottles, belts, and military equipment such as helmets, shields, and slings. A tentmaker (or leatherworker) had first to skin the animal, then remove the hairs from the hide, make it supple for use, and sometimes dye it as well. The hairs were removed by a combination of scraping, soaking, and the application of lime. The hides were then soaked in water containing oak galls and sumac leaves, rubbed with dog manure, and hammered. The smell of the work was so bad that the tanner had to work outside the town in the direction of the prevailing wind, and it was so bad personally that it could become grounds for divorce. When the servants of Cornelius came looking for the house of Simon the tanner at Joppa, it would have been easy to find (Acts 10:6).

Linen and woollen cloth developed very early. Among Jews, woollen cloth was the norm. After the wool from the sheep had been washed, it was

Opposite: Leatherworker makes sandals outside his workshop; notice the special tools on his bench.

Left: Raw wool and sheepskins outside a merchant's shop in Hebron.

Weaving weights from Kadum, Israel. See them in use on a loom on p. 165.

combed so as to prepare it for spinning. Spinning was done by using a wooden stick or spindle that had a notch or hook at one end. The other end was weighted with a heavy stone with a hole through its centre, called a *whorl*. The whorl was made of clay, stone, or bone and gave the stick momentum when it was given a spin. The spinner pulled out some strands of wool from the combed wool held under her left arm and attached the strands to the notch or hook. She then gave the spindle a twist and let it fall until it nearly reached the ground. In falling and twisting the spindle had pulled out a woollen thread that was then wound round the stick before the process was repeated again and again. Although natural colours were used in weaving, it was possible to dye the thread. The yarn was cleaned with nitre and soap (Jeremiah 2:22) before dyeing.

Dyeing

Scarlet dye (Exodus 25:4) was made from lice eggs that had been ground into powder. Indigo was obtained from pomegranate rind. Purple was obtained from the murex shellfish (Acts 16:14). The shells were crushed, cooked in salt, and left in the sun so that the secretion would turn purple (see also Numbers 15:38; Esther 8:15). Blue was also made from

Below: A bedouin woman spins wool in preparation for weaving.

the murex but another substance was added during the cooking. Yellow was made in Egypt from the safflower, and the Romans extracted it from crocus flowers. The dyes were made by preparing a solution of water, potash, and lime. After two days the pigments were added, and the dyeing was done in earthenware pots or in stone basins. The yarn or skin being dyed was then washed in clear water and hung up to dry.

Weaving

Weaving developed throughout the period of the Old Testament. At first a horizontal loom was used, which was pegged out on the ground. Later, an upright loom was developed, although there were times and places where both types of loom were used side by side. The horizontal loom was pegged out on the ground with the long warp threads running the length of the required piece of cloth. The yarn, held in a pointed stick, was then pushed alternately between the warp threads. The process was aided by the use of a flat piece of wood that was already passed through alternate threads. When it was put on edge, the warp threads were separated out so that there was plenty of room for the weft thread to be passed through on its stick. On the return journey the stick had to be passed over and under each successive thread.

Eventually it was realized that if the same warp threads that were pushed down by the flat piece of wood could be pulled up for the return journey by fastening them with loops to another piece of wood, the stick could be passed rapidly in the other direction, too. This made it possible for the stick to be replaced by a shuttle. The shuttle was certainly in use by the time of Job (Job 7:6), and the horizontal loom was in use in the time of the judges because it was used by Delilah to weave Samson's hair into a piece of cloth (Judges 16:13). The "pin" mentioned in this story was used for beating down the weft so that the threads became compacted together.

A woman weaves at an upright loom. Notice the loom weights hanging from the warp threads.

The problem with the horizontal loom was that the width of the cloth was limited to the arm span of the weaver, because the weaver had to sit or crouch at his work. The invention of the upright loom enabled wider material to be made because the weaver could walk across the face of the cloth. In this case a heavy wooden framework (see 1 Samuel 17:7) was built like a square archway, and the warp threads were hung from the crossbeam and weighted down with a series of pierced stones or clay balls known as loom weights. The material was then made top to bottom, and the pin was used to push the weft thread together at the top of the loom.

The final development of the loom was one in which the weights were replaced with a roller that could wind up the finished cloth. The weaving was then done bottom to top. Such looms did not lend themselves to the making of complicated coloured patterns, and even "embroidered cloth" may refer to different cloths that had been sewn together (Judges 5:30; Ezekiel 26:16). It did, however, mean that cloth could be shaped on the loom by varying the required number of warp threads.

Bedouin women weaving at a village near Hebron.

Stone masons at work in Jerusalem.

Workers with stone

Masons were the partners of carpenters in building. Masonry was another craft that had to be learned by the Jewish people. The Jews destroyed the large and well-fortified cities of the Canaanites (Numbers 13:28), and they did not learn how to rebuild them until, at a later date, they were helped by the Phoenicians. The mason's work started at the foundations, where a trench was filled with rock and lime and allowed to settle (Luke 6:48). The walls were then erected on the foundations. Paul's point that in preaching he did not build on another man's foundation is probably based on a contemporary custom that the man who built the foundation also built the walls (Romans 15:20).

Opposite: The Roman aqueduct at Caesarea Maritima.

In a good building, cornerstones were placed at each corner, large and square. It was because such large stones were not suitable for the rest of the building work that they could be left to one side by the builders, only to have the builders discover that the stones were necessary to give strength and direction to the building (Psalm 118:22). Such stones or "chiefs" became metaphors for the prominent and stable men in the community (Judges 20:20; 1 Samuel 14:38).

When a good building was being erected, limestone blocks were cut in the quarry. The limestone was always softer when it was hewn underground; it hardened on contact with the air. The general practice was therefore to cut the blocks roughly to size in the quarry and then finish them by chipping away the surface on site. When Solomon's Temple was built the blocks were finished in the quarry where a more accurate finish could be obtained because the blocks were still soft (1 Kings 6:7).

Part of the massive stonework around the Dome of the Rock. The huge stones making up the lower part of the wall date from Herod's time.

The walls were kept true by reed and plumbline. The reed was a straight cane about twenty feet (seven metres) long (Ezekiel 40:3). The plumbline consisted of an inverted lead cone attached by a line to a wooden rod of the same diameter as the base of the cone. When the rod was held on the side of a building, the edge of the base of the cone should just barely touch the wall lower down if the wall was true (Amos 7:8). A line was used from corner to corner, and a layer of stones was built up to the line before proceeding to the next course (2 Kings 21:3).

Stone was not used for many houses. Amos regarded stone houses as a luxury made possible by the exploitation of the poor (Amos 5:11). Only public structures such as the Temple, city walls, and the store cities such as Megiddo were normally built of stone. Phoenician builders probably helped on all those projects. The quality of the building was clearly to be seen.

"Stretchers" and "headers" were used to strengthen the walls, and the stones were often so accurately fitted that there were no gaps between and no need for mortar. Masons in Bible times found problems, however, in providing windows in a stone wall. Jeremiah considered windows to be unacceptable luxuries (Jeremiah 22:14).

Most houses were built of mud brick, made from mud and straw in wooden moulds and left to harden in the hot sun. Mud was then used both as mortar and as a plaster for the inside and outside of the work. Other cruder houses were constructed from a mixture of stones and mud. The mason was also involved in the building of silos, wells, cisterns, public buildings, arches, roads, and aqueducts (the latter three in Roman times). With the development of the arch, it was the odd-shaped keystone that held the arch together. Perhaps Simon Peter had this concept in mind when he put forward Jesus as the one who will hold the Jewish faith together and stop it from falling down (Acts 4:11).

Workers with medicine

Jews were promised health if they obeyed God's laws (Exodus 15:26), and they were given a number of health laws (regular rest and relaxation, suitable food, avoidance of contaminated water, marriage regulations, cleanliness, separation from contagious disease), which when followed led to a high level of good health. If the laws were disobeyed, disease resulted (Deuteronomy 28:60–61). There was no call for doctors, and anyone who resorted to them came under criticism for going against the will of God. This happened to King Asa in 2 Chronicles 16:12. The correct procedure in illness was regarded to be prayer to God (Numbers 21:7; 2 Kings 20; 2 Chronicles 6:28–30; Psalm 6; 107:17–21).

But there was a different attitude in other countries. In Egypt and Babylon, disease was looked upon as the result of evil spirit activity, and doctors were required to counteract this. Although medical work was sometimes at the level of magic, it also brought about surgery and the development of medicine through herbs. There were even laws that controlled the work of doctors. The Hammurabi Law Code said that if a man operated on another man's eye using a copper lancet, and that man lost his eye, then the doctor's eye was also to be put out with a copper lancet.

The Egyptians were skilled in brain surgery. They bored holes into the skull "to let the evil spirit out," but in so doing they relieved the pressure within, which sometimes led to cures; this was also done in Lachish. The Egyptians also practised dentistry and some of the Phoenicians had gold teeth.

Despite the theological attitude of the Jews, much of the attitude of the surrounding nations seems to have rubbed off on them. At the popular level people seem to have worn charms to ward off evil spirits, and doctors were around, as King Asa knew. Exodus 21:9 seems to indicate the use of a crutch when a limb was injured, and Hezekiah made a poultice to treat his boil (2 Kings 20:7). By the time the book of Job was written, attitudes were changing, because one of the important points of the book is that Job's sickness was *not* the result of sin. In the second century before Christ, Ecclesiasticus says that although God is the healer, he gives gifts of healing to men. Isaiah said that Judah's condition needed cleansing, bandaging, and ointment (Isaiah 1:6); wine mixed with myrrh was used as a painkiller (Matthew 27:34); mandrake roots were believed to aid conception (Genesis 30), and midwifery was practised throughout Bible times (Exodus 1:15; Ezekiel 16:4).

Medicine in Jesus' time

By the time of Jesus there was therefore an uncertain attitude toward medicine. Mark 1:32–34 seems to indicate that disease was a major problem. Diseases included leprosy, diseases of diet and pollution (dysentery, cholera, typhoid, beri beri [dropsy]), blindness (dusty climate), deafness, and crippling diseases. Epilepsy and other nervous disorders were also present. Reference to these diseases can be found in 2 Samuel 12:15; 1 Kings 17:17; 2 Kings 4:20; 5:1–14; Daniel 4:33. When looking at this situation the Jews were still uncertain about doctors. They believed there was a connection between disease and sin (John 9:2) and cited sayings such as "Physician heal yourself" (Luke 4:23). But for all that, every town was required to have a physician (which is why the woman with the issue of blood was able to consult a number of them, Mark 5:26) and there was always a doctor in the Temple to look after the priests who had picked up things through their habit of walking barefoot. Mark clearly didn't think much of doctors (see above, Mark 5:26).

Jesus' attitude did not contradict the Old Testament. He seemed to regard disease as the result of Satan's evil activity in the world, and that as such it must be combated. However, Jesus did not believe that disease was necessarily the result of individual sin. This is clear in John 9:2–4a, if we repunctuate the sentence:

> As he went along, he saw a man blind from birth. His disciples asked him, "Rabbi, who sinned, this man, or his parents, that he was born blind?"
> "Neither this man nor his parents sinned," said Jesus. "But this happened so that the work of God might be displayed in his life."

Jesus accepted that some diseases were the result of spirit possession and dealt with them accordingly (e.g., Matthew 12:27), but he did not treat *all* disease by this method. It was this attitude toward sickness that accelerated the Christian acceptance of physicians in the early church. Luke, as a doctor, was the traveling companion of the apostle Paul (Colossians 4:14). He was, of course, a Greek doctor, and in Greece medicine had been developed considerably. Following the teaching of Hippocrates, doctors took an oath that the life of a patient

Below: A Roman surgeon
tends a flesh wound.
Notice his set of specialist
instruments, which include
a small saw.

should come first, that they would never take advantage of women, that they would never procure abortions, and that they would never reveal confidential information. There was a large school of medicine in Alexandria.

Very few Jews were therefore likely to become physicians, but they were often glad of a physician's services despite the many misgivings.

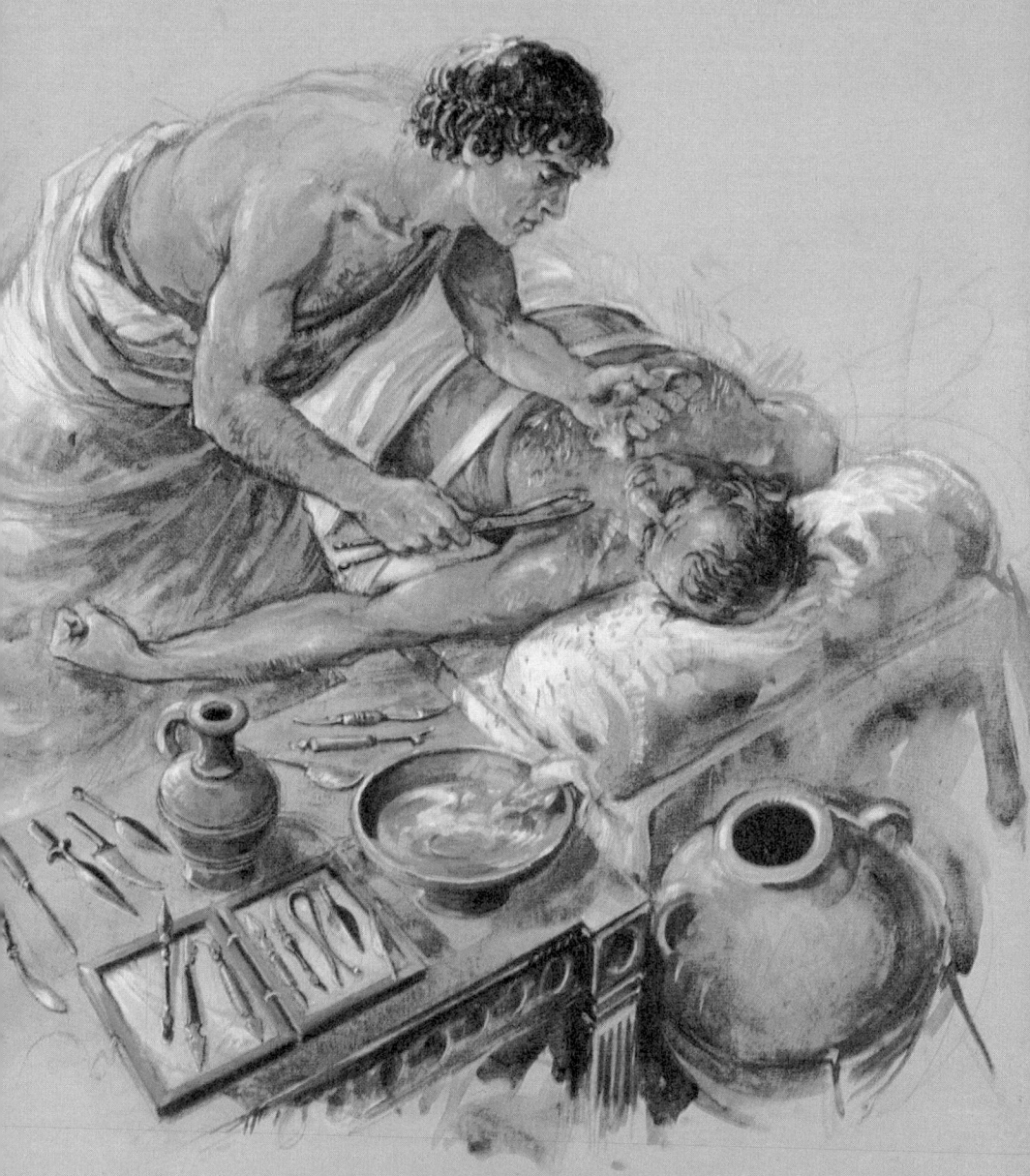

Workers with Money and Goods

Traders were concerned with measurements and money. Before we look at the way traders worked and lived, we will examine the measurements and money of the Bible.

Shekel

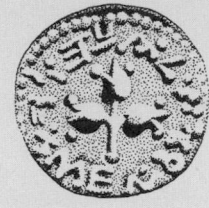

Half shekel

Linear Measurements

Linear measurements were developed from the proportions of the human body, the finger, the palm, the span (distance from spread thumb to little fingertip), the cubit (distance from the elbow to the middle fingertip), and the rope or fathom was the distance from the tip of one middle finger to the other middle finger with the arms extended. This gives a table of length as follows:

4 fingers	= 1 palm
3 palms	= 1 span
2 spans	= 1 cubit
4 cubits	= 1 fathom

This system was not without its problems. Body measurements vary from person to person, and there is evidence that there were differing lengths of cubit, from about 17.7 inches to about 20.5 inches. There was a long or "royal" cubit of 7 palms or 28 fingers (all royal measurements were larger than standard); there were also old cubits (2 Chronicles 3:3) and new ones (Ezekiel 40:5). In general, however, the system was easily understood, and approximate measurements could be calculated.

Longer distances were vaguely worked out in terms of several days' journey (e.g., Genesis 30:36). Much later, the Greeks used a measurement called a *stadion* (plural, *stadia*), which was just over 200 yards and is mentioned in the book of Maccabees. Distance was not used for calculating area as in our system. An acre was the amount of land that could be ploughed by an ox in a day (Isaiah 5:10). The maximum distance that could be walked on the Sabbath (a Sabbath day's journey, Acts 1:12) was 2,000 paces, a there-and-back distance (each way) of a Roman mile (1,000 paces).

Capacity

Capacity was originally measured in a similar, homely way, the name of the container giving its name to the weight. The largest dry measure was the homer, which means "donkey load," and was used for cereals (Leviticus 27:16). The ephah was a large container with a lid and according to Zechariah 5:6–7 was large enough to hold a woman. It was one tenth of a homer (Ezekiel 45:11) and was also used to measure cereals (Ruth 2:17). The omer ("the sheaf") was the smallest measure for cereals and was a tenth of an ephah (Exodus 16:33). It was probably the same size as an issarion, which actually means "tenth," and was used to measure meal (Exodus 29:40). The liquid equivalent of the ephah was the bath. This gives a table on base ten:

10 omers/issarion	= 1 ephah/bath
10 ephahs/baths	= 1 homer

Quite unrelated to this decimal table was the hin, which was used to measure offerings of oil and wine (about seven pints). A sixth of a hin was the minimum amount of water needed each day (Ezekiel 4:11).

Greater accuracy seems to have been developed in later times. The Assyrians developed a system on base six. Their system was:

6 qa	= 1 situ
30 situs	= 1 gur

The words sound very close to the Hebrew words *qab, seah,* and *kor,* and it may therefore be that the Jews adopted the system and used it side by side with the old one. This would mean:

6 qab	= 1 seah
30 seahs	= 1 kor

The qab is mentioned in the siege of Samaria, in which a quarter qab of doves' manure (or seed pods) was sold for five shekels of silver (2 Kings 6:25). The seah was used to measure flour for cereals (2 Kings 7:1), and the kor measured large quantities of liquid and was the equivalent of the homer (Ezekiel 45:14). We cannot work out the exact English equivalents, but the donkey-load or kor is estimated to have been about two hundred twenty litres (about fifty-eight gallons).

Weight
The verb "to weigh" is *shaqual* (shekel) in Hebrew, and for this reason the "shekel" became the basic weight. Absalom's hair weighed two hundred of them (2 Samuel 14:26). From the figures given in Exodus 38:25–26, we can work out that a beka was half a shekel, and a talent was three hundred shekels. At a later date another weight was added, called a *mina*, which was probably fifty shekels. This gives the following table:

2 bekas	= 1 shekel
50 shekels	= 1 mina
60 minas	= 1 talent

The names in the preceding table were adopted in other countries, but the multiples and the actual weights were different. Added to this was the complication that there seem to have been two sets of weights used by the merchant. A light set was used when purchasing and a heavy set when selling (Deuteronomy 25:13). This gave the trader a legitimate percentage profit and was not wrong in itself. It was *mixed*

Left: Coin of the procurator Pontius Pilate, A.D. 30.
Right: Coin of the procurator Antonius Felix, A.D. 59.

weights that were the problem, or the deliberate use of *false* weights in order to cheat people (Leviticus 19:35–36; Micah 6:10–11). Weights themselves were often shaped stones, carved into animals and other subjects, and marked with their weight. They were used in scales and balances (Isaiah 40:12). It is estimated that the talent weighed between seventy-five and eighty pounds. It took its name from the large, heavy lid of a container.

Coinage
In the earliest days of the Bible, trade was done through barter, but it was soon recognized that it was more convenient to exchange something that in its turn could be exchanged for something else. This was done through weighed quantities of metal. Abraham therefore weighed out four hundred shekels of silver in payment for a burial place for his family (Genesis 23:16). The metals used in exchange were mainly gold, silver, and copper. At one point metals were made into standard shapes such as discs, bars, and rings, but true coinage did not start until the seventh century BC. The king's mark was then put on a piece of metal to

guarantee its weight and purity and therefore its value.

Coins are not mentioned until quite late in the Bible. Only in Nehemiah's time do we read about "darics of gold" (Nehemiah 7:71), which were minted by Darius of Persia and took his name. Coins became more plentiful in New Testament times, but there were so many types that money was quite confusing. Three systems of coinage were in operation. The Roman coinage had international currency and was made in coins of copper, bronze, silver, and gold. When Jesus told his disciples to take no gold, silver, or copper in their purses (Matthew 10:9), he was probably referring to the coinage.

Roman coinage

4 quadrans	= 1 as (copper coins)
4 as	= 1 sestertius (bronze)
4 sesterces	= 1 denarius (silver)
25 denarii	= 1 aureus (gold)

The Roman coins are very familiar in the New Testament. Jesus said that if we are sent to prison by an adversary, we will not get out until we have paid the

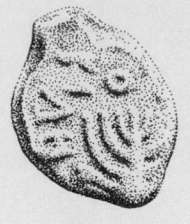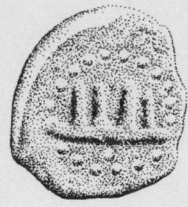

Two dilepton coins from the period of the Jewish Revolt, A.D. 66–70.

Denarius of the Emperor Tiberius.

last quadrans (Matthew 5:26). Matthew 10:29 tells us that two sparrows were sold for a sestertius. The workers in the vineyard of Matthew 20:1–16 each receive a denarius, which was the standard wage for a labourer. Two denarii were paid to the innkeeper by the good Samaritan (Luke 10:35), and Jesus called for a denarius when he was asked questions about the tribute money (Mark 12:15).

Jewish coinage
The Romans allowed local coinage to circulate in addition to their own. There was a very limited Jewish coinage. Coinage seems to have been minted by Nehemiah, probably to pay the Temple tax. Nothing else was heard of coinage until one of the descendants of the Maccabees wrested the privilege from the Syrian overlords (1 Maccabees 15:6). In New Testament times the sole Jewish coin was a copper *lepton*, which means "thin." The widow put them in the treasury (Mark 12:42). It was equivalent to about half a quadrans. The first "real" Jewish coins were produced at times of revolt, between AD 66 and 70, and between AD 132 and 135.

Greek coinage
The other coinage in use was Greek money, originally from the mint set up by Alexander the Great at Acco and subsequently minted at several centres. This table of coinage was:

2 drachm	= 1 didrachm
2 didrachm	= 1 tetradrachm (or stater)
2 tetradrachm	= 1 mina
A large number of mina	= 1 talent

The drachm was the equivalent of a denarius. The stater was therefore four denarii. Again, the coins are mentioned in the New Testament. It is a drachm that the woman loses from her headdress in Luke 15:8. The didrachm was the equivalent of the half shekel that the Jews needed to pay for Temple tax; but because the coin was not very common, a tetradrachm was used for two people. This is the coin that Peter found in the fish's mouth to pay the tax for himself and Jesus (Matthew 17:27). It was probably thirty tetradrachms that Judas received for the betrayal of Jesus (Matthew 26:15). The mina was the "pound" that was given over

to servants by their king (Luke 19:13). The talent was a large amount of money, not a coin. It was used to describe an impossible debt (10,000 talents, Matthew 18:24) and in the parable to which it lends its name (Mathew 25:14–30).

Moneychanging

Those who worked with money had plenty of opportunity for employment. Moneychangers were needed when specific coinage was required and ten percent was normally charged for the exchange. Most important was the money used in the Temple, where it was needed to pay the tax and to pay for sacrificial animals that had been certified as ritually clean. Some people believe that Nehemiah minted special coinage for this purpose (Nehemiah 10:32) and that this practice had been continued. Twelve percent was charged for such exchanges.

When Jesus drove out the moneychangers in the Temple he seems to have been acting out the principle of two messianic prophecies (Psalm 69:9; Malachi 3:1–4; see John 2:17). It was not that the moneychangers were doing anything criminal but that it was not an activity good enough for the house of God (Matthew 21:13).

People who exchanged money were also able to make loans (in fact the table over which money passed was called a "bank"). Jesus suggested in his story of the money entrusted to the king's stewards, that it might have been invested so as to make interest (Matthew 25:27; Luke 19:23). There is an issue here that needs to be understood. In Old Testament times, life was based upon a simple agricultural economy. Nobody needed loans for investment; loans were needed to tide a person over hard times. For this reason, charges of interest was not allowed because that would have been making a profit out of a brother's plight (Exodus 22:25; Leviticus 25:53; Deuteronomy 23:19). But such profit from interest could be made out of a foreigner (Deuteronomy 23:20). By New Testament times, the economy had changed, and it was possible to lend money to support a business venture and to expect a return for it, as in the parables. But Jesus still disapproved of private loans at interest (Luke 6:34).

Taxation

Others were employed in taxation. In the early days of Israel's history, taxation was used only to support the Tabernacle and Temple (Deuteronomy 14:22–27; 18:1–5). When the people wanted a king, Samuel warned them that they would face increased taxation (1 Samuel 8:15), and so it proved. Solomon's building programme and life-style (1 Kings 4:22–28) demanded heavy taxation. Tax commissioners were appointed by the king for twelve districts (1 Kings 4:7–19), and the burden of taxation was so high that it caused a rebellion that divided the kingdom very soon after Solomon's death (1 Kings 12:4).

There is evidence that this form of taxation continued in the kingdoms of Judah and Israel. Ostraca found in a Samaritan storehouse included receipts for oil and wine, and the handles of jars found throughout Judah indicated that the jars contained oil and wine sent to the king. Even the first cuttings of the grass seem to have been taxed during the time of Amos (Amos 7:1).

The most objectionable form of taxation was the payment of protection money. It was the practice of powerful kings to force their neighbours to pay them taxes. Any infringement would be regarded as rebellion and would be followed by a punitive expedition from the army of the more powerful state. Tiglath Pileser of Assyria extracted such tribute from Israel while Menahem was king (2 Kings 15:19–20), and Necho of Egypt did the same thing to Jehoahaz of Judah (2 Kings 23:33–35).

In New Testament times, tribute by taxation had to be paid to the Roman Empire. Roman officials would sell the right to collect taxes in an area to the highest bidder. The tax commmissioner (chief publican) would then have to supply a certain amount of money. He would employ local people as the collectors (publicans), and both commissioner and collectors would tax excessively so that they made a good living as well as passing on what was required by the government. Zacchaeus as chief publican admitted fraud by restoring goods fourfold (Luke 19:8). Levi would have been a local collector (Luke 5:27). The Jews hated the publicans, not only because the publicans took the Jews' money, but because publicans were regarded as traitors to the occupying power. The name was therefore a name of derision. Jewish leaders could not accept Jesus' friendship with such people (Matthew 9:11; 11:19; 21:31). Dislike of the publicans was not entirely unjustified. John the Baptist spoke generally of the need of the publicans not to be greedy (Luke 3:12).

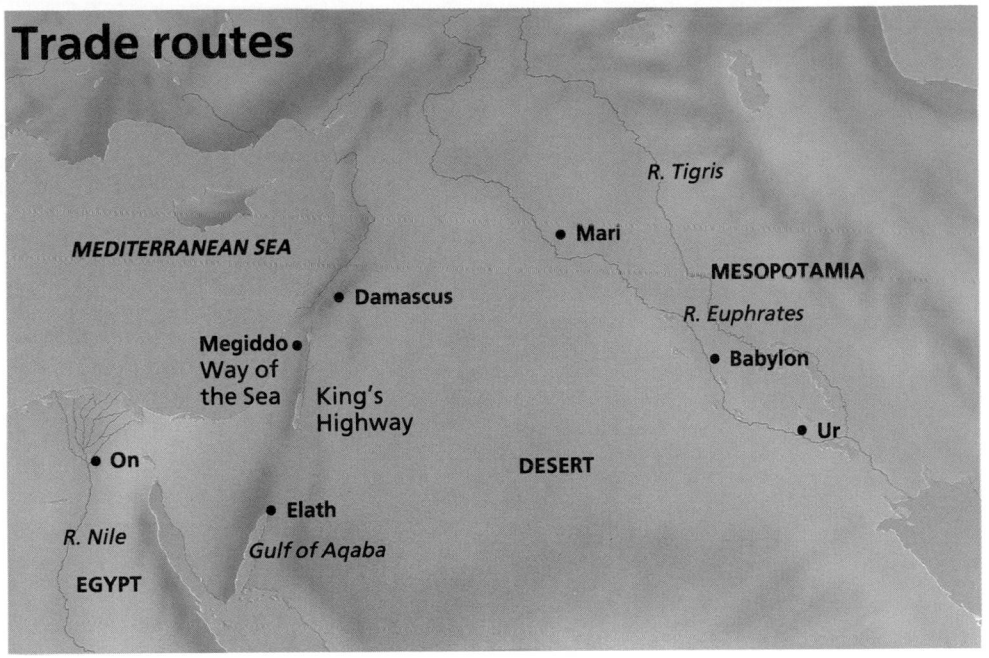

Trade routes

(map labels: MEDITERRANEAN SEA; R. Tigris; ● Mari; MESOPOTAMIA; ● Damascus; R. Euphrates; Megiddo ●; Way of the Sea; ● Babylon; King's Highway; ● Ur; ● On; DESERT; ● Elath; R. Nile; Gulf of Aqaba; EGYPT)

Trading

A living was also made from the profits of trading. This did not happen in early days because the simple agricultural economy not only gave no profit margin to make trading possible, but the prevailing attitude was that the simple life was the right life (Proverbs 31:10–17). Yet by the time Ezekiel 27:17–24 was written, there was extensive trade in agricultural produce — wheat, olives, early figs, honey, oil, and balm being traded with Tyre. Oil and wine were also exported to Egypt, where there was a surplus of grain. Wool and woolen cloth were exported to many areas, and in return there were imports of timber, metals (tin, lead, silver, and copper), and luxury goods (spices, silk, jewels, and gold). This trading had been brought about by the expansion of the kingdom under Solomon. The expansion made it possible for the king to claim taxes on the goods that passed through his territory and on tribute from subject states.

The most important trade route was the "Way of the Sea," which followed the coast from Egypt through what had been Philistine country. It then turned northeast to Megiddo and Hazor and went through to Damascus. The hill route from Egypt passed through Beer Sheba, Hebron, Jerusalem,

Bethel, and Shechem and then divided, either toward Beth Shan and out to Damascus or to Samaria and on to Megiddo. But it was a difficult route used only in wet weather when other routes were made impossible.

East of the Dead Sea and the River Jordan, the "King's Highway" connected the Gulf of Aqaba with Ammon and Damascus. Sea routes were controlled by the Phoenicians, who were in alliance with Solomon.

As the major trade routes went through areas controlled by the Jews, it was possible for those with any capital both to import and export goods. Solomon seems to have imported horses from Cilicia and chariots from Egypt and to have exported them both (2 Kings 10:28). Arrangements were also made so that kings could have an open market for their goods in neighbouring cities. Ahab had such an arrangement in Damascus (1 Kings 20:34).

The problem with such trading is that those with capital tend to acquire more and more wealth while those without capital get relatively poorer. This seems to have happened individually and nationally. Individuals were condemned by Amos, particularly where this kind of wealth was joined with oppression of the poorer people (Isaiah 5:8–12; Amos 6:1–7; Micah 2:1–2). Tyre was condemned for giving a bad return to the poorer nations that needed her goods (Ezekiel 28:2; see also Isaiah 23). By New Testament times, trading was a way of life, and the *Pax Romana* (the peace and unification the Romans had brought to the Mediterranean) increased the possibility for trade because travel was much safer. Rome became the centre of wealth and commerce as "all roads led to Rome." In this period, increased quantities of olive oil were exported from Judaea, while Greek wines, glass, apples, cheeses, linen, and cotton became common in the country.

The marketplace

We know little of the way that trading was done locally. There was normally an open place inside the city gate that served as a market square, and streets leading from the square would have served as dwellings for traders. There was a street of the bakers in Jeremiah's time (Jeremiah 37:21), and the valley between the eastern and western ridges of Jerusalem was known as the valley of the cheesemakers. It is clear that there must have been stalls to service people who lived in the city, because fresh food had to be purchased each day. A weekly market was available for people from the surrounding villages to buy and to sell produce. Nehemiah had to regulate things so that there were no such markets on the Sabbath (Nehemiah 13:15–22).

The form of the market was for the goods to be displayed at ground level, while the seller sat among the goods. Special markets would be set up when a caravan arrived. Prices were seldom fixed, so that every purchase needed some form of bargaining. Proverbs 20:14 sees the person who, while in the market, grumbled at the high price he had to pay, but when he got home boasted of the bargain. Goods in kind were accepted as exchange, as well as weighed amounts of metal or coinage (see Luke 16:5–7). Measurement was always full. When Jesus was describing how a measure should be pressed down with grain, shaken together, and topped up until it overflowed, he was describing the standard practice for giving goods of dry measure in the market (Luke 6:38; "bosom" in old versions means "lap.")

Now look at your Bible

The first smiths

Genesis 4:15. Metalwork was taken up by the Jews so that metalsmiths became the elite of all craftsmen and were taken into captivity by the Babylonians (2 Kings 24:15–16). Solomon used his metalsmiths to create the implements for use in the Temple (1 Kings 7:45–47). It is not clear, however, where the Jews learned the craft. Some scholars believe that they learned it from traveling metalsmiths of the Kenite clan, whose people traveled throughout the land with their bellows strapped onto donkeys. The traveling smith was recognized by a metal cross worn on his forehead. It has been suggested that this was the "mark of Cain" given by God to indicate that the descendents of Cain (which means "smith") should be artisans, not rulers of tribes.

Health laws

God gave the Jewish people a number of commandments, and their medical significance has been appreciated only in recent years. Deuteronomy 23:13 ensured that the soldier carried a spade so that all human excrement could be buried. Leviticus 13 ensured isolation for people who had leprosy. It has been suggested that the insistence on circumcision has led to a very low incidence of cancer of the cervix among Jewish women, and that the forbidden degrees of marriage were given to control a number of hereditary diseases.

Jewelry making

Exodus 28:9–14. The Jews developed the craft of jewelry making and engraving. Ivory was carved and used for inlay (1 Kings 10:22; 22:39; Amos 3:15). Small cylinders were engraved and were used as personal seals. This craft developed naturally because as nomads it was not possible to carry a lot of material around.

Unglazed pots

Matthew 10:42. Unglazed pottery was extremely important. As water evaporated through the clay, it cooled the liquid inside. This lies behind the description of water as *cold* water.

Designation of money

The terms used for money in the New Testament illustrate the problems Bible translators actually face. If they use the original term, it might be meaningless to the reader. If they substitute the name of a current coin, or a monetary value, then inflation might make the substitute completely out of date in a short time. "Pieces of silver" or a "day's wages" does not always indicate the value of the coinage because amounts vary in different societies.

Israelite ivory carving from Samaria. The Jews developed the crafts of making jewelry and carving ivory.

Part 2

National Institutions and Customs

Towns and Villages

When people moved away from caves and began to cultivate the land, they settled in places where the land was fertile and where there was a ready supply of water. This sometimes led to conflict with nomadic groups who wanted to share the water. This conflict made it necessary for the new farmers to live near one another for mutual protection, and it was for this reason that the village came into being.

If the village was vulnerable, it would sometimes be built so that the blank walls of the houses formed a defensive village wall, with access only through one gap or gate. If the village was on an easily-defended site and if it was on a trade route, then at the time when the invention of the bronze ploughshare made it possible to cultivate the land more intensively and so brought more wealth, the village was ringed with a defensive rampart. It was this, rather than sheer size, that turned the village into a town (see Leviticus 25:29–31, "But houses in villages without walls round them are to be considered as open country..."). Even cities as important as Jerusalem and Megiddo were only about thirteen acres in extent in Old Testament times. If the rampart was replaced by a wall of solid construction, it became known as a "fortified city" (Jeremiah 34:7).

There was a two-way link between towns and villages. In times of warfare, the villagers would flock to the town for the protection of its walls. In the summertime, people from the town and city were glad to leave for the country, where they would get involved in the harvest and so have a "working holiday." Towns and villages were therefore clustered together (Joshua 15:32, 36, 41).

The centre of the village

The "centre" of the village was the water supply. People went to the well to get their water, taking their own leather buckets and pitchers (see John 4:11), and as they did so they met others from the village for conversation and relaxation at the beginning and end of the day. The well was not always a deep hole with a wellhead. The well was quite often in a dried-up river bed. About four feet (a metre) square and four feet (a metre) deep, it filled up with water and was known as a pit (literal meaning of Jeremiah 14:3). Winter rains always filled the dry bed. When there were quarrels, the pits were sometimes filled in (Genesis 25:15).

Town walls

The most important feature of the town was its wall. Initially, the walls of important towns appear to have been made of stone. The ancient walls of Jericho were six-and-one-half feet (two metres) thick and had towers of thirty feet (ten metres) in height — and that was in 5000 BC. In the bronze age, when building became more extensive and agriculture more intensive, the foundation stones of the

The ancient well at Beer Sheba.

Opposite: Part of the seven metre wide wall dating from eighth century B.C. Jerusalem. This is the wall referred to by Isaiah in his words to King Hezekiah: "you broke down the houses to fortify the wall" (Isaiah 22:10).

walls were made of stone, but the walls themselves were made of bricks. The walls tended to follow a particular contour, so that, although the town had an irregular shape, it always had to be approached uphill.

Walls varied in type. Some walls sloped from bottom to top, with bases up to twenty-six feet (nine metres) in thickness. Some were casemate walls — two parallel walls with rooms built in the space between. Others were double walls, filled with rubble. The walls did not always keep the invaders out. Therefore, after cities were taken and destroyed, it was necessary to rebuild on the ruins of the old, because inevitably the old one was built on the best site in the area. This happened so many times in some towns that when archaeologists dig into a site, they find successive levels like layers of a cake, corresponding to the times of destruction and rebuilding. Such a site is called a tell, and by accurately dating each layer, the archaeologist can often write the history of the city.

Remains of the wall of the Jebusite city of Jerusalem, dating to the eighteenth century B.C.

In practical building terms the development of a tell meant that the lower part of the defensive wall

Tel Beer Sheba. This area was occupied from the fourth millennium B.C.

had to be built as a retaining wall to hold in the higher level inside. The *glacis* was therefore developed — a steep slope of beaten earth and rock, up to the level of the new building line. The glacis was often prefaced by a wide ditch, which had the additional advantage of supplying more soil to make the glacis even higher. The wall was then erected on top of the glacis.

As techniques of siege warfare advanced, casemate walls had to be replaced by solid walls — normally effected by infill. Systems of salients and recesses were built into the walls, and towers provided for defense (2 Chronicles 26:15). The defenders could then shoot at those who were attacking the walls. In some cases, such as at Lachish, two separate walls were built, one inside the other, to give a double line of defenses. We cannot be sure how the walls were finished on the top. Rahab's house may have been built on the top, because the spies hid on the roof, but it may have been the top dwelling in a casemate wall (Joshua 2:15). There are some indications that the tops of the walls were hung with shields (Song of Songs 4:4; Ezekiel 27:11).

The gate

In the early days the gate was the potential weak point in the defenses, and it therefore became a matter of particular concern. To possess the gate was to possess the city (Genesis 22:17). It was therefore common practice for the Canaanites to offer a human sacrifice when setting up a gate. There seems to be a reference to this in 1 Kings 16:34 when Hiel's son Segub died when his father rebuilt Jericho; God had said that anyone who rebuilt the city would lose his son.

The doors of a gate were made of wood covered with metal (Psalm 107:16). Iron bars held the doors in place (1 Samuel 23:7; Isaiah 45:2). As warfare became more sophisticated, such gates did not offer enough protection. One early design for providing that protection called for building overlapping walls with two gates, forming a courtyard between. Another was to build walls at right angles to the main walls, again forming a courtyard. If the outer gate was penetrated there was still another, and in the meantime the defenders could pour down liquids and shoot down things on the attackers in the courtyard below. Both forms of gate made it

The strongly protected gate to the stronghold of Megiddo.

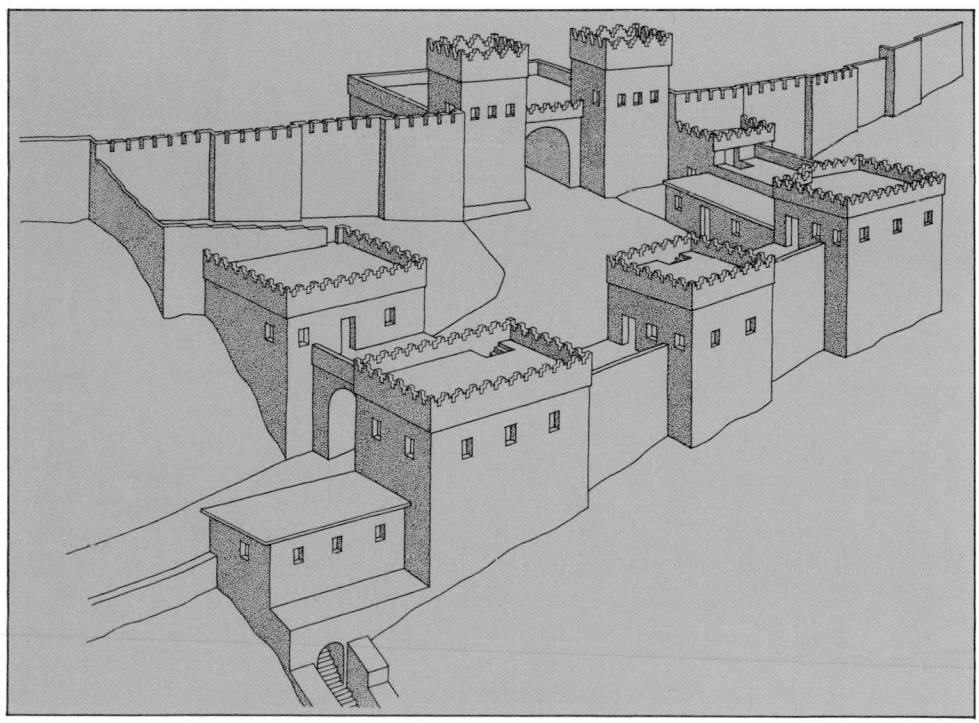

The busy Damascus Gate into the city of Jerusalem.

possible for the defenders to sally forth in sudden sorties against the enemy.

The gates were heavily defended and were provided with towers to serve as lookout posts. In 2 Samuel 18:24–26 David is sitting between the two gates at Mahanaim, and the watchman in the tower above is able to see a runner coming with news of the battle with Absalom's forces.

The gates became still more sophisticated when the two pairs of gates were made at 90° to each other so that the attacking soldiers had to make a turn. The gates were arranged so that the attackers had to turn left. This exposed their right-hand side, which was not covered with a shield, to the defenders above. More complex designs of zig-zag entry and

of three gates instead of two were also developed.

The elaborate construction of the gate was useful in peacetime. Rooms were provided in the walls for merchants to stay, and the shade provided by the high walls made it a good place for meetings. The gate was therefore a place for public speaking, the listeners sitting on stone benches (Proverbs 1:21; 2 Chronicles 32:6; Jeremiah 17:19), and for conversation (Psalm 69:12). It was useful for resting (Esther 2:21), and was the place where local justice was dispensed (Ruth 4:1–2), or should have been (Amos 5:15). Gates were always shut at night, which gives rise to the joy that in the New Jerusalem there will be no night — the gates will always be open (Revelation 21:25).

The market

The market normally opened off the gate and was associated with it (Acts 16:19). It was the area where the villagers brought in their produce to sell and where traders from other parts of the country brought their wares. It was normally open every weekday (see Nehemiah 10:31) for in the absence of refrigeration it was necessary for people to purchase food on a daily basis.

A market of Bible times. Notice the camels with their packs of merchandise, the traders with their booths and the beggar in the foreground.

An Arab merchant on market day in Beer Sheba.

There were other special "market days," and almost festive occasions when a caravan arrived. It was not possible to bring trucks or even camels through many gateways, and therefore the porter was engaged to carry the wares into the marketplace. Jesus used the great loads carried by the porters as a picture of the burden of legalism the lawyers put on the people of his day without lifting a finger to help (Luke 11:46). Paul may have had the same practice in view when he told us to bear one another's burdens (Galatians 6:2).

The marketplace was generally a busy and happy place, as there were many people about. It was therefore a place where public speaking and teaching could be done (Acts 17:17), where children played games of "weddings" and "funerals" (Matthew 11:16–17), and where the unemployed would go in hope that someone would give them work (Matthew 20:3). Houses surrounding the marketplace might provide a place to call out the news (Luke 12:3) and places where craftsmen could work and sell their wares. Somewhere in this area, the public oven would be sited.

Town streets

In Old Testament times, streets ran off the market. They were so narrow that it was possible only for people to walk in single file. The houses were built hard up against each other and the "street" was the space left between. From the street led equally narrow alleys to gain access to areas behind (Proverbs 7:8). This system created a network so complex it was almost impossible for a newcomer to know so that he could find his way about. The streets were unpaved and were full of rubbish — mud bricks, broken pottery, and refuse — often higher than the floor level of the houses themselves.

During the wintertime the whole system turned into a quagmire and in the summer the smells made

Narrow street in the old city of Jerusalem.

it necessary for people to work out of the city (see Psalm 18:42; Isaiah 10:6). It was no wonder that one of the delights of the city of New Jerusalem is that it will be paved (Revelation 21:21).

The narrowness and darkness of the streets, together with the odd corners, made the cities centres of violence (Psalm 10:8), and dogs, wolf-like and savage, roamed the area. David could hear the dogs barking in the night (Psalm 59:6), and Jesus knew they would come for the scraps under the table (Matthew 15:27; Luke 16:1). Dogs were not popular. The price of a dog could never constitute a monetary offering (Deuteronomy 23:18), and to call a person a dog was an insult (Revelation 23:15).

Towns built by the Greeks and Romans tended, by contrast, to be well-planned and with paved streets. Squares were formed where major streets crossed one another, and there were many open squares before public buildings. Caesarea, the port Herod built to bring the Romans to Judaea, had a main street, with shops on either side, and baths and theatres. Houses were built in blocks of four, and there were major buildings of administration and entertainment. Antioch, which Paul used as his

The Roman theatre at Caesarea Maritima. In its ruins was found an inscription with Pontius Pilate's name.

The Citadel, Jerusalem. The lower portion of this tower dates back to Herod's time, and formed part of his palace.

base, even had street lighting. The question arises as to why there was so great a contrast. Basically it was that when the Jews began to build, they did so on the foundations of the Canaanite cities and there were few master builders of the type of Solomon, Omri, and Ahab.

Central fortress

In some towns a central castle was built as a royal residence and as a means of last defense for the remainder of the population if the outer walls were breached. Omri seems to have done this in the city of Samaria (1 Kings 16:24). The Akkra, Herod's palace, and Castle Antonia were all castles of this type in Jerusalem. A temple could also be used for defense. The "tower" of Shechem seems to

The entrance to the water supply system at Hazor, which dates from the reign of King Ahab.

have been of this type (Judges 9:46). When Jerusalem fell to the Roman armies in AD 70 the final stand was made at the Temple. It became the practice to build additional walls in the castle area so constituting an "upper city" and a "lower city."

Water supply

Water provision was a necessity if a city was to withstand a siege. Some cities had easy access to water. Jericho had a spring, and the water used by Mary at Nazareth is still flowing in the city today. Other places had some difficulty in providing an adequate, secure water supply. In some cases provision was made by digging down to water level. This was done to begin with in Jerusalem. In Megiddo and Hazor, huge pits that went down to water level were dug inside the city. Then a tunnel was built out to the source of the water beyond the city walls.

Cisterns supplied much of the domestic water needs. There is still a huge one in use in the garden tomb in Jerusalem, which in the time of Jesus was in the northern suburb of the city. It still supplies all the water needed for the garden throughout the dry season. The water cisterns of Bethlehem were well-known for their cool water. When lime plaster was developed, the water was retained for even longer.

But cisterns and pools were also provided publicly too. The pools of Gibeon (2 Samuel 2:13) have been excavated. One is rectangular, thirty-five by fifty-five feet (twelve by eighteen metres), and another is thirty feet (ten metres) in diameter and sixty feet (twenty metres) deep. There was a pool in Samaria (1 Kings 22:38), and there were others in Jerusalem (2 Kings 18:17; Isaiah 22:11). One of the most remarkable water works is the tunnel Hezekiah constructed to bring water from an underground spring through a ridge to a pool inside the city walls, the pool of Siloam. As the standards of water engineering were improved, aqueducts and clay pipes were used to bring water from Solomon's Pools, near Bethlehem, into Jerusalem. Similarly two aqueducts were built to bring water into Caesarea.

Solomon's Pools, near Bethlehem, served as reservoirs for the city of Jerusalem.

The development of the city of Jerusalem

Jerusalem provides a good example of the development of a city, and because it is so important in the

Bible, we shall look at the development of the city throughout Bible times. It was first built by the Jebusites, a Canaanite tribe, for protection in the mountains of Judaea. It was situated on the winter trade route, which passed north-south along the watershed between the Jordan valley and streams that flowed down toward the Mediterranean. The earliest settlement was built at the southern end of a steep-sided ridge bounded by the Kidron on the east and another small stream on the west. A defensive wall north of the settlement and across the ridge was the only artificial defense line needed.

Although the town stood on the hill road from north to south, there was no geographical reason that it should have developed into a major city. It did not have a major water supply, a great river, or a great trade route. Sometimes it was called Jebus and sometimes Jerusalem (Yara-Salem), which means "Founded by Salem." Salem was a Canaanite god, either of dawn or of twilight, and the reference might be to the beauty of the place in early morning or in evening light.

By the time of Abraham it was ruled by a "king"

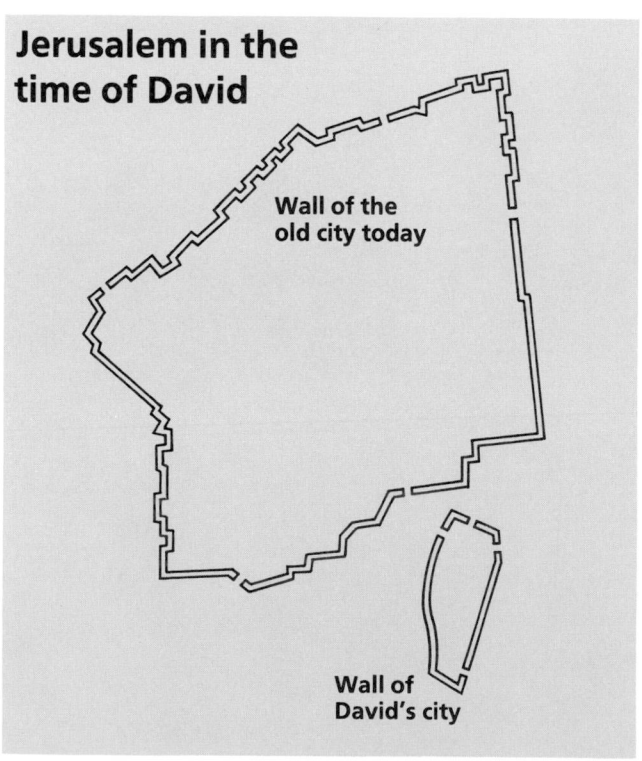

Jerusalem in the time of David

Wall of the old city today

Wall of David's city

Remains dating from the Jebusite city and David's Jerusalem can be seen in this view of the Ophel ridge.

(Melekh) who was understood to be the representative on earth (Zedek) of El Elyon — the Most High God. The Melchizedek of the time of Abraham's rescue of Lot from his captors came out to meet Abraham to offer him hospitality (Genesis 14:18). If Moriah is the area immediately north of the city, then Abraham went back to Jerusalem to obey God's command to sacrifice Isaac (Genesis 22:2; 2 Chronicles 3:1). At the time the Jews entered Canaan at the conquest, probably about five hundred years later, the ruler of Jerusalem was still regarded as a priest-king and was then called Adoni (Lord) Zedek (Joshua 10:1).

David's capital

Jerusalem would probably never have developed in importance had it not been that the Israelite tribes split into two groups at the time of the occupation of Canaan. The tribes that settled in the south had their centre at Hebron and came to be strongly pro-David. The tribes that settled in the north came to be strongly pro-Saul. When Saul's remaining son, Ishbosheth, had been murdered (2 Samuel 4) the tribes in the north asked David to be their leader. It was

The Ophel ridge, site of the earliest city, is on the left in this view of Jerusalem from Mount Scopus.

not in the interests of national unity to choose a capital in either north or south or to select a capital already associated with one of the tribes.

Jebus/Jerusalem was a logical choice. It was placed between the northern and southern grouping of tribes, and it was associated with neither group. The king of Jerusalem had been defeated in battle (Joshua 10:1), and though the place had been held for a time by the tribe of Judah (Judges 1:8), it had regained its independence as a Canaanite city (Judges 19:11–12).

David therefore set out to conquer it and to make it his capital. He accomplished the capture in two spectacular ways — by defying a curse and by overcoming a seemingly impassable natural barrier. The Jebusites had brought out their blind and lame as part of a ritual display to curse David's troops with blindness and lameness if they attacked the city. Also, the Jebusites had removed the wooden steps in the shaft leading from the inside of the city to the water supply below (2 Samuel 5:6–8). These actions did not deter David and his forces. Led apparently by Joab (1 Chronicles 11:6), they pursued the attack through the narrow water shaft and showed

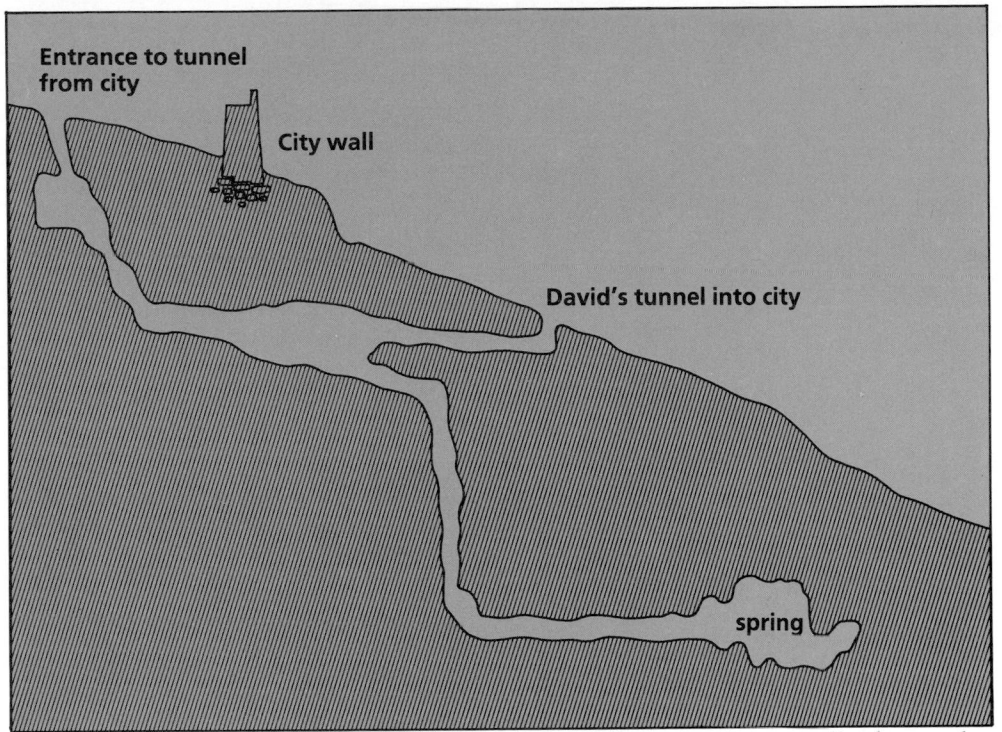

Entrance to tunnel from city

City wall

David's tunnel into city

spring

David seems to have captured the Jebusite city of Jerusalem by sending men through a tunnel which gave access to the Gihon spring.

their fearlessness of the curse by actually despatching the blind and the lame.

David then built up Jerusalem, expanding its area by means of retaining walls and narrow terraces (2 Samuel 5:9; 1 Chronicles 11:8), which today we know as the "millo" (1 Kings 9:15, 24). It may have been at this time that the Jews reinterpreted the name of the city so that it became known as "The City of Peace," Ieru-shalom, an understanding that has remained with it ever since. Jesus referred to this name when, knowing the conflicts that were to overtake the city, he said, "If you, even you, had only known on this day what would bring you peace" (Luke 19:42).

It was not enough, however, to use a neutral city as a capital; it was necessary to develop Jerusalem as a religious centre. David achieved this by bringing the Ark of the Covenant to the city (1 Chronicles 13:25–26), making plans to build a Temple to contain it (2 Samuel 7; 1 Chronicles 21–22). North of the city was a threshing floor where the angel of God had stopped a plague from going any further (1 Kings 9:15, 24). It was the place believed by the Jews to be the spot where Abraham had so nearly sacrificed Isaac. It seemed to be the ideal spot for a Temple. David was to leave this development to his son Solomon, but he does seem to have expanded the city northwards up to what was to be the Temple site. This involved taking the fortified tower or royal fortress known as the Ophel (2 Chronicles 27:3).

Solomon's Temple

When Solomon began to build the Temple, he found it was not an easy thing to build on so steep a ridge. David had achieved construction at the southern end by erecting a series of walls and terraces, but Solomon needed to do much more than that. Solomon solved the problem by creating large terraces. These terraces were supported by arches beneath, which were themselves anchored to the hillside, and by massive retaining walls at the edges. The terraces descended from the highest point southward toward Ophel and the main city (1 Kings 6–7). The Temple was erected on the highest point, and administrative and royal buildings were built on the lower terraces. During the building operations, large numbers of workmen were employed, and large amounts of building material were required; as a result there was commercial development. The country itself was divided into twelve districts, each district responsible for the upkeep of the royal court for one month of the year, for the provision of workmen for the buildings, and for taxes. Jerusalem, Bethlehem, and Hebron were not taxed, presumably because of the historical links with David's family. The high level of taxation, the exemptions, and the old history of division between north and south led to a permanent division of the kingdom. The influx of workers and traders probably led to settlements growing on the large flat hill to the west of the city.

Hezekiah's pool

Because of the division of the kingdom, we would have expected the city to have declined in importance after the reign of Solomon. Ten tribes declared their independence and set up a capital city first at Shechem (1 Kings 12:25) and eventually at Samaria (1 Kings 16:23–24). Jerusalem remained the capital for the tribes of Judah and Benjamin. But it still retained great importance because of the Temple buildings, despite the rival shrines set up in the northern kingdom of Israel at Dan and at Bethel (1 Kings 12:29).

During this period, when there was civil war between Israel and Judah and when there was deportation to Assyria and Babylon respectively of the most skilled of the population of Israel (712 BC) and Judah (586 BC), there were two remarkable building developments in Jerusalem. One was undertaken to secure the city's water supplies, which at the time were outside the city walls, at the pool of Gihon. King Hezekiah bored through the ridge under the city to cause the water to flow through to a new pool built inside the city walls. Then he appears to have blocked off access to the spring from outside the city

Warren's Shaft, Jerusalem; the vertical shaft cut by the Jebusites to give them access to water when the city was besieged. It may have been through this shaft that David's men entered the city.

walls (2 Chronicles 32:30).

The other building development during this period was to enclose by a defensive wall the hill to the west of the city, where there had been large-scale settlement. That project had the effect of more than doubling the size of the city of Jerusalem (2 Chronicles 32:5). It is difficult to be certain either of the exact line of the wall or of the builder. We do know that after the city had been destroyed by Nebuchadnezzar and Nehemiah was sent from Persia to rebuild the city walls, the line of the wall he repaired included the deep valley to the west of the city of David and the hills on the other side.

Jerusalem rebuilt

Jerusalem would have remained a heap of ruins after the Babylonian destruction had it not been that the Persian ruler, Cyrus, who had brought the Babylonian Empire to an end, wanted to restore the religious life of his subject peoples. A contingent was therefore allowed to return to Jerusalem under a man called Zerubbabel to restore the Temple. Ezra came to restore the people's knowledge of the law and religious practice, and Nehemiah through personal contact with the Persian emperor was allowed to rebuild the walls as the governor of the city.

The walls were rebuilt with the labour of the local people and against great discouragement and opposition from outside. The Temple was repaired and people once again lived in the city, but the royal buildings and porches were left in ruins so that the Temple in effect was an isolated building in the middle of a very large courtyard. Jerusalem thus became the spiritual centre of a small Persian province on the fringes of the Empire.

Jerusalem under the Seleucids

As Babylon had come to the end as a great power in 538 BC, so in 332 BC, the Persian Empire came to an end, falling to the Greeks under Alexander the Great. This did not have a great political effect on the Jews at Jerusalem, but it had a profound religious effect. Allegiance was switched from Persia to Greece, and Greek ideas and philosophy came to influence many of the religious ideas of the Jews. A Hellenist party developed that denied bodily resurrection, for example. But the more formidable prob-

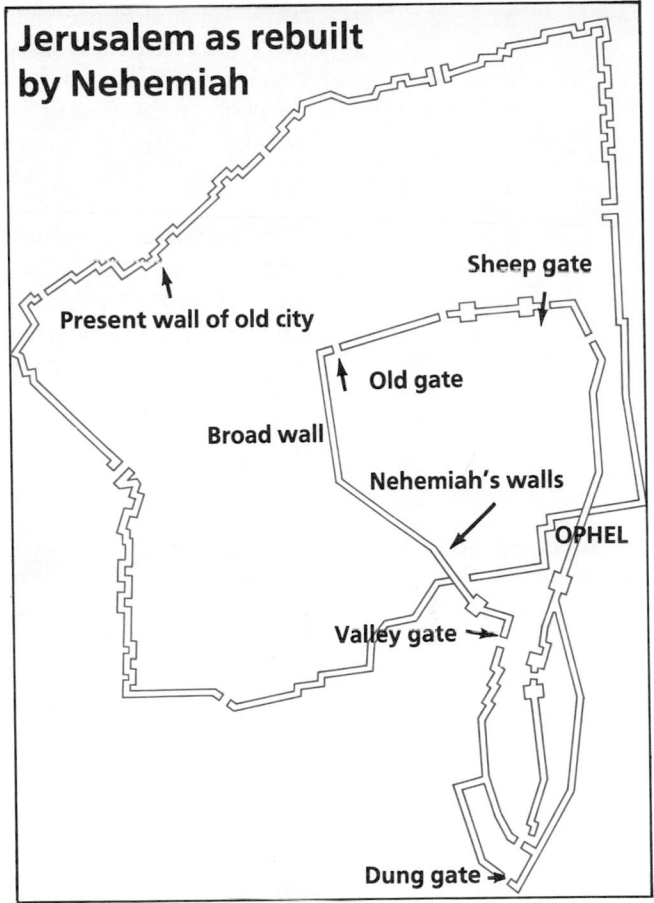

Jerusalem as rebuilt by Nehemiah

Sheep gate

Present wall of old city

Old gate

Broad wall

Nehemiah's walls

OPHEL

Valley gate →

Dung gate →

lems in political life for the Jews came later, after Alexander died and his empire was divided up among his generals. Egypt came under the control of Ptolemy, Syria came under the control of Seleucus, and Jerusalem was caught between the two.

As long as Jerusalem was under control of Ptolemy the problem was moot, except that large numbers of Jews were exiled to Alexandria and became the most important Jewish community outside of Jerusalem. But in 198 BC Jerusalem came finally under the control of the Seleucid king, Antiochus. One of his successors, Antiochus Epiphanes, decided that the time had come for all Jews to convert to the Greek religion. He plundered and desecrated the Temple, built a fortress on the now-deserted hill to the west called the Akkra, and systematically sought to destroy the Jewish faith. Jewish reaction led to a revolt under the Maccabees, a name taken from the nickname (Maccabeus means "the hammer") of one of the resistance leaders. It took many years of conflict and the death of all the rebel leadership before the Akkra was defeated and the office of priest and ruler was combined in the family succession.

The Hasmoneans rebuild

The new rulers, known as the Hasmoneans because they retained the family name of Hashmon, were able to expand the size of their territory until they occupied the area once held by Judah and Israel. The city of Jerusalem became prosperous through trade. A new element affected its prosperity; there were now so many Jews scattered throughout the Middle East that when they came to the Temple to take part

The Garden Tomb, Jerusalem.

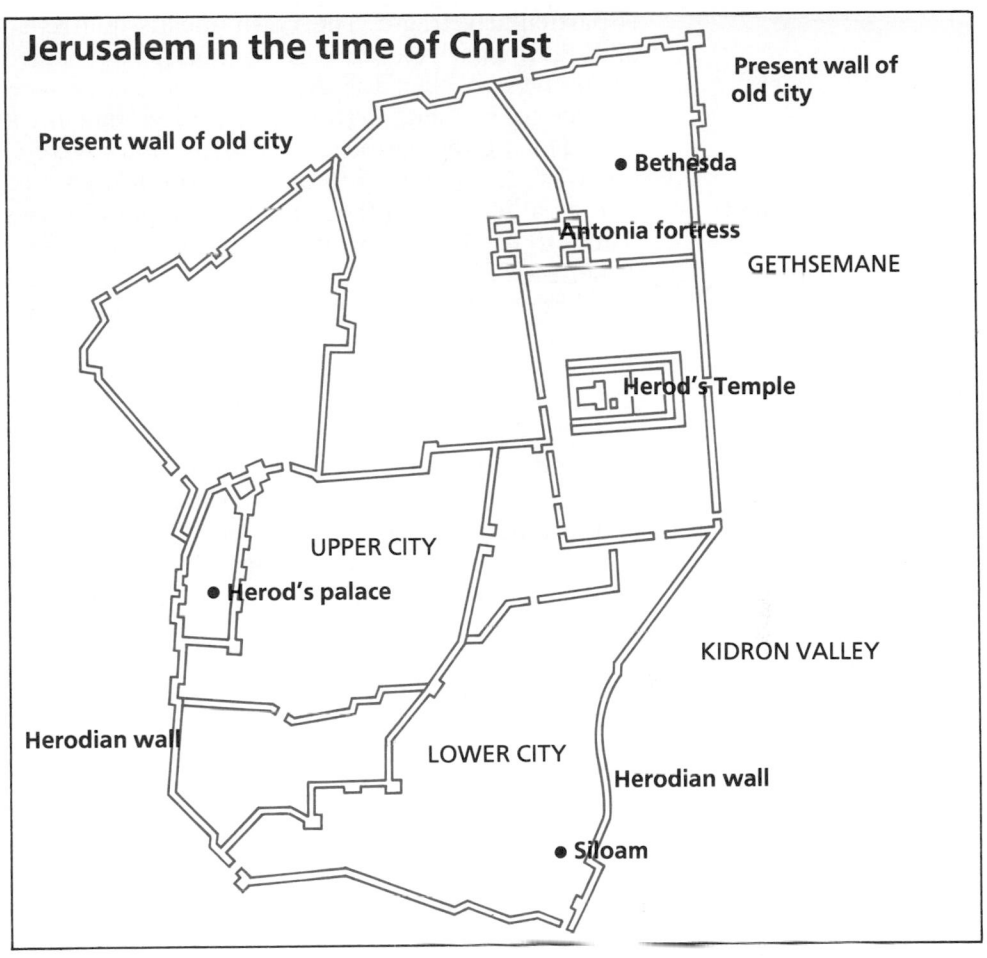

Jerusalem in the time of Christ

Present wall of old city

Present wall of old city

● Bethesda

Antonia fortress

GETHSEMANE

Herod's Temple

UPPER CITY

● Herod's palace

KIDRON VALLEY

Herodian wall

LOWER CITY

Herodian wall

● Siloam

in the pilgrim feasts, they brought much of their wealth and goods with them.

In rebuilding the city, the Hasmoneans again enclosed the western hill, and they dug a deep fosse, sixty feet (twenty metres) deep and two hundred fifty feet (eighty metres) across, beyond the northern wall of the Temple. They built their own palace opposite the Ophel over what had become known as the Tyropoean Valley. It is in the south-facing, northern side of the fosse that the "garden tomb" is to be found today. It is revered by Christians as a place similar to that in which Jesus was buried and from which he rose from the dead.

Herodian Jerusalem

The history of Jerusalem between the establishment of the Hasmonean priest-kings and the time of Jesus is particularly tragic. The Hasmoneans quarrelled among themselves, and in seeking power allied themselves to alien forces, so that Jerusalem was subject to Roman, Parthian, and Herodian invasion. During the period the Roman armies were in the area, Antipater, king of the Edomites, entered into an alliance with the Romans to support a contender to the Jewish throne and thereby made himself effective ruler of the area under the Romans (63 BC). Antipater was driven out by the Parthians, who supported another contender, and Jerusalem at last fell to his son Herod, who was granted legions from Rome to retake the city. So Herod the Great became "king of the Jews."

Herod had a perennial problem of insecurity because he was hated by the Jews. One resolution of that problem was through bribery. So as to ingratiate himself with the Jews, he decided to rebuild the Temple. He cleared the entire site of Solomon's Temple and royal palaces, extending the work south so as to produce a platform four hundred yards (three hundred and sixty metres) long and three hundred yards (two hundred and seventy metres) wide. On this he built a Temple twice as high as

Herod the Great built his palace of Herodion on a volcano-like peak between Bethlehem and the Dead Sea.

Herod the Great's stronghold of Masada. The cone-shaped slope in the centre is the artificial ramp constructed by the Romans to force an entrance in A.D. 74.

was Solomon's. The courtyard was surrounded by magnificent colonnades, and the whole place was one of the building wonders of ancient times. This was the Temple that featured so often in the life of Jesus.

Herod's other approach was to build fortified palaces. Masada and Herodion were built in the country, and Jerusalem itself was fortified by two great castles. One of these, Castle Antonia, named in honour of Mark Antony, was built at the northwest corner of the new Temple and overlooked it. It was in this place that Jesus appeared before Pilate (John 18:33) and where steps led down into the Temple and provided a convenient rostrum for Paul to speak to the Temple crowds (Acts 21:37, 40). A further fortified palace was built on the western wall on the edge of the western hill. It was built around three towers, and it was here that Herod received Jesus on the morning of the crucifixion (Luke 23:7).

Finally, Herod built a large wall from Castle Antonia to his own Citadel, the wall arching out into the northwestern area beyond the existing city. The wall enclosed settlements, markets, the pool of Bethesda, and domestic dwellings. It had to come

Model of the Castle Antonia, Jerusalem.

back at an angle to avoid an ancient quarry now made into a garden. The quarry, with a spur out to the centre, which the quarrymen had left, became the public place for crucifixion. In the quarry wall was a tomb that was as yet unused. It was to become the site for the victory of Jesus.

At a later point in history, another wall was built to bring in other domestic dwellings north of the city. It linked the Citadel to Antonia again, but there is still a great deal of argument as to whether it included Herod's northern wall, or whether that was even farther out to the northwest.

Jerusalem was destroyed by the Roman general Titus in AD 70, after a rebellion led by the Zealots. After yet another revolt in AD 135, the emperor, Hadrian, ploughed up the land south of the Temple and rebuilt a new city to the north, which he called Aelia Capitolina. Effectively Jerusalem had moved north, with the Temple now at the southeast corner, the position it holds today.

Now look at your Bible

Water for King David

2 Samuel 23:13–18. David longed for water from the well of Bethlehem, and three of his men fought their way to the well to get it. Instead of drinking the water, David poured it out "to the Lord." This story is often not understood. It is based on two things. First, it is sometimes possible to give a person something so expensive that he says, "I'm sorry, I really cannot accept it." David felt that way about the risks his men had taken and the blood that had possibly been spilled. The water was too precious for him to accept. Second, a person's most precious things were offered to God. David was giving to God the most precious thing he had.

A city amidst hills

Psalm 121:1. Jerusalem is on a ridge surrounded by hills. It was easy for the defenders of Jerusalem to feel that their city was safe because of those hills. The psalmist was challenging that attitude when he wrote, "I will lift up my eyes to the hills — where does my help come from?" The writer knew that his help came from God and so he wrote, "My help comes from the Lord." One of the hills overlooking Jerusalem on the west is Kiriath Jearim. It was there that David brought the Ark and let it rest so that it could overlook Jerusalem. He was too afraid at that time to bring the Ark into the city because the Temple was not yet built and because of the problems the Ark had caused on the way from the Philistines. Above Jerusalem to the west is the Mount of Olives. It was there that Jesus looked down on the city and wept, and it was there that he told his disciples of the coming end of the world.

Jesus' yoke

Matthew 11:28. It is commonly thought that Jesus was talking here about the yoke that harnessed animals together when they were pulling a plough or a load. He was instead referring to a piece of wood that was fitted over one's shoulders so that loads could be hung on it. The device was similar to the yoke used by the milkmaid of a byegone age when she was carrying two pails. The reference in Matthew 11 is to a porter. Often he was asked to carry loads impossible for a human being, but when he was given a yoke, the burden became much easier. Jesus does not say that he will take our burdens away but that he will give us the means of carrying them so that they are not too much for us.

Following after Jesus

Matthew 16:24. In our culture, to "follow after" a person means to put oneself in a secondary position, but the phrase did not mean that in Bible times. The streets were so narrow that if two people went together, they had to go single file. To follow after a person was to go *with* them. We would therefore say, "If anyone *comes* with me..."

Let's Look at Jerusalem

More and more people are visiting Jerusalem, and others would go if they knew that there were things to see that would bring the Bible alive to them. The following suggestions are made for anyone who is hoping to visit Jerusalem, so that he or she can make the most of his or her visit.

The Temple site

You can explore the Temple site. Outside, on the southeast corner, you can see where Herod extended the retaining wall first built by Solomon and

An artist's reconstruction of Jerusalem in Jesus's time.

repaired by Zerubbabel. The drop from the colonnade built at the top of the wall was so great that the devil tempted Jesus to throw himself down from it (that is, down from the pinnacle). Farther along to the north is the Golden Gate, built on the site of the western entrance into the Temple and at present completely blocked up until the Messiah returns. The western retaining wall, deliberately allowed by Titus to stand when he destroyed the city, flanks a piazza that is now the centre of Jewish worship. The courtyards into which it is divided are similar to those of Bible times. It is possible for men to enter a synagogue on the northern side and to stand under

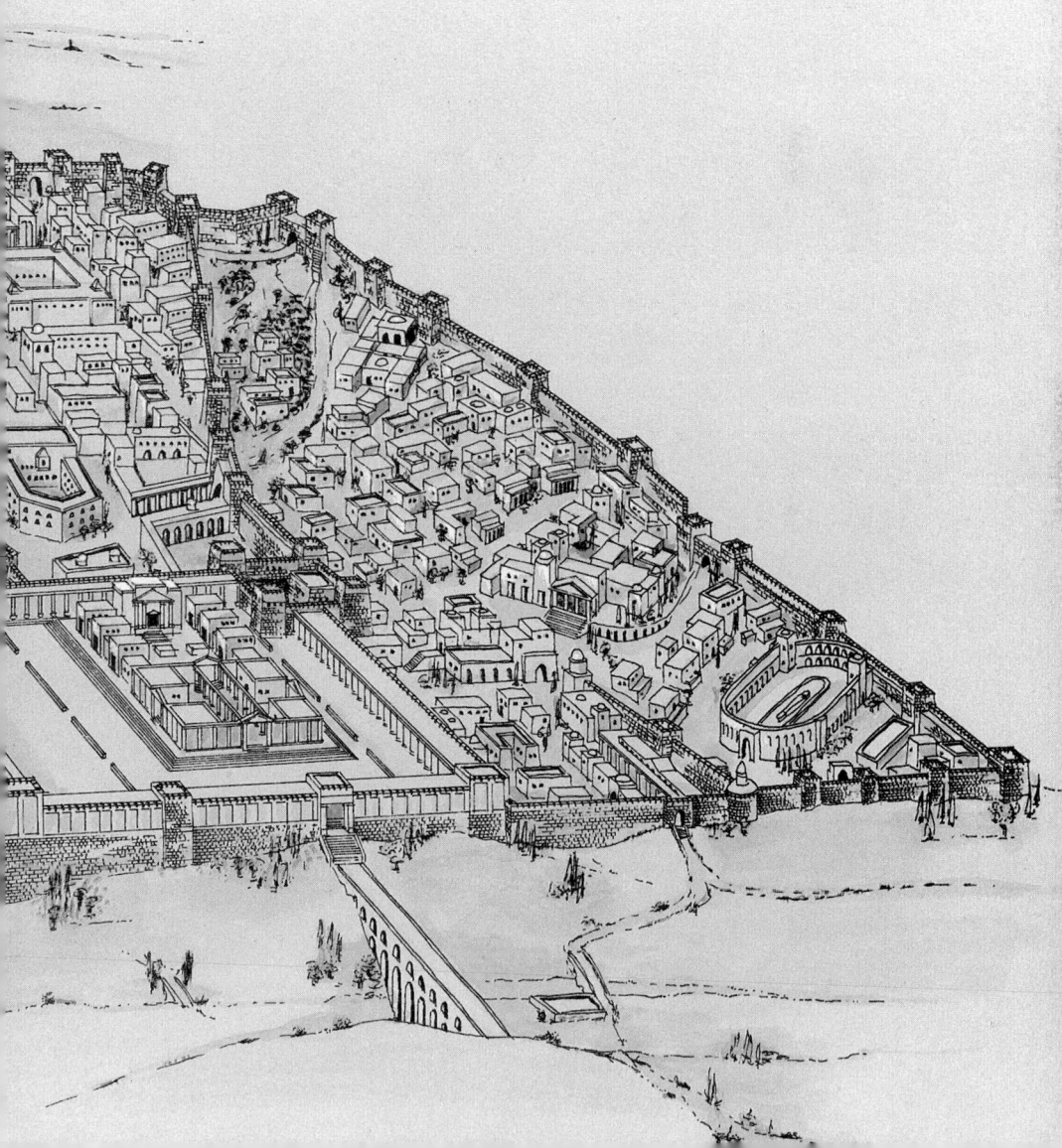

Jerusalem and the Dome of the Rock from the Mount of Olives.

the archways of a viaduct built by Herod to cross the Tyropoean Valley. The Temple site itself is a Muslim centre of worship. The authorities will very occasionally allow a visit beneath the platform so that the arches that support it can be seen. They are known as "Solomon's stables." One can also see the threshing floor of Araunah, the rock Moriah, which is inside the Dome of the Rock.

The place of crucifixion

You can see the places of the crucifixion, burial, and resurrection of Jesus. Many Christians find these places upsetting to visit because of the changes that have been made in them over the years. The original spur of rock where Jesus was crucified has been cut down to a cube of about twelve feet (four metres) and has been covered with elaborate ornamentation. Also the rock that once surrounded the tomb has been cut away, leaving the tomb itself isolated; it too has been covered with ornamentation. The two sacred places are housed in a large Crusader church, the Church of the Holy Sepulchre, where predominantly Orthodox worship is carried on. But this is the place.

Many Christians often find it helpful to follow a visit to the Church of the Holy Sepulchre with a visit to the Garden Tomb about four hundred yards (three hundred and sixty metres) north of the Damascus Gate. The garden was there in the time of Jesus and recreates the atmosphere of Easter Day.

The Mount of Olives

You can take a bus to the eastern side of the Mount of Olives, to the village of Bethany and then walk over the ridge back to Jerusalem. In Bethany itself there is a modern church to remind people of the home at Bethany where Jesus went to visit Mary and Martha and where Lazarus was raised. Outside, villagers will show a tomb marked with Lazarus's name, although it is unlikely to be the real tomb. It can be entered.

At the top of the steep hill is Bethphage. To get there is to follow the path which Jesus walked. There one finds a simple church commemorating the Palm Sunday walk. The descent from Bethphage leads to the stunning view of Jerusalem from the east. It is worth stopping at Dominus Flevit ("The Lord wept") church on the way down. The church is

The Church of the Holy Sepulchre, by tradition the site of Jesus's crucifixion and burial.

The Mount of Olives from the walls of Jerusalem.

small and exquisite, built in the shape of a tear to remind us that near the spot, Jesus wept. At the bottom of the hill is the Kidron valley and the Garden of Gethsemane. Inside the Church of All Nations is the rock where, traditionally, Jesus prayed in the garden. Outside is a simple garden kept by the Franciscans, which contains very ancient olive trees.

Places linked with the Judgment

You can look at the places associated with the last twelve hours of Jesus' life. On Mount Zion is a beautiful church built on the ruins of Caiaphas's palace. Beside the church are the ancient steps that at one time led to the palace, steps on which Jesus must have walked. The church is called St. Peter Gallicantu — "St. Peter of the cockcrow."

It is also possible to stand in the courtyard where Peter warmed his hands and to see the cistern where Jesus was almost certainly held overnight after his first trial. It is possible to walk across to Castle Antonia, where Jesus stood before Pilate. Part of the remains are built into the Ecce Homo convent. You can see the huge water cisterns that supplied the castle, stand on the original Via Dolorosa — the way of sorrows, and see Gabbatha.

The "Western Wall" of the Temple area is today the centre of Jewish worship.

Most moving of all at this spot is to see the markings on the ground where the Roman soldiers used to play the gambling game King, with a skittle, and to realize that here Jesus was given the sceptre, crown of thorns, and the robe, as he replaced the skittle in their cruel game. It is also possible to stand in the elevated playground of a Christian school opposite and look down into the Temple courts, as Paul did when he made his defense to the Jews. It is then possible to walk across to Herod's palace. The Citadel later became a Turkish fort and is now a museum, but it is built on the ruins of Herod's fortified palace, and the foundations of one of the three great towers can still be seen.

Hezekiah's tunnel

Provided you have beach shoes, shorts, a towel, a flashlight, and a change of lower clothing, you can walk through the water in the tunnel from the spring of Gihon to the pool of Siloam. Leaving the city by the dung gate above the Hinnom valley (Gar Hinnon gave its name to Gehenna, the Old Jerusalem rubbish dump where the fires never went out), one can walk down to the spring. Walking through the tunnel, it is possible to see the shaft Joab climbed and the place where Hezekiah's workmen, tunneling from opposite ends, actually met. After about half a mile (one thousand metres) one comes out into the present pool of Siloam.

Other sites

There are other, scattered, sites about Jerusalem that are also of biblical interest. Out on the west of the old city, by the King David Hotel, is a garden that was the burial place for Herod's family. Taking a flashlight, one can scramble down and see the short tunnels and the ledges where the dead were once laid. In the northeast corner of the city under the ruins of an ancient church is the pool of Bethesda. Only one of its porches has been uncovered, but one can clamber down some steep steps and stand by the now murky water. Outside the walls at this point are Solomon's quarries, where much of the stone for the Temple was quarried, and on some days the sheep market is open, as it has been for three thousand years.

On the Mount of Olives is the Paternoster Church, so called because of the renderings of the

The Paternoster Church, on the Mount of Olives.

The Herod family tomb, Jerusalem. Notice the great circular stone serving as a door.

Pater Noster — Our Father — prayer into every conceivable language. The church is built on the ruins of one built in its turn in the fourth century. It marks the spot — a cave in its crypt — where Jesus taught the disciples about the end of Jerusalem and the end of the world. Outside the wall to the south-east are tombs built by the Hasmoneans.

Bethlehem

You can take a local bus to Bethlehem (ten minutes) to see the cave, under the Church of the Nativity, where the early Christians believed that Christ had been born. The church itself is one of the oldest in the world, and the cave is in the crypt. The decorations and the crowds of people often give it an air of unreality for many Christians. It is therefore worthwhile asking a taxi driver to take you to the two

This cave under the Church of the Nativity, Bethlehem, is believed to be the site of Christ's birth.

shepherds' fields sites. One is at the Y.M.C.A., where there are ancient shepherds' caves, and the other is a beautiful church with equally beautiful paintings to remind people of the Christmas story. It is also worthwhile asking the taxi driver to go on to Herodion, Herod's fortified palace outside Jerusalem, which is believed to be his burial place.

There are countless other things of interest to see in Jerusalem. Some are sites associated with the life of Christ — the Via Dolorosa, the Cenacle (house of the Last Supper), and Church of the Ascension, for example; but they are not authentic sites. There are other sites of architectural, artistic, and historical interest, as well as places sacred to Jews and Muslims. A stay in the city is an unforgettable occasion. A useful guide (which is sometimes available and in print) is Herbert Bishko's *This Is Jerusalem* published by the Heritage Publishing Company in Israel.

Journeys and Travel

Travel in Bible times was very difficult. It was never a pleasure. When people traveled it was either for government affairs, business, or necessity. Travelers on government business were protected (Acts 23:31), and the wealthy businessmen who could afford it sent others in a caravan on their behalf. They had to take a calculated risk as to whether or not their goods would arrive and return safely. Paul summarizes (2 Corinthians 11:26–27) the problems he had when traveling, "I have been constantly on the move. I have been in danger from rivers, in danger from bandits, in danger from my countrymen, in danger from Gentiles, in danger in the city, in danger in the country, in danger at sea."

Things were so difficult that people settled their affairs before setting out on a journey. It was safer to stay at home, or if travel was absolutely necessary, to travel in a group. Jesus' own group of twelve disciples was not simply a matter of a fellowship for teaching; it was a necessity. The same could be said for the pilgrim group that traveled to and from Jerusalem when Jesus was twelve years old, a group large enough to prevent Mary and Joseph from spotting him during the day (Luke 2:44).

Sea travel
Sea travel was dangerous. Even in New Testament times, boats would scarcely have been called "ocean-going," and there were neither charts nor even primitive compasses until about this period. The Egyptians had developed craft for use on the river Nile. The current bore the boats northwards to the delta, and a single large sail took advantage of the prevailing north wind to take them south again. It is true that boats made of papyrus entered the

Mediterranean and at least one actually crossed the Atlantic, but the development of boats was primarily as river craft and for use in a flood plain, not for trading.

Israel had no natural harbours on the Mediterranean coast except north of Mount Carmel, where Haifa stands today, and the Red Sea outlet was not always in Israelite hands. The Jews therefore made poor sailors, and needed Phoenician help (1 Kings 9:27–28). When the Jews went it alone, their fleet was wrecked in port in a storm (1 Kings 22:48).

Even when better ships were built in Greek and Roman times and the lighthouse was established at Alexandria, voyages were very difficult. Passengers were extras to the goods that were being carried. They had to take their own food and seek lodgings ashore each night, since there was no accommoda-

This large stone was used as a ship's anchor in Bible times.

A Roman merchant ship is depicted on the top of this pottery oil lamp.

tion on board (see Acts 21:3, 7, 8.) At certain times of the year no ships sailed at all. Roman law forbade sailings between November 10 and March 10. The only "safe" period was from May 26 until September 14. The periods between were regarded as dangerous. A sailing might be made in an emergency or if a trader was willing to take a chance. Acts 27:9 refers to "the fast" day when travel was dangerous — November 10; Acts 28:11 refers to a boat that had been at sea when it was overtaken by the danger period. It had wintered at Malta.

How risky sea travel could be can be seen from the example of what happened to Paul. He was traveling on an Alexandrian grain ship, loaded and on its way to Rome (Acts 27:6). The boat was caught in a northeasterly storm wind, and in order to try to save the boat the crew lowered the mainsail and used a small sail at the bow, threw the grain

overboard, ran a cable from the prow to the stern to help to prevent the ship from breaking its back, and finally passed another cable over and under the ship for its length to keep the timbers together.

Grain ships were of no small size. They were two hundred feet (seventy metres) long and had a dis-

Roman coin of the Emperor Augustus, showing a merchant ship.

A Roman merchant ship. Notice the 'eye' on the sail (see p. 240). The ship was steered by means of the large rudders at the stern of the boat; the steersman can be seen in the illustration.

placement of twelve hundred tons. The faster boats, men-of-war, that were propelled by rowers, were much lighter and could not survive a storm.

Even after the Romans had dispersed the feared Mediterranean pirates, sea travel was still far from safe. Paul had to be very careful when he took the famine collection money to Jerusalem. He started off on a Jewish pilgrim boat making for Jerusalem for the festival of Passover. It was then that he discovered that a plot (to kill him and take the money) had been hatched (Acts 20:3), and therefore he spent the festival of Passover at Philippi (Acts 20:6). It was easy for anyone to disappear over the side (Jonah 1). In all, sea travel was so unpleasant that it must have been a relief for early Christians to read of a new heaven and a new earth where there would be no more sea (Revelation 21:1).

Land travel

If travel by sea was dangerous, travel by land was little better. There were many reasons that it was good *not* to travel. In the first place, the roads themselves were poor for the ordinary traveler. The roadway was either so faint it was difficult to make out (Psalm 107:4–7 tells of a group that lost its way, prayed to God for help, and were led by him to a city), or the surface was uncomfortably bumpy.

The wheel had been invented in Mesopotamia. It was a small, heavy disc of wood, and it replaced the runner on a sledge. The development of the wheel led to the need for roads so that the wheels would not disintegrate on large stones or in deep hollows, for wheels could not pick their way around obstacles in the way that animal feet could. But even with the need for good roads, there was little development in road building. Initially a road was simply a track where the stones had been removed, the bumps flattened, and the holes filled in. When an important person was to arrive, it was the practice to "prepare the way for the Lord." All the mountains (bumps) were made low, and the valleys (ruts and holes in the road) were exalted (see Isaiah 40:3–4; Matthew 11:10).

It was the Persians who first developed a good road system, because without it they could not maintain communications and government throughout their empire. But even though the roads

Cross-section of a Roman road. The bottom level was sand, then came stone and rock set in concrete, then crushed stone in concrete, and finally the paved surface.

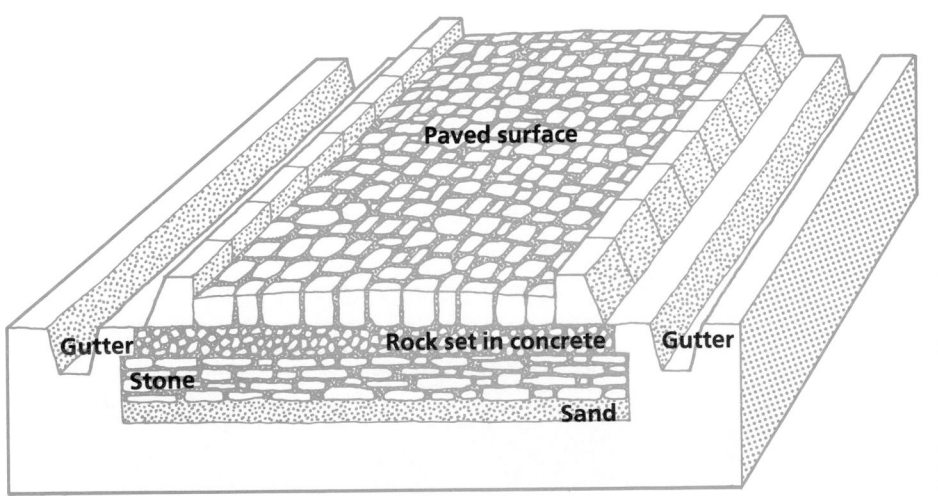

**Roman milestone at
Capernaum.**

they made were broad, fairly level tracks and even
though there were staging posts with fresh horses so
that important messages could be got through, it
still took three months to cover the 1,600 miles
(2,576 kilometres) from Sardis to Susa.

Roman roads
The Romans were the finest road builders — "all
roads lead to Rome." Roman roads were straight
and level and were made of four layers. First was
sand, then pieces of stone and rock in concrete, then
crushed stone in concrete, and finally a paved surface. Drainage was provided, and where the roads
went into the cities, there were raised walkways for
pedestrians.

Milestones were placed along the roads (4,850
feet to the Roman mile). These stones gave an indication of distance, but journeys were still reckoned

Busy traffic on a Roman road of Bible times. Notice the Roman officer on horseback, the various horse-drawn carriages, and the donkey with its load.

in days' journey as they had been centuries before (Genesis 30:36; 31:23). The stones served another purpose, though. Roman law made it possible for a soldier to compel a civilian to carry his pack from one milestone to the next. Jesus had this in mind when he said that if anyone compels us to go one mile we should be willing to go the extra mile (cf. Matthew 5:41). Fifty thousand miles of roads were built in this way through the Roman Empire, and road maps were on sale in the shops in Rome.

A courier could cover 75 miles (121 kilometres) in one day, but distances were so great that it still took 54 days to travel from Rome to Caesarea. The courier service was highly developed and involved vehicles, horses, and staging posts. The roads themselves were continuously maintained by local supervisors.

Wagons were drawn by oxen, and lighter vehicles could be hired outside city gates. The *cisium* was a light open carriage with two wheels. It could take two people — the driver and the passenger. The *essedom* was driven by the hirer, and it had a pair of horses. Some of the wagons, known as *reda*, were covered and provided with seats for passengers. Chariots, too, were available (Acts 8:29), as were litters, the latter for use by only the most important people. The litter was carried by human hands or was placed on a sling between animals. The Roman system of roads may not sound too bad, but if one was not an official nor a Roman, one could take little advantage of it.

A horsedrawn chariot from a Greek relief.

Accommodation

Another reason people did not like traveling — both in Old and in New Testament times — was that travelers were in danger from bandits (Judges 9:25; Luke 10:30). Another, similar, reason was that travelers were completely at the mercy of the local people (Judges 19:15; Job 31:32). Staging posts for the ordinary traveler did not develop until Persian times, and they were often dubious places. The inn, khan, or caravanserai was built around a central courtyard. Stabling for animals was provided at courtyard level, and other accommodation was above. It was the ancient equivalent of a motel.

Although in theory the staging posts provided free accommodation, food, provender, and other services were paid for (Luke 10:35), and it was a feature of most of the inns that prostitution was part of the system. This explains why Jesus told his disciples to seek accommodation in private homes (Matthew 10:11), and why it was so important that first-century Christians be given to hospitality (Romans 12:13; 1 Timothy 3:2; 1 Peter 4:9).

Since services were so doubtful it was necessary to take food for the journey (Joshua 9:4–6; Judges 19:19). Normally this would be bread, parched grain, and dried fruit for about two days. It was therefore unusual for Jesus to send his disciples out on a journey without such provision (Matthew 10:10). On the other hand, when he was aware that crowds had been following him for three days, he knew that the people had nothing to eat (Matthew 15:32).

Taxes

Yet another problem was that taxes had to be paid on a journey. There may have been one language for communication (Greek) and no frontiers to cross, but payment on goods, wheels, axles, and persons all had to be made as one passed through successive tax districts.

Another problem was heat. Summer temperatures were extremely high, so that it was unusual to travel at midday (Acts 26:13). Travel was most comfortable in the morning and the evening, and the wise men from the East took advantage of their knowledge of the stars to travel at night (Matthew 2:9).

The basic pack animal of Bible times was the donkey.

Another, surprising, problem was the time taken in greetings. The actual salutations on a journey took an inordinate amount of time. It was not considered polite simply to pass the time of day. It was necessary to ask and receive answers to questions such as "Where are you going? ... Where are you from? ... What is your name? ... How many children have you?" and so on. Jesus considered these salutations to be so great a problem that he told his disciples "do not greet anyone on the road" (Luke 10:4). He was equally scathing about the time some of the religious leaders of his day took in such greetings (Luke 11:43; 20:46). He would have had little patience with the small talk of conventional social gatherings today.

The donkey
The final, and perhaps the biggest, problem was that animals had to be cared for on the journey. The basic pack animal was the ass or donkey. This was the first animal used by nomadic people and ensured that in the early days travelers were never far from centres of population. The pack animal was used to

carry people as well as goods. The saddle was made of three layers — felt, straw, and haircloth. Sacks were either roped together and slung over the saddle, being tied together underneath for security (Genesis 42:25–28), or else they were hung from a cradle that had been put across the saddle. Boxes or baskets were also hung from the cradle (1 Samuel 16:20; 25:18), and children were sometimes carried in the boxes.

Donkeys were even used for pulling a plough (Isaiah 32:20), but they could never be paired with a larger animal such as an ox (Deuteronomy 22:10). Donkeys were also harnessed to corn mills and to water wheels. Although some breeds of donkey were marked out for royal usage (Judges 5:10) and though they were used by important people for transport (Genesis 22:3; 1 Samuel 25:23), donkeys were replaced by mules as the status symbol, and the horse later became the mount for going to war. The donkey gradually became a symbol of labour and peace, although always the mount of ordinary people (Zechariah 9:9; John 12:15).

The camel

The camel was domesticated about 2000 BC and gave the nomadic tribes independence of settlements. It enabled them to live in the desert far from scattered oases, because the camel was able to store enough water for several days. Abraham lived at a time when there was a transition from the use of donkeys to camels (Genesis 12:16; 24:35; 30:43), Abraham used the camels only for long journeys (Genesis 24:3, 64), and so did Jacob (Genesis 31:17). Camels were frequently in use in later times by nomadic tribes such as the Midianites (Judges 6:5) and the Amalekites (1 Samuel 15:3). It became the animal for long distance travel.

Not only could the camel travel great distances, but it was the means of bringing international news from place to place (Proverbs 25:25), and it was an excellent beast of burden. The donkey load, or ephah, was the largest unit of volume, but the camel could take more, and there was an informal measurement known as a *camel load* (cf. 2 Kings 8:9). Camels traveled in caravans of up to fifteen hundred beasts, groups being roped together and led by a rider on a donkey at about three miles (five kilometres) per hour. The use of the donkey was not simply to reserve carrying space on the camel — the camel was not at all comfortable to ride. It is easy enough to mount when it is in a kneeling (resting) position, but when one rides it the swaying movement induces travel sickness.

A camel was a considerable investment, and it was cared for appropriately. The camel furniture — saddle, saddle bags, and bridles — were of considerable value and were kept in the tents (Genesis 31:43). The decorations of the bridle were valuable enough to be taken as spoil in war (Judges 8:21). In return for the crushed straw from the threshing floor, which constituted its staple food, the camel gave meat (although the Jews were not allowed to eat it, Leviticus 11:4); milk (Genesis 32:15); and hair, which was woven into coarse but soft camelhair cloth and was then used for clothes such as those worn by John the Baptist (Matthew 3:4). The skin was useful too. When it was tanned it could be made into bags and trousers.

The most common type of camel was the single humped camel, sometimes known as the *dromedary*. It had long wiry legs and little fat to store

The camel was an important beast of burden in Bible times.

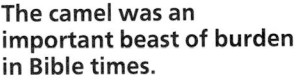

water. What it lacked in endurance it made up in speed. It could travel at nearly ten miles (sixteen kilometres) an hour.

The mule

Mules were not much used until David's time, because an animal bred from mixed parentage was contrary to the law (Leviticus 19:19). Presumably the Jews of the time believed that so long as they were not doing the breeding themselves it was allowable to purchase the animals. The mule was initially rare enough to be a royal mount. The king's sons have them in 2 Samuel 13:29, and when Solomon rode David's mule it was a sign that he was the heir apparent (1 Kings 1:33, 44). Mules were brought as presents to Solomon when he became king (2 Chronicles 9:24), and Ahab was worried about his mules when there was a period of drought (1 Kings 18:5), but by the time of Isaiah they had become much more common (Isaiah 66:20).

The horse

The horses of the Bible were similar to the Arabian horses of today. They were used for war (see Revelation 19:11, 19), though not so much to provide a mounted cavalry as to provide a means of pulling chariots (Genesis 41:43; Exodus 14:9). Horses were not above working on a farm, however, when the need arose (Isaiah 28:28). The Jews were warned against the acquisition of horses (Deuteronomy 17:16). Their neighbours had chariots, however, and although God helped the Jews to overcome those neighbours, the Jews were anxious to have chariots of their own (Joshua 11:6, 9; Judges 4:3). David therefore used horses and chariots (2 Samuel 8:4), but it was Solomon who really developed their usage (1 Kings 4:28; 2 Chronicles 1:14; 9:25). Their possession tended to make people trust more in the chariots than in God (Isaiah 31:1).

A chariot was a semicircular box on wheels, open at the back. The floor was made of rope to give a degree of spring, and two people stood in it — the driver and the soldier. But horses had a place in peacetime too. It became a status symbol to have a horse, particularly if one had a chariot to go with it. By Roman times chariots were raced against one another in the games. Horses therefore became

An Arab farmer ploughs using a horse.

symbols of power (Psalm 147:10). For all the value of the chariot and horse, the charioteer was greatly dependent upon good roads. It was easy for the narrow chariot wheels to get stuck in mud (Exodus 14:28; Judges 5:21–22), and this explains why Ahab was so anxious to get back to Jezreel (1 Kings 18:44).

Now look at your Bible

The woman of Shunem

2 Kings 4:24. That the great woman of Shunem saddled a donkey and went to visit Elisha, was unusual, because it was normal for a man to ride and a woman to walk. It gives us some idea of her status that she was able to do this. If Mary rode the donkey and Joseph walked alongside, which is traditional in Christian art, then Joseph would have been a laughingstock to fellow travelers.

The eye of the needle

Matthew 19:24; 23:24. Many stories have been told to indicate that the "eye of the needle" is a small postern gate that was opened at night when the city gate had been shut, and that a camel could get through it provided it had been fully unloaded. It is a nice story but not true in biblical terms. The eye of a needle is a surgeon's needle. In both Matthew 19 and Matthew 23, the point was that the camel was the largest animal with which people of the day were familiar. Jesus was using the term much as we would use the word *elephant* as the largest creature in our experience. Jesus may also have used the camel as an illustration because it was ritually unclean.

The room in the inn

Luke 2:7. The "inn" where there was no room for Mary and Joseph was not a *khan*. The Greek word is *kataluma*, which means a "temporary shelter." The Romans erected large marquees for shelter when there was insufficient accommodation for people and shelter was needed. They were erected around Jerusalem, for instance, at Passover time. The *kataluma* was a noisy place, bustling with animals and people, and sometimes the odd cooking fire. No "innkeepers" were at hand. Since there was no room there for Mary and Joseph, then it is more than likely that Jesus was born either outside (the idea of the writer of the carol "Away in a Manger" — "The stars in the bright sky look down where he lay") or in a shepherd's cave. This last is more likely. Such a cave has been shown from antiquity as the birthplace of Jesus. It is now under the Church of Nativity in Bethlehem.

The eyes of a ship

Acts 27:15. Ships were often personified, and eyes were painted on each side of the bow. This seems to have been done to the ship Paul was on, because the literal meaning of the original is "when we could not look the wind in the face."

Hospitality

Entertaining others to eat and to stay was important for the people of the Bible; the urge to give hospitality seems to have been rooted in their experience of nomadic life. Nomadic people are conscious of the loneliness of the desert and that the provision of food is often a matter of life and death. Because Esau was too weak to prepare a meal for himself after he had been hunting, his brother, Jacob, was able to extract the birthright from him (Genesis 25:29–34). Even an enemy could not be allowed to die of hunger. Paul wrote, "If your enemy is hungry, feed him" (Romans 12:20), and he was repeating what was always done among nomadic people.

If a person came within one's tent or home, he was absolutely safe under the protection of the family (Genesis 19:8). When David wrote, "You prepare a table before me in the presence of my enemies," he was referring to this kind of safety and protection (Psalm 23:5). The custom was taken up by God in the giving of the law so that it was reinforced by divine sanction. Because the Jewish people had received protection from God, they were to give protection to others. It was therefore a sin to eat alone (Job 31:17) or to refuse to share one's food with the poor and needy (Isaiah 58:7). The Ammonites and Moabites were condemned for such a lack of hospitality (Deuteronomy 23:4).

Angels unaware

The Jews believed that God sometimes sent angels in disguise to test whether people were obeying the law of hospitality. They knew that this had happened to Abraham (Genesis 18:2–13) and to Gideon (Judges 6:17–22), and they believed therefore that the same thing might happen to them (Hebrews 13:2). This style of thinking gave rise to problems as well as opened the way for revelation. Many Jews thought that if they were in the house of God then they would be under God's protection, and as a result tended to be careless in their daily living (Jeremiah 7:14). They did not realize that the glory of God had departed from the Temple and that it was no longer, therefore, the house of God (Ezekiel 11:23).

So important was hospitality that Jews looked upon the final blessing as a great banquet held by God himself (Zephaniah 1:7) and the same theme was taken up by Jesus in the parable, "The kingdom of heaven is like a king who prepared a wedding banquet for his son" (Matthew 22:2–14).

In New Testament times, refusal to give hospitality amounted to rejection (Matthew 10:14), and it was therefore essential for Christians to give hospitality (Galatians 6:10; 1 Peter 4:9). Although such a practice gave moral protection in view of the character of many inns (see p. 234) and in view of the fact that many Christians had to leave their own homes because of persecution, it was more than this: "hospitality" is *philoxenia*, a "love for others." It was particularly important for preachers of the time who had given up their livelihood so that they could preach the gospel (3 John 5–8). They were to be given hospitality for several days, and then encouraged to move on to another place (e.g. Acts 9:43; 16:15; Romans 16:2). One could not be recognized as a leader in the church unless one was hospitable (1 Timothy 3:2; Titus 1:8).

Greetings
Greetings have changed little over the centuries. Then, as now, there were three types of greeting, which corresponded to the closeness of the other person. First there was a face-to-face greeting, which could be, but need not be, verbal, and which involved a gesture with the hand, without physical contact. Sometimes the word used was "Rejoice!" or "Greetings" (Matthew 28:9) and at other times "Peace be with you" (John 20:21). This word was used in mockery by the soldiers when they put on the crown of thorns (Mark 15:18). "Peace be to this house" was the first greeting the Seventy made when they went to the home of a stranger (Luke 10:5).

Second, there was a formal kiss given much as we might give a kiss to a friend or a guest. It involved the laying on of hands on each other's shoulders then a pulling together and the giving of a kiss, first on the right cheek and then on the left. Samuel kissed Saul when he anointed him (1 Samuel 10:1), Simon the Pharisee failed to greet Jesus in such a way when he came as a guest to his home (Luke 7:45), and Paul wrote, "Greet one another with a holy kiss" (Romans 16:16).

There was also the mouth-to-mouth kiss of greeting to demonstrate affection (Genesis 29:11). This appears to have been the kind of kiss Judas gave to Jesus, because the Greek words indicate that Judas kissed Jesus several times. It was this greeting that prompted Jesus' question in Luke 22:48.

Another form of greeting was the bow, which was given to a particularly honoured person or guest (Genesis 18:2–3; 23:12). It might be an inflection of the head forwards or a movement from the waist; it could even become an act of prostration at the guest's feet (Matthew 18:26). There were dangers in this — it could look like worship. In one sense such obeisance was proper because it was acknowledging someone to be of great worth (or giving them worth-ship), and we use the word *worship* in this sense when we say, "He worships the ground she walks upon." But if our thinking goes beyond this conventional use of the term, we are giving to man what rightly belongs to God (Revelation 19:10). When Cornelius fell down before Peter to give him such a greeting, Peter was anxious to stop him in case it should be any kind of worship (Acts 10:25–26). In Revelation 3:9, the expression "bow down" is used, but it refers to the prostration of respect.

Guest accommodation

There were a number of kinds of accommodation where one could stay in New Testament times, apart from the inn. A stranger would normally go to the gate or wait by the well until an invitation to stay had been given by someone locally (Genesis 19:1–2; 24:13–14; Judges 19:15). When a person was invited to sleep it was not normally alone. Other members of the family slept with him because it was believed to be discourteous if a person lacked company through the night. In the simple, one-roomed peasant house, there was only one place to sleep, and the guest would sleep on the raised platform with the family or upon the roof if the weather was good (1 Samuel 9:26). In the case of the bedouin tent, the visitor was invited to sleep in the open tent entrance with the men. The visitor was never allowed into the inner, closed-off part of the tent, which was the women's quarters.

In a larger house and in later times, a guest room would be provided, sometimes at the quiet end of the inner courtyard or in a room near the entrance. When householders with smaller rooms could not provide a guest room but wanted to entertain, several families might join together to maintain a guest room and employ a servant to keep it prepared. A family's guest would sleep in and be fed in that guest room. But such rooms were available only for men; anyone traveling with a family had to sleep in a family house (Judges 19:4). This is probably because, when not used for guests, the guest house became the men's social centre. Elisha's experience was unusual. He was given a well-furnished room on the roof away from the rest of the family, although there were a number of unusual things associated with the "great woman" of Shunem (see p. 240 and 2 Kings 4:20, KJV).

Feasting

Provision of meals was an important part of hospitality. Almost any excuse was given for a party — a weaning, the arrival of a guest, and, almost certainly, birthdays. That was because life and food was often tedious and monotonous, and it may explain why the Hebrew word for "feasting" is the same as the word for "drinking" — they wanted a merry time!

When a friend arrived at midnight and the host had no food to meet the needs, the host would be persistent in waking his neighbour and asking him for food, not simply because the neighbour was a friend but because the obligation to offer a meal to a guest was so great in that culture (Luke 11:8). Meals were an important aspect of friendship. To eat a meal with someone was to be at peace with him (Genesis 26:28–30). Salt had a particular function as part of the meal. To "eat salt" was to be at peace — perhaps because it healed wounds (Mark 9:50; when Jesus tells us to be "salty," he is therefore telling us to be at peace with others).

If the guest was coming to carry out an errand that might not be approved by the host, it was necessary to speak about the errand before the meal was begun (Genesis 24:33). A covenant of peace made at such a meal was binding (Joshua 9:14, 15), and thus a meal was a means of reconciliation (Genesis 31:53–54). That is probably why Jesus appeared to his disciples after the crucifixion and ate with them: it was a means of reassuring them that if they had failed him, there was no loss of relationship between them (Luke 24:30; 24:41–43; John 21:9).

Religious festivals were also great social occasions. After a sacrifice had been made, the family sat down to eat part of the sacrifice that was being burned on the altar. The family was literally having a meal with God as a sign of peace (Deuteronomy 12:5–7).

An invitation to a formal meal in New Testament times followed an established procedure. Double invitations were always given. Initially a formal invitation was refused as a matter of course. ("I could not possibly come: I am not worthy.") Then the guests would be urged to come until the invitation was accepted (Luke 7:36; 14:23; Acts 16:15). Later, the message would come that the meal was prepared (Esther 5:8; 6:14).

When a guest arriving for the meal had been greeted, a slave would remove the guest's sandals in preparation for washing his feet and so that the sandals would not bring in dirt that had been picked up along the way. Then the feet were washed by a servant, water being poured over them, which were then rubbed with hands and dried with a towel (Genesis 18:4; 19:2; 24:32; 1 Samuel 25:41; John 13:3–5; 1 Timothy 5:10). Next the guest's head was anointed with olive oil scented with spices. David refers to this custom in Psalm 23:5. It was another of the courtesies Simon the Pharisee neglected when Jesus arrived at Simon's house for the banquet (Luke 7:46). Water was then produced for a drink. It indicated that the guest was worthy of peaceful reception; to ask for a drink of water was to be received (Genesis 24:17). The Samaritan woman found it incomprehensible that Jesus, a Jew, had asked for water when there was generally such animosity between Jews and Samaritans (John 4:9).

A formal meal in New Testament times. Notice the couches arranged on three sides of an open square.

The formal meal

The placings at table were extremely important. In large houses there was a raised platform for the "top table" where honoured guests would be received (Matthew 23:6; Luke 14:8–10). The chief guest sat on the right-hand-side of the host and the second guest on the left-hand-side (see Mark 10:35–37). The largest and best plates of food were always given to such guests.

In early Old Testament times guests usually sat on their feet, cross-legged on a carpet, but by the time the kingdoms of Israel and Judah were established, guests sat at tables on chairs or even on couches. By New Testament times the triclinium was beginning to come into use. This was an arrangement of three tables set around a square, with access to the middle gained through the open side of the square so that servants could come and go to bring in food and to take away the left-overs. Couches were arranged on the outside of the three tables, close to one another, so that the guest could recline to eat. The guest was given a cushion and lay on his left arm with his head

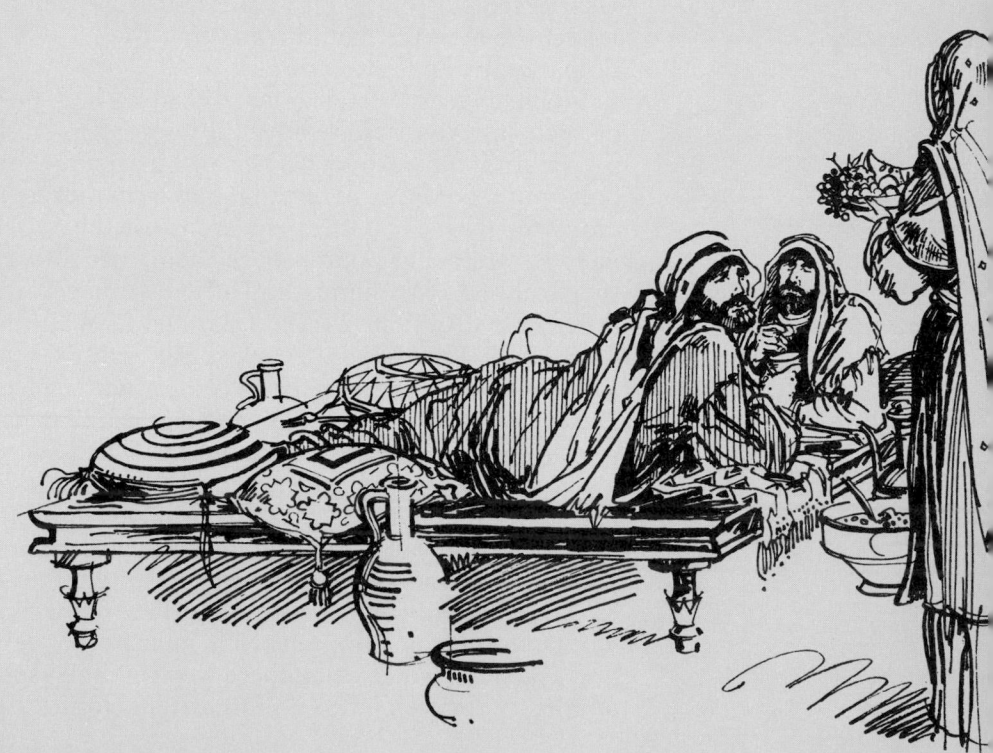

towards the table, leaving his right arm free to take what he wished. This made it possible for servants to rinse the feet while the guests continued the banquet. Jesus was therefore probably using a couch at a triclinium when his feet were washed (Luke 7:46).

The arrangement of the triclinium meant that, although it was relaxed, it was not necessarily easy to make conversation. If one wished to speak to the person on one's left it was necessary to lean back and nearly lie on him in order to talk. One would therefore "recline" on someone's "breast" (John 13:23–25; see also Luke 16:22).

At a formal meal there was a "starter" of wine diluted with honey to drink. The main dinner, called the *cena*, followed. It was of three courses arranged on trays and often beautifully decorated. Guests ate with their fingers, except when soup, eggs, or shellfish were included, in which case they used spoons. There were no forks. Finally there was a dessert of pastry and fruit. We can now begin to understand what Martha was trying to do, and why Jesus said that "only one" thing was "necessary" (Luke 10:42). The most honoured guest was given a

Relief of a Roman banquet.

"token" meal by the host. A piece of bread was dipped into the food and was used as a spoon. The "bread spoon" and contents were put into the mouth of the favoured guest. This was known as the "morsel" and was given by Jesus to Judas during the Last Supper (John 13:26), providing a final, loving appeal to him.

Entertainment

During and after the courses of the meal entertainment was provided in which readings of poetry and prose were given and in which there was music and dancing (Amos 6:4–6). Dancing was normally individual — men and women dancing together had not arrived by this period — and occasionally a display as in a cabaret act was performed (Mark 6:22). It may have been for this reason that it was possible for local people to look in at what was happening. It was probably in this way that the woman who poured ointment on Jesus' feet was able to gain access (Luke 7:37). The occasions were brilliantly lit so that they could be seen from the darkness outside. To be put out of the lighted room into the darkness could lead to despair (and so, "gnashing of teeth" Matthew 8:12; 22:13; 25:30).

When the entertainment was finished and the meal had been cleared away, there was a long period for conversation. Traditional stories were told from memory. Local gossip was another feature of the conversation, and there are sufficient warnings in the Bible against gossip (Matthew 12:36; Ephesians 5:4) for us to recognize that it was a frequent occurrence. Proverbial sayings were also shared. Departure was delayed as long as possible, for once a person had accepted such hospitality it was looked upon as insulting to leave it early as if it were not good enough (see Judges 19:5–10).

Now look at your Bible

Removing the shoes
Exodus 3:5. When one entered a house it was the usual practice to take off one's shoes, because otherwise the dirt from the unpaved streets and pathways would defile the house. If the floors were carpeted, the carpets would be ruined. Removal of shoes was therefore a mark of consideration and respect, and since God can be given no less respect, the removal of shoes is a mark of respect toward God. This practice continues in Muslim places of worship in contemporary society.

Entering women's quarters
Judges 4:17–22. The story is normally told as an example of Jael's treachery, for when an enemy was at rest in a tent, he was supposed to be completely safe. But there may be more to the story than meets the eye, and we are probably not given all the details. A guest in a tent slept in the porch and was never allowed inside, which were the women's quarters. Invasion of the women's quarters was punishable by death.

The Levite and his concubine
Judges 19–21. This is one of two appendixes to the book of Judges that illustrate the spiritual chaos into which the people had fallen. The book is set in a period when the twelve tribes of Israel were united in their allegiance to Yahweh — a relationship called an *amphictyony*. When the Levite was returning home with his concubine, they went to Gibeah — within the tribal territory of Benjamin — to look for a place to stay for the night, but the house was raided and the woman taken away and murdered by repetitive rape. The division of the woman's body was the call to the twelve tribes to assemble at the central sanctuary. It became clear to the assembly that the attitude of the men of Gibeah was not just lust, but was part of an attitude that lay claim to independence on the part of the whole tribe. Benjamin wanted to be out of the amphictyony. It was because the tribes believed that the protection of God depended on their loyalty to one another that they took such drastic action against the show of independence.

The drink of water
Mark 9:41. One of the first things done for a guest was to give him a drink of cool water. It was a pledge of friendship. (Abraham's servant Eliezer looked for a welcome by waiting for a drink of water, Genesis 24:17–18). When Jesus said "Whoever gives you a cup of water to drink because of your name as followers of Christ" he was saying that if we pledge a person our friendship for Christ's sake we shall not lose our reward.

The broken tile
Revelation 2:17. Christ tells the angel of the church at Pergamum that "To him who overcomes ... I will give ... a white stone, and a new name written on the stone which no one knows but him who receives it." This statement may be an allusion to a common practice between friends. A tile was taken and broken in half. One friend wrote his name on one of the halves, and the other friend wrote his name on the other. The two halves were then exchanged. Often the pieces were handed down from father to son. To be able to produce the counterpart of a piece of tile held by another person, even years later, was to guarantee friendship and hospitality.

Social and Political Groupings

Whereas many people do not adopt a particular "party line" either in religion or politics, others become members of a pressure group or a political party and become involved in it. This was true of life in Bible times — of the period when the Jews returned from exile in Babylon and rebuilt the Temple in Jerusalem and of the time in which Jesus lived. In order to understand the New Testament groupings, we have to look back to the events that took place after the fall of Jerusalem and the Exile in 586 BC.

The Samaritans

The Samaritans took their name from the city of Samaria, the capital of the Northern Kingdom of Israel from the time of the kings Omri and Ahab (1 Kings 16:24). The city of Samaria was destroyed by the Assyrians in 721 BC, and about twenty-seven thousand people of the ruling classes and those who were useful artisans were deported to Assyria and dispersed (2 Kings 17:24). As part of Assyrian pol icy, leadership of the city was taken over by other subject peoples, so that lack of communication with the local working people combined with the new rulers' gratitude to the Assyrians for placing them in charge would result in a stable, peaceful situation.

Things did not go well — wild animals increased in the country at an alarming rate, killing many people. The newcomers believed these attacks to mean that they were not worshiping the God of Samaria in the right way. One of the priests in exile was sent back to teach the Jewish faith, and he set up a religious sanctuary at Bethel. As a result, a syncretistic religion was formed between the worship of Yahweh and the worship of the local gods from the original homes of the new rulers of Samaria (2 Kings 17:25–34).

Some of the people from the Northern Kingdom

who had not been taken into exile worshiped at Jerusalem, where they were welcomed (2 Chronicles 35:17), and when the city of Jerusalem was itself destroyed by the Babylonians this link was still maintained (Jeremiah 41:5). When the Persian Empire succeeded the Babylonian, and the Jews were allowed to rebuild their religion — their Temple and eventually the walls of Jerusalem — there was a mixed reception from the Samaritans. There were Samaritans who wanted to join in with the work so that the worship of Yahweh could be renewed (Ezra 4:2), but they were strongly rebuffed by the returned exiles, who regarded the Samaritans as impure because of the syncretistic nature of their religion (Ezra 4:3). Other Samaritans were alarmed that Jerusalem was being rebuilt, for Jerusalem had always rivaled Samaria. These Samaritans did everything they could to hinder the rebuilding of the city (Nehemiah 4:1–2).

All the old antipathy between North and South came to the fore. Those feelings had a long pedigree, going back to the time when the twelve tribes had originally occupied the hill country of Canaan after the Exodus. The tribes in the north had been separated from those in the south by a line of Canaanite fortresses, and when David became king, it was to be king of two united kingdoms rather than of one kingdom (see p. 268). When the kingdom of David and subsequently of Solomon was divided during the period of their successors, the division followed the old historic line. The Samaritans were regarded not only as political enemies but as unclean people whose presence would defile the newly-returned exiles (see Nehemiah 13:23–30).

At a subsequent time, there seems to have been a group of Samaritans who, having been prevented from worshiping Yahweh in Jerusalem, and wishing to dissociate themselves from the continual infighting, withdrew to set up a place of worship of their own at Shechem (see John 4:19–20), centred on Mount Gerizim, which had been of great importance in the history and religion of the Jewish people (Deuteronomy 11:29; Joshua 8:33). A temple was built on Mount Gerizim, and a distinctive faith gradually developed. The Samaritans accepted the five books of Moses in their own language as their authority (the Samaritan Pentateuch), and this posi-

Tel Balata (biblical Shechem); Mount Gerizim can be seen in the background.

tion was reflected in their creed: There is one God; Moses was his prophet and will one day be returning as the Taheb ("restorer," sometimes called "Messiah"; see John 4:25); there will be a Day of Judgment; and Mount Gerizim is the place appointed by God for sacrifice. The last element was the tenth commandment in the Decalogue of the Samaritan Pentateuch (John 4:20).

At least some Samaritans held to a traditional belief that Moses had hidden sacred vessels on the mountain, for in AD 36 a Samaritan gathered a crowd on the mountain with the promise that he would show them the vessels. The whole group was massacred by Pontius Pilate.

Because of the difference in creed, there was strong religious distrust between those who worshiped on Mount Gerizim and those who worshiped at the restored Temple in Jerusalem. In 128 BC, one of the Jewish Hasmonean rulers (John Hyrcanus) captured Shechem and destroyed the temple, and somewhere between AD 6 and 9 a group of Samaritans defiled the Temple in Jerusalem by scattering bones there during Passover.

There are explicit and implicit references to the hostility of Jews and Samaritans in the New Testament (John 4:9, 33). Jesus went out of his way to indicate the good in Samaritans (Luke 10:33), which he had experienced (Luke 17:16), but he followed Jewish tradition and did not normally pass through Samaria when traveling from Galilee to Judaea. The normal route for Jews who did not wish to defile themselves was to cross the River Jordan at Beth Shan (to the north) and Jericho (in the south) traveling on the eastern side of the river (Luke 18:31, 35). Many Samaritans became Christians (Acts 8:25).

Hellenists and Hasidim

The Hellenists and Hasidim became distinct during the period of Greek culture when the Greeks controlled the country. After Alexander the Great had conquered the East, there was always likely to be strong Greek influence in Israel. The settlement of Greek soldiers, the use of Greek as an expressive language, and the emphasis on Greek life-style and entertainment led to the appropriation of Greek thought and ideas. Had not the Greek civilisation led to unprecedented conquest and culture?

Since the leaders of the Jewish people came into contact with the Greek rulers in Antioch in Syria, and since they had sufficient wealth to be able to bribe their Greek rulers to give them armed support when they needed it, the ruling class in Israel generally accepted the Greek mode of life. A critical point came for the Jewish people when they sided with the Greco-Egyptian rulers against the Greco-Syrian rulers in the hope of gaining some independence.

The Greco-Syrian ruler, who wanted to establish peace in his empire through the establishment of Greek cultural centres, decided that he would go much further than that in the case of the Jews and would eliminate opposition to Hellenism by eliminating Judaism itself. In general, the Jewish rulers went along with this. They accepted the high priesthood of one called Jason, who built a gymnasium in the city and encouraged the young people to wear Greek clothes. After the Maccabean revolt, when it was necessary for the priest-kings to enter into a political compromise with the Syrians, the Hellenistic rulers were still in a position of power and influence.

But among the ordinary people there was a strong reaction against the process of Hellenization. The people believed that Greek ideas were corrupting their religious faith, and out of inborn conservatism they rejected institutions such as the gymnasium, Greek games, and Greek clothes. They believed as well that the youth were being drawn into a decadent Greek life-style. Most of the reaction against Hellenization came from the countryside where there were a number of middle class people able to think their position through. They became known as the Hasidim, which means "godly" or "gracious." The Hasidim were mocked as "the tender ones" because they had a tender conscience about the new approaches.

When the Maccabeans revolted against the Syrians, the Hasidim were prepared to join in the fight for religious freedom. As soon as the Hasmonean successors of the Maccabees became involved in a struggle for political power and worked with the Hellenists in their own community and the Greeks in Antioch, they were abandoned by the Hasidim, who wished to be true to their religious faith. The Hasmoneans thus needed the support of the Hellenists, and they therefore continued to move in that direction. Hellenists and Hasidim are not found in the New Testament, but their successors are very familiar.

The Sadducees

The Sadducees were the successors of the Hellenists. Still the wealthy, ruling class, they were identified with the high priesthood and with Greek thought. Their group name, Sadducee, may be derived from Zadok, to indicate their high-priestly connection. They found the world a good place in which to live and were interested in the here-and-now rather than believing in a resurrection, a judgment, or an afterlife. They rejected ideas of resurrection in favour of the Greek idea of immortality of the soul and believed they could show that the idea of a bodily resurrection was ridiculous. They limited the canon of Scripture to the five books of Moses, which is why Jesus confined himself to those books in refuting their arguments against the resurrection (Matthew 22:23–32). The Sadducees rejected any belief in angels or spirits and followed "common-sense" morality — good and evil, they believed, resulted from personal action.

In the time of Jesus, the Sadducees were the majority party in the Sanhedrin, and the intensity of argument between them and the Pharisees over the resurrection was to be exploited by Paul when he stood before the Sanhedrin (Acts 23:6–10). The Sadducees would have opposed Jesus because they recognized his teaching to be contrary to their own. It was after the teaching about the resurrection and the raising of Lazarus that the chief priests (Sadducees) decided that Jesus must die (John 11:45–53). They would have seen him as an agitator who could upset things for them (the ruling class) and who must be stopped at all cost (John 11:48–50).

The Herodians, Pharisees (with their scribes), Essenes, and Zealots seem to have been derived from the Hasidim. When these groups faced the fact that their country was still under domination, this time of Rome, they reacted in different ways.

The Herodians

The Herodians supported the family of Herod as rulers. The Herods were originally an Edomite family, and they ruled the country for the Romans. The Edomites, after all, had some affinity with the Jews as descendants of Esau and the Jews believed that intermediary rule by the Herods was better than direct Roman rule. The Herodians accepted the good that Herod the Great had done for Jerusalem by providing a new Temple, although they sided with the Pharisees in objecting to paying taxes to Rome (Mark 12:13–14). They reacted against Jesus when he healed the man with the withered hand on the Sabbath day (Mark 3:5). Like the Sadducees, Herodian opposition to Jesus was probably because they believed he would upset the status quo and because his clear moral teaching was as big a challenge to their life-style as had been the teaching of John the Baptist.

The Pharisees

The Pharisees followed a direct line from the Hasidim. Their name means "those who separate themselves." There were some six thousand of them at the time of Jesus. They were concerned, above all else, for their religious faith and believed that the

Exile had been the result of their ancestors' breaking God's law. They wanted to be legally pure, separate from any form of defilement. They believed that the difference between being "clean" and "unclean" depended upon that law. What was "clean" was obedience to the law; what was "unclean" was disobedience to the law.

This position regarding the law created problems, however, for although there are six hundred and thirteen commandments in the Torah (the books of Moses), they are not always specific. If the Sabbath day is to be kept "holy," then exactly what may be done and what may not? There were lengthy discussions on such subjects as whether or not it was lawful (or "unclean") to eat an egg laid on the Sabbath.

The Pharisees developed a set of regulations designed to save people from breaking the law itself, and they tried to apply the ancient law to new situations. It was necessary that stories be told illustrating the principles of the law (the Haggadah), and it was necessary for decisions about the law to be transmitted to others. The people responsible for this side of the work were the scribes, and there were several different schools of interpretation. The strict school of thought was led by Shammai, who came from a wealthy aristocratic family. The lenient school of thought was led by Hill'el, who came from the middle classes and understood the people. The differences of interpretation became live issues, so that Jesus was asked to give his opinion about the disputed divorce laws (Matthew 19:3–12).

The interpretations of the law were of little importance to the common people, who refused to join the Pharisees, the result being a great deal of bitterness between the two groups. The Pharisees believed in the historic doctrines of Judaism — in the unity, holiness, and providence of God; in the resurrection, the immortal soul bringing about a revival of the body; and in final judgment and the election of Israel. They tithed all they possessed, and they lived moral lives. The Pharisees survived all of the other groups, and as their traditions developed they became the founders of modern Judaism.

It is difficult to understand why there was so great a conflict between the Pharisees and Jesus, though there were probably a number of reasons. Jesus was popular with the common people, whereas the

Pharisees had made little headway (Mark 12:37; John 12:19). The crux of the matter seems to have been that in seeking to live according to the law, the Pharisees had failed to understand what the law was all about.

When God originally gave the law he did so as an act of supreme grace. People were in darkness, not knowing what God required. The law said: "This is my standard; if you live according to it, I will save you." (See for example the story of the rich young ruler in Matthew 19:16.) The Pharisees seem to have taken the law and changed it from an act of grace into a great burden — "This is what you have got to do; if you fail, God will punish you; if you do not fail, then you are righteous enough so that God has to receive you." It was so out of tune with what God intended that Jesus attacked it. One line of attack was to show that even the upright living Pharisees could not keep the law. They were corrupt (Matthew 23:27; Luke 11:39) play-actors (Matthew 23:23–36) who did not act according to the spirit of the law (Luke 11:39; 18:9–14). Because this false spirituality was the centre of their faith they turned against Jesus along with the other groups.

The Essenes

The Essenes withdrew from the world into communities of their own — about four thousand of them in all. The last straw preceding their withdrawal came when a particular priest-king was deemed to be so evil that a "Teacher of Righteousness" led people away from the "Wicked High Priest." The Essenes undertook basic agricultural craft and spent much time together in the study of religious and moral questions and in interpreting the sacred books. All property was held in common, they held to a program that ensured ritual purity, were unmarried, and rejected animal sacrifice.

When possible they formed communities of their own and lived in a way reminiscent of the monks in the monasteries in medieval Europe. People who wanted to withdraw from society joined their communities. There was a two-stage novitiate. At the end of the first period (one or two years) there was a ritual of purification, and at the end of the second period (one or two years) the novice was made a full

The Dead Sea Scrolls were discovered in caves in these cliffs near Qumran.

member of the community, was allowed to take a number of oaths and, more important, to participate in the common meal.

The Essenes believed that God would bring the evil age to an end in response to their good lives and their prayers and that the longed-for end would be marked by the appearance of a prince of Aaron's line, a warrior prince (the Davidic Messiah) who would defeat the forces of evil, and a prophet would reveal God's will. The community that lived in the monastery by the northwest corner of the Dead Sea was probably an Essene community.

It has been suggested that, as well as being important in preserving ancient texts of the Old Testament (the Dead Sea Scrolls), they may have had another influence. John the Baptist was born to aging parents — Elizabeth and Zechariah — and many people believe that he was brought up at the Qumran community when his parents died. Part of their charitable work was to care for the orphans of the priests.

There are reflections of the Essenic message in the message of John — the need for repentance and for

Qumran monastery

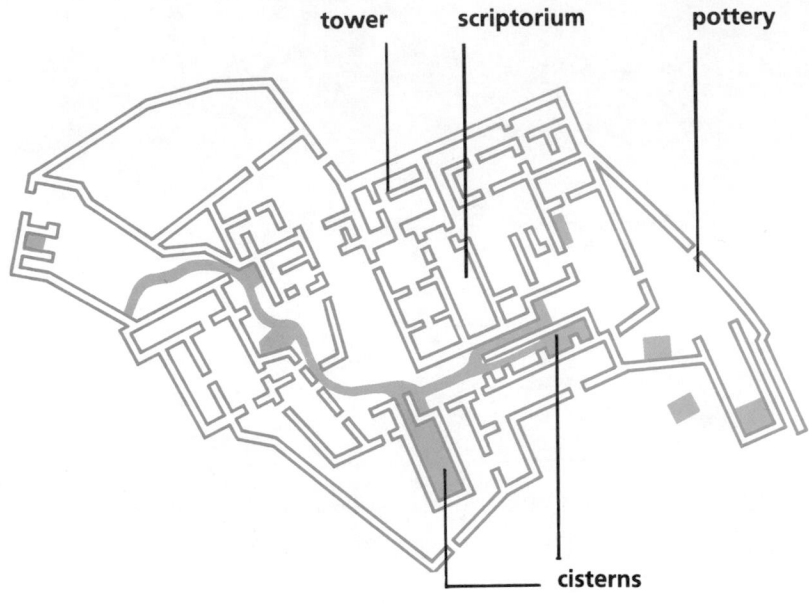

tower   **scriptorium**   **pottery**

cisterns

Plan of the community buildings at the Qumran monastery.

ritual washing (baptism), and a looking forward to the coming of the Messiah. It is unlikely to be an accident that the traditional site of John's baptism is within sight of the monastery at Qumran. The monastery was destroyed by the Romans in the campaign that followed the rebellion of AD 66. The Essene community took the most valuable manuscripts they possessed and hid them in almost inaccessible caves in the area where they were discovered in the twentieth century.

The Zealots

The Zealots reacted to foreign influence by seeking to destroy the enemy. They believed that only when the Romans were driven from the soil would God redeem his people. The Zealots were founded by Judas of Galilee in AD 6. The Zealots held that paying taxes to the Roman Empire was treason against God. They took their name from the zeal shown by the Maccabeans when they threw off the Syrian yoke. The Romans referred to the Zealots as "sicarii," or "dagger men," because they were continually in action with this weapon.

Some people believe that the Zealots tried to stimulate Jesus into leading a popular revolt. According to this view, Judas Iscariot worked with the Zealots to try to get Jesus into an impossible position where he would need to use his divine power to save himself. At such a display of power the common people would immediately follow him. Judas supposedly arranged the débâcle at the same time as he was lining his pockets. Those who hold this view look upon Judas as blind rather than evil. They claim that only by seeing Judas in this way can we understand how Judas could have given Jesus an affectionate kiss at the time of Jesus' arrest or understand Judas's subsequent suicide. On the other hand, Jesus referred to Judas as the son of perdition (John 17:12).

The Dead Sea Scrolls were discovered in pots like this.

Opposite: Herod the Great believed he had found an impregnable site for his palace at Masada.

Herod's stronghold of Masada, above the Dead Sea.

The Zealots were involved in the revolt that brought about the destruction of Jerusalem in AD 70. They retreated to their last stronghold, Masada, by the Dead Sea, which they had wrested from the Romans at the beginning, and finally perished when Masada fell in AD 74. Zealots were still active in the time of the final rebellion of Bar Cochba in AD 135 that led to the banishment of the Jews from their own country and the final destruction of Jerusalem.

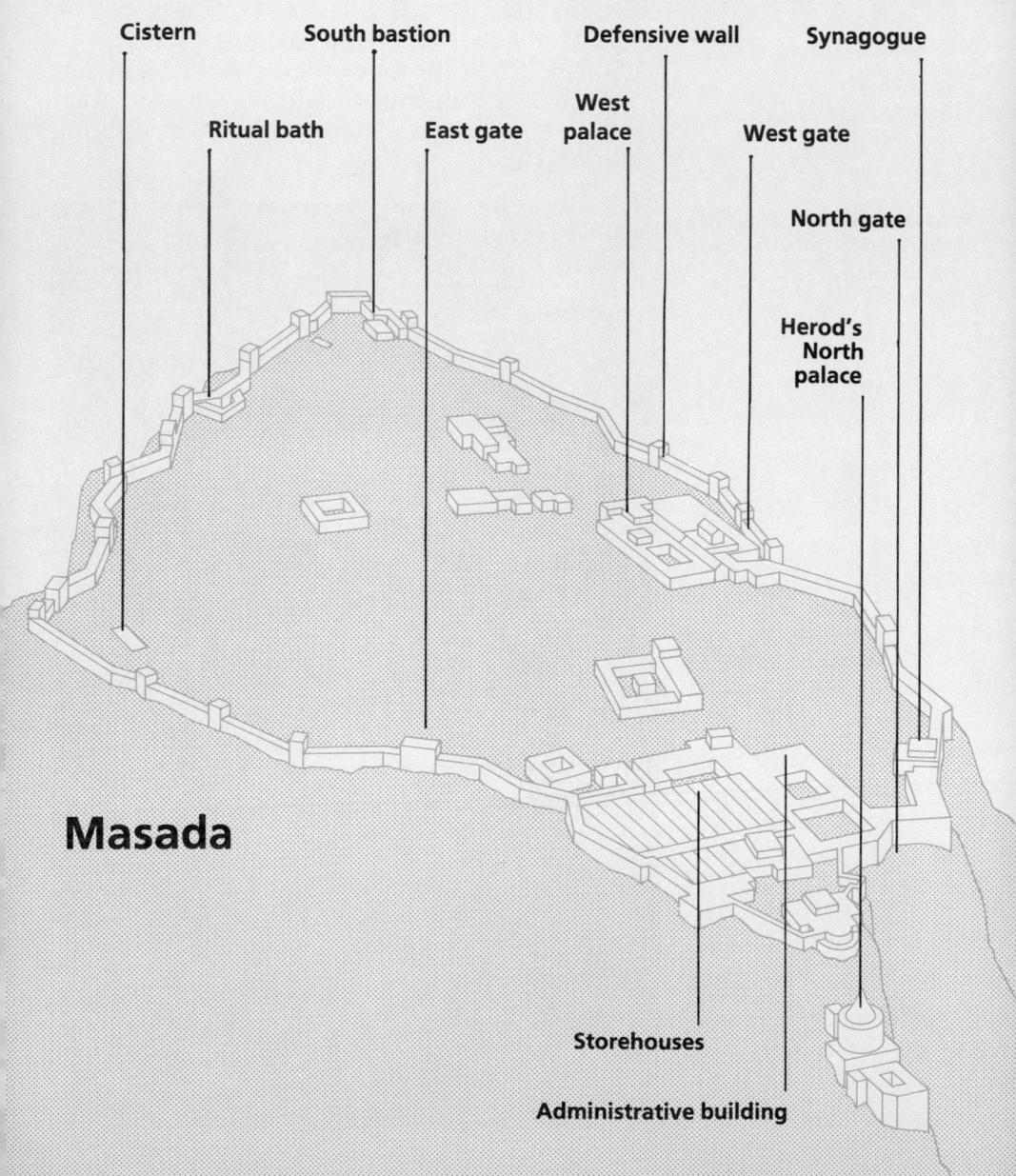

Cistern South bastion Defensive wall Synagogue

Ritual bath East gate West palace West gate

North gate

Herod's North palace

Masada

Storehouses

Administrative building

Government and Society

Government varies from country to country, and it varies in the same country over a period of time. It might be a democracy or a dictatorship, or the form of government might change to meet a new situation. While this is true of the twentieth century, it is also true of Bible times. Government varied among the Jewish people from the patriarchal family leadership in the time of Abraham to the uniting of clans under Moses, to the monarchy from King Saul onward, to the priest-kings of the period between the Old and New Testament. At the same time the kingdoms of Israel and Judah were in the centre of great empires — Egypt, Assyria, Babylon, Persia, Greece, and Rome. It is not possible within the scope of this book to deal with all the forms of government in detail; the bibliography will need to be consulted. But there are two forms of government that are of key importance to an understanding of the Bible — the period of the monarchy and the period when the Jews were part of the Roman Empire.

Divisions in society

There were no divisions within society during the period of the patriarchs (Abraham, Isaac, and Jacob) because everyone was a member of a family. Even slaves were looked upon as members of the family, so that Abraham could expect his slave Eliezer to inherit his possessions (Genesis 15:2–3). Even when clans developed from the families there were still no social divisions, because a clan is simply a family that has settled to form a village. In such a society the laws were upheld by the clan elders, who presided over village affairs. There were seventy-seven elders at Succoth in Gideon's time (Judges 7:14). By the time the monarchy arrived the term *elder* was used for the ruling class. The servants of

Amon who killed him were elders (2 Kings 21:23), and Zedekiah was concerned that Jeremiah should not repeat their conversation to the princes, or elders (Jeremiah 38:24–25).

Another group in society in the days of the monarchy was the wealthy. Some wealthy people were believed to have their wealth as a blessing from the Lord (Psalm 1:3; Proverbs 10:15–16), but others gained their wealth in evil ways. Deuteronomy 10:17 seems to compare the justice of God, who is impartial and takes no bribe, with those who show partiality and accept bribes. Proverbs 22:22–23 warns against the crushing of the poor and afflicted. Although some land changed hands because the original owners were better craftsmen than farmers, other land changed hands because of false accusation and confiscation (1 Kings 21:10–16). Those people became wealthy landowners, and as such they were taxed by King Menahem to help him pay protection money to the Assyrians (2 Kings 15:19–20).

Besides the elders and the landowners, there were the "people of the land." They were the freemen of the country with basic civil rights, and we meet them throughout the Old Testament (2 Kings 16:15; Jeremiah 1:18; 37:2; Ezekiel 22:29). A distinction was made between the sin offerings that had to be brought by one of the nobility (Leviticus 4:22–26) and the offering that had to be brought by one of the people of the land (vv. 27–31). The nobility had to bring a male offering, and the people of the land a female one.

In addition to these classes of Jewish people there were considerable numbers of resident aliens who were free, but without land. They therefore had to sell themselves into service in order to live. They were allowed to pick up the fallen grapes in the vineyard (Leviticus 19:10) and the gleanings of the grain harvest (Leviticus 23:22). It would have been very easy to take advantage of such a person, but Exodus 22:20 forbade that because the Jews themselves had been aliens in Egypt. In other respects, however, resident aliens were like the people of the land (see Leviticus 25:47; Numbers 35:15; Deuteronomy 14:29).

Alongside the freemen there were several classes of slaves. Personal slaves were often part of a family as a result of captivity in warfare (Judges 5:30; 2 Kings 5:2; Joel 3:6). King Pekah of Israel actually enslaved some of the people from Judah until Oded the prophet made a strong protest (2 Chronicles 28:8–15). It was expected that the Jews would take captives of other nations (Deuteronomy 21:10–14), although it was also possible for them to purchase slaves from the slave market (Leviticus 25:44–45).

Jews themselves were never supposed to become slaves, but they could sell their labour to make restitution after theft (Exodus 22:3) and to earn enough money to pay off a debt (Leviticus 25:47–53). They had to be released at Jubilee, or after seven years (Leviticus 25:40; Deuteronomy 15:12–18). In addition to personal slaves, there were state slaves known as the Nethinim and used for building (2 Samuel 12:31), for maintaining the merchant fleet (1 Kings 9:27), and in some cases for working in the Temple to assist the Levites (Ezra 8:20). Ezekiel said that God did not approve of this third practice (Ezekiel 44:7–9), but it had begun when Joshua enslaved the Gibeonites for such a purpose (Joshua 9:27).

The amphictyony

Before the monarchy was instituted, the relationship between the clans could best be described as an amphictyony, or an associaton of neighbors to defend a common religious centre. There was a formal agreement made at Shechem under Joshua's leadership (Joshua 24). It involved the worship of the same God at a common shrine and the keeping of a common code of law that was inscribed upon a stone and left at the shrine. When Joshua died, the clans accepted the leadership of any person who, like Joshua, was clearly endowed with the Spirit of God for military purposes (Judges 13:5) and sometimes for peaceful purposes (Judges 10:3). Some exercised their authority in a small area, but others were national leaders. Only Samuel seems to have been recognized by all the clans (1 Samuel 7:15).

There was therefore no properly organized government and little political unity. It was not very easy to live like this when the Jews were constantly under pressure from other military powers. The recognition of a leader endowed with God's Spirit implied the willingness to wait for God to act and the

During the period of the Judges, Shiloh became the permanent resting-place for the Ark of the Covenant.

ability to exercise spiritual discernment. Many of the people believed, however, that it would be easier if they had a king like other nations. The king would always be on hand to lead them, and his offspring and heir could easily be identified. This idea was reinforced when there was general dissatisfaction with Samuel's own sons (1 Samuel 8:5) and the people asked for a king.

Saul became the first king, but he was not king in the sense of being a true monarch. He was transitional between the judges and a true king. Like a judge, he was appointed by God (1 Samuel 9:16), received the Spirit (1 Samuel 10:6), and delivered his people (1 Samuel 11:1–11). But at the same time he was recognized by everyone, was given a coronation, and Saul expected his son Jonathan to succeed him (1 Samuel 11:15; 20:31). When David eventually succeeded Saul, he was acceptable not because he was a relative of Saul's but because it was recognized that he too had been chosen by God (2 Samuel 5:2). He had been anointed (1 Samuel 16:1) and endowed with the Spirit (1 Samuel 16:13). David was still at a stage before the true monarch, even though there were more trappings of monarchy than Saul had.

David and Solomon

The kingship of David and Solomon is unique in the history of Israel. First they were actually kings of *two* kingdoms rather than one. David was first made king of Judah (2 Samuel 2:4) and later was made king of Israel (2 Samuel 5:3). He was therefore called king of Israel and Judah (2 Samuel 5:5; 1 Kings 1:35) and not king over a single kingdom. The same was true of Solomon, which is why the two kingdoms went their separate ways after his death (1 Kings 12:16–17). Yet at the time, David and Solomon ruled over an empire that required considerable administration (2 Samuel 20:23–26). At a time of general weakness among the great powers, it was possible for Israel-Judah to fill the power vacuum (2 Samuel 8:1–14).

After the reigns of David and Solomon, when the two kingdoms had lost most of their empire, they differed from each other in an important way. In Israel there was no hereditary monarchy, but a number of dynasties. Like the judges, the king could be individually chosen by God (1 Kings 11:31; 19:16). In Judah, the kings were all members of a chosen dynasty (David's), which had itself been chosen by God (2 Samuel 7:11–12). When the monarchy came to an end and the kingdoms of Israel and Judah were simply the provinces of a greater power, the Jews formed a religious community because there was no possibility of a political one. God was their king (Isaiah 41:21; 43:15) and the high priest became his representative on earth. Within this development of the kingdom there were several common strands of administration.

The coronation

The king's reign commenced with a coronation. The first ceremony of the coronation took place in the Temple on a raised platform (2 Chronicles 6:13). There the king was given his crown (2 Samuel 1:10) and some kind of document, or "testimony," (2 Kings 11:12) that said he was king and stated how he was to exercise his kingship (Psalm 2:7–9). The king was then anointed (1 Kings 1:39; 2 Kings 23:30) to separate him to God (see 1 Samuel 24:6).

Israel in the time of David and Solomon

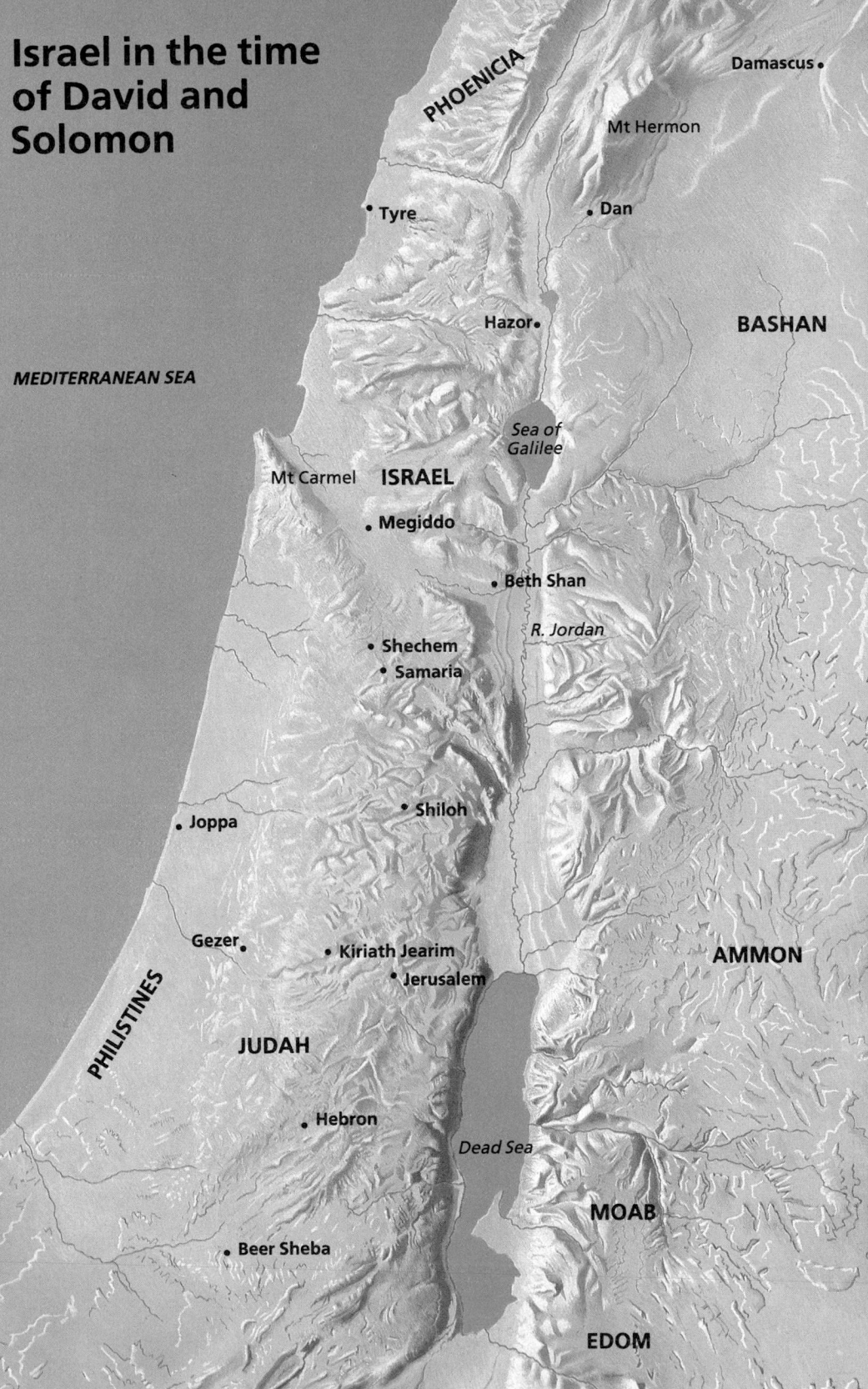

PHOENICIA

Damascus

Mt Hermon

Tyre

Dan

Hazor

BASHAN

MEDITERRANEAN SEA

Sea of Galilee

Mt Carmel   ISRAEL

Megiddo

Beth Shan

R. Jordan

Shechem

Samaria

Shiloh

Joppa

Gezer

Kiriath Jearim

AMMON

Jerusalem

PHILISTINES

JUDAH

Hebron

Dead Sea

MOAB

Beer Sheba

EDOM

God could then give his Spirit so that the role of kingship would be fulfilled. A trumpet was sounded and everyone cried, "Long live the king," in recognition of the king's authority (1 Kings 1:34; 2 Kings 11:12, 14).

The second stage of the coronation took place at the royal palace when the king sat on his throne (1 Kings 1:46; 2 Kings 11:19). The king may then have received a special coronation name. Eliakim had his name changed to Jehoiakim (2 Kings 23:34), Mattaniah became Zedekiah (2 Kings 24:17), Shallum became Jehoahaz (1 Chronicles 3:15; cf. 2 Kings 23:30), and Solomon's earlier name might have been Jedidiah (2 Samuel 12:24–25).

Special songs were sung. The second psalm may have been used at the coronation — the occasion when God looked upon the king as his son (Psalm 2:7) — although prophetically Psalm 2 speaks of the Messiah. Psalm 72 was a prayer for the king, and Psalm 110 was an enthronement psalm that again looks forward to the Messiah. It was therefore a religious as well as a civil ceremony because the king was to have special place in the religion of the Jewish people (see 2 Samuel 24:25; 1 Kings 3:4; 12:28–29; 2 Kings 16:12–16).

The royal household

There were important elements in the royal household, although this seems to have developed to a greater extent in Judah than in Israel. The harem was an important status symbol. Even Saul had a small harem (2 Samuel 3:7; 12:8), and David seems to have increased it (2 Samuel 5:13; 15:16). Solomon's harem was the greatest of all (1 Kings 11:3). The harem was not just a matter of status. It was also politically useful, because a king could make many alliances as he received the daughters of other royal families into the harem (1 Kings 3:1; 16:31).

The possession of the harem was the symbol of the right to the throne, which is why claims to the harem were treated as treason (1 Kings 1:5; 2:13–22). The harem was ruled over until she died by the gebirah, the "great lady," on the succession of her son to the throne (1 Kings 15:13). This is why the king's mother's name is often referred to in connection with the kings of Judah (see for example, 2 Chronicles 20:31). Daughters would stay in the harem under the care of the women until they were married, but princes left the care of the women to set up homes of their own (2 Samuel 13:7).

Court attendants

There were a considerable number of attendants — nobles and servants. There were singers (2 Samuel 19:33–35; Ecclesiastes 2:8) and people to look after the provision of food (1 Kings 10:4–5), which was often for a large number of people who were fed at the palace (1 Kings 18:19). The king had a squire, or armourbearer (1 Samuel 16:21), who shared the king's chariot in battle (2 Kings 7:2; 9:25), a "friend" who had no special function but who was available for the king to talk to and sound out (2 Samuel 15:32), people who looked after the estate (2 Samuel 9:10), and a bodyguard.

In addition to such staff, the king also had a number of high-ranking officials. Lists of such officials are given in 2 Samuel 8:16–18; 20:23–26 and 1 Kings 4:1–6. They included the army commander, the captain of the guard, a herald, a secretary, someone who controlled the twelve prefects (see below), the "chief of the levy" and the master of the palace.

Some of these officers of state were extremely important. The herald was in charge of palace ceremonial functions and introduced people who sought an audience with the king. Joah was herald (or recorder) at the time of Hezekiah (2 Kings 18:18; see also Isaiah 36:3, 11, 22). The secretary was responsible for all correspondence and collected the Temple repair money (2 Kings 12:10). It was when Shaphan was secretary that he discovered the law book that he read to King Josiah (2 Kings 22:10). The master of the palace was senior to the secretary (Shebna was demoted from master of the palace to secretary, Isaiah 22:15; compare 36:3). He was a kind of vizier, as Joseph had been in Egypt, literally running the kingdom on behalf of the king. Obadiah held this position in Ahab's court (1 Kings 18:3).

The prefects were each in charge of an administrative district that supplied a month's amount of food for human beings and fodder for animals at the court (1 Kings 4:7–19). Two of the prefects were sons-in-law to King Solomon at one time (vv. 11, 15). The twelve prefects were controlled by an officer. A parallel post was held by an officer who organized the levy by which able-bodied men for part of the year were forced to give their labour for building projects (2 Samuel 20:24).

Finances

It is clear that such an organization required a great deal of expenditure. Yet finances during the monarchy were organized quite differently from finances today. The king's expenses were the kingdom's expenses. The king paid for the army, but he collected the revenue (2 Chronicles 17:5). There was little or no distinction between the civil treasury and the Temple treasury. The king would put money into the Temple treasury after a successful military campaign, as had Joshua (Joshua 6:14), but he used money from the Temple treasury when he needed it (1 Kings 15:18; 2 Kings 12:18).

The legal system

One of the remarkable institutions of Bible times was the Jewish legal system. It was quite different from anything that existed in any contemporary society of the time. There was no written law in Egypt at all, and the legal systems of Babylon and other nations were not documents to which judicial reference was made but rather were collections of the king's judgments for the use of the people. Judgment was the action of the king who not only made the law but actually *was* the law. No other nation had a legal system to which kings and rulers were subject and to which reference had to be made.

The legal pronouncements given to the Jewish people were of two kinds. One had the structure, "If ... and ... then ..." which is sometimes known as casuistic law (laws of conduct and resolving questions of right and wrong). For example, "If a man strikes his slave and the slave dies under his hand then he shall be punished" (Exodus 21:20). Most of the laws of this kind were similar, if not identical, to many of the judgments made by rulers in surrounding society. God was in effect taking the customary law that people understood and putting his approval on specific laws so that they formed a legal code.

The other kind of law is direct "Thou shall not kill" and "Remember the sabbath day, to keep it

King Jehu of Israel pays tribute to Shalmaneser III of Assyria; detail from the Black Obelisk of Shalmaneser.

holy," — and is called apodeictic law (of absolute truth). This form of pronouncement is not found in any other legal system, but it is found in contemporary suzerainty treaties used by the Hittites. A suzerainty treaty was drawn up when a conquering king (the suzerain) imposed his will on a subject people. It always took a standard form in which there was a description of the king and the good things he had done. This was followed by a set of statements of the relationship that should exist between the conquered people and himself, and between the conquered people and other people. This was followed by a set of casuistic laws and a list of blessings and cursings for those who kept and those who failed to keep the treaty.

A careful look at the Ten Commandments in Exodus 20 will reveal that they are part of such a structure, commencing with "I am the Lord your God who brought you up out of the land of Egypt" (Exodus 20:2) and finishing with blessings and cursing (Exodus 23:20–33). Although the form is familiar, the content is unique. It is a religious law and at the same time a body of teaching. There are several other ways in which the Jewish legal system stood out from contemporary law of Bible days:

1. Justifying motives are given for some of the laws. Exodus 23:9 says that the Jews were not to oppress aliens because they had been aliens in Egypt. Exodus 20:5 says that idols are not to be made because God is a jealous god.

2. There are severe penalties for crimes against God (idolatry, blasphemy) and against those things that spoiled the relationship between people and God (bestiality, sodomy, incest). The death penalty was incurred for them all.

3. In general, the punishments dictated were humane. There was no bodily mutilation, and flogging was limited to forty strokes. Special arrangements were made for manslaughter. The avenger, or *go'el*, was very limited as to what he could do through private justice. Cities of refuge were set aside where a man's case could be put to the elders. If he was found to be a murderer, he was put to death; but if it was a case of manslaughter, he was given his liberty within the city but not outside it (Numbers 35:9–34; Deuteronomy 4:41–43; 19:1–13). The sanctuary of God, either the Tabernacle or Temple, was also a place where a person was safe from the avenger of blood when the person had committed a crime (Exodus 21:12–14).

4. The king did not enact law so there was no state law. Although he was a judge (see 2 Chronicles 17:9; 19:5–7), he had to be subject to the law as well.

The Old Testament law was therefore in actual fact a gift of grace from God.

The judges

In the days before the monarchy, every tribal chief was a judge (Joshua 7:19–26), and during the time of the amphictyony, there were local and even "circuit judges" to whom appeal could be made (1 Samuel 7:15–17; 12:3–5). But generally, justice remained in the hands of the local elders who dealt with local matters in the town gate (Amos 5:10). They could pronounce the death penalty if it was merited, and the execution was carried out by witnesses (Deuteronomy 21:18–21). This local system prevailed throughout the history of Israel, but the personnel were added to. The king was always an "appeal judge" (2 Samuel 12:1–6; 15:2–4; 1 Kings 3:16–18), and when the task became too great, as it did for Moses, he delegated some of the work to professional judges (Exodus 18:13–27; Deuteronomy 16:18–20; 2 Chronicles 19:5–11).

There seems to have been a Jerusalem court made up of priests, Levites, and the heads of families that dealt with legal cases in the city, but which also acted as an appeal court. The high priest presided over religious matters and the chief of the house of Judah over civil matters. This may have been the model for the Sanhedrin, which we meet in New Testament times (see for example Acts 4:5–7). If the court could not decide, God was asked to decide (Exodus 22:8). This, in effect, could mean the bringing of a curse upon one's self, trial by ordeal (Numbers 5:11–31), or revelation through the casting of lots (Joshua 7:14–15; Proverbs 18:18). At times the sacred lots, the Urim and Thummim, held in the high priest's breastplate were probably used for the purpose.

The Roman Empire

The Roman Empire was a second period of great importance to the people of Bible lands. The birth of Jesus is clearly set in Roman times: "In those days Caesar Augustus issued a decree that a census should be taken of the entire Roman world. (This was the first census that took place while Quirinius was governor of Syria.)" (Luke 2:1–2). Rome had only recently acquired an emperor. For hundreds of years it had been a republic, governed by a senate of people who had proved themselves in public office. Two senior magistrates were elected to lead the republic on an annual basis, after which they returned to the senate. They represented the two main social groupings of the Roman people.

As the Republic began to expand through wars and through conquest, army commanders, supported by their loyal troops, became the most powerful people in the Republic. About fifty years before

The Roman Empire in the time of Christ

ILLYRICUM

ITALY

• Rome

SICILY • Syracuse

• Carthage

TRIPOLITANIA

MEDITERRANEAN SEA

Cyr

AFRICA

Coin portraits of the Emperor Augustus (top) and the Emperor Tiberius (bottom).

the birth of Jesus three powerful generals dominated Roman politics, and the senate dared not disregard them — Pompey (who was responsible, among other things, for bringing the Jewish people into the Roman realm), Crassus, and Julius Caesar. It was inevitable that there would be a power struggle and civil war.

Julius Caesar was the ultimate victor and in effect became sole ruler. Before he was murdered in the forum, Julius had willed that his place be taken by his nephew, Octavius. Again, there was a power struggle between those who supported a republic (and had therefore planned the downfall of Julius Caesar) and Octavius. Octavius Caesar won, and the people, grateful for peace, gave him the title "Augustus" when he became emperor.

Provincial rule

In controlling the Empire, it was agreed that Augustus should govern those areas where there was unrest among the local people or a threat of invasion from outside. This plan was devised because the emperor had sole control of the army. In effect this meant that he governed through army commanders, or legates, who held their positions for five-year periods. Quirinius was a legate (Luke 2:1). When smaller areas were involved, procurators were appointed who were responsible to the legate. Syria (which included Judea) was under the emperor's control because there was considerable unrest among the people, and because the Parthians were a continual threat on the eastern frontier of the Empire. In provinces where there was no such danger, the senate appointed a proconsul (formerly a consul) each year as governor.

Vassal kings were allowed to rule in some areas if they followed Roman policy. Herod the Great ruled from 40 BC until AD 4 as a vassal king (Matthew 2:1). When Herod died, his kingdom was divided among his sons. Galilee and Perea were governed by Herod Antipas; Herod Philip governed Ituraea and Trachonitis; and Archelaus governed Samaria, Judaea, and Idumaea (Edom). Archelaus (Matthew 2:22) could not keep order and so a Roman procurator (initially called a prefect) was appointed, subject to the legate of Syria. Pontius Pilate was the fifth procurator and controlled the area formerly

Roman columns from a public building at Caesarea Maritima, capital of Palestine for six hundred years.

run by Archelaus, but he had no jurisdiction over Herod Antipas's area of Galilee and Perea (see Luke 23:5–6).

This was not the end of the interplay between the family of Herod and the Roman procurators. When Herod Philip died and Herod Antipas was deposed, another younger member of the family, Herod Agrippa I, took over Galilee, Peraea, Ituraea, and Trachonitis. Because Agrippa I had been brought up in the court at Rome, he was allowed to become king of the Jews again like his grandfather Herod the Great and take over the procuratorial area as well. All this went to his head and, as well as persecuting the early Christians (Acts 12:1–5), he imagined himself to be a god and for this blasphemy was struck down (Acts 12:20–23).

His son, Herod Agrippa II, did not have the patronage of Rome in the same way as his father. He was allowed to look after Ituraea and Trachonitis but procurators Felix (Acts 24:2) and Festus (Acts 24:27—25:1) took over the remainder of the country. Agrippa II appeared as an expert in Jewish affairs to help Festus assess the position of Paul (Acts 25:13–27).

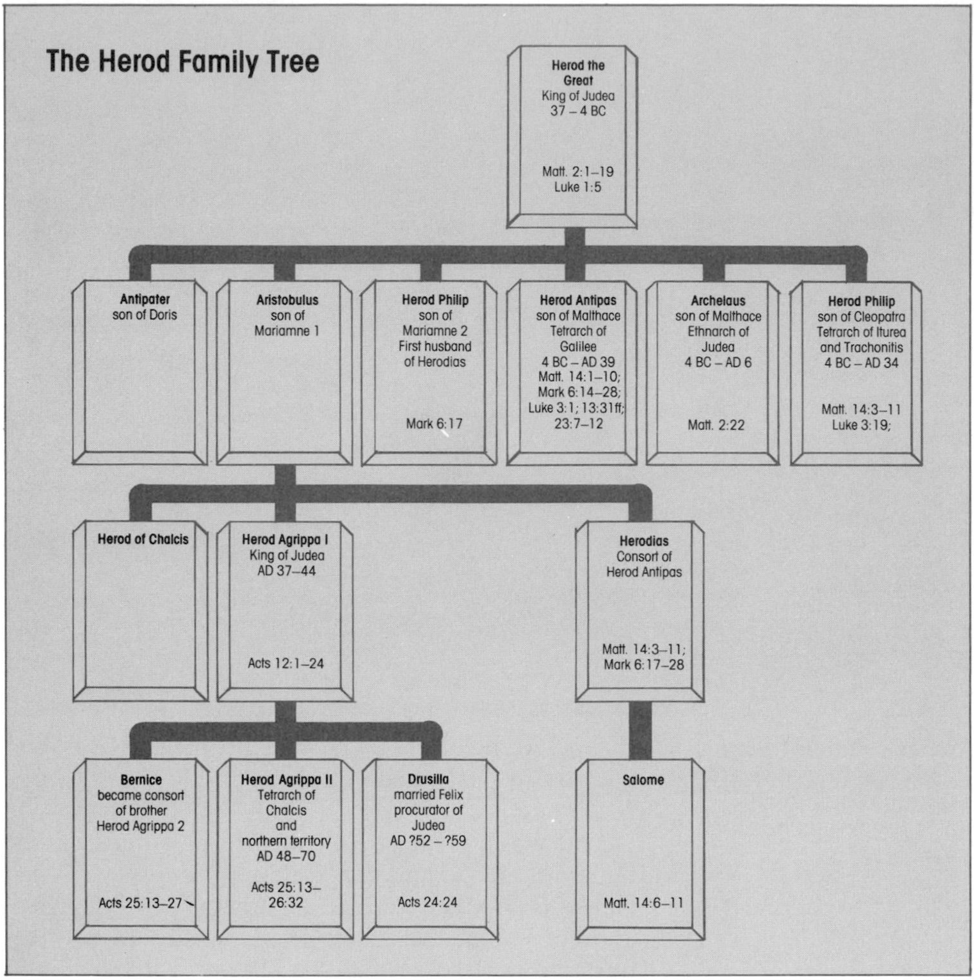

The Herod Family Tree

Herod the Great
King of Judea
37 – 4 BC

Matt. 2:1–19
Luke 1:5

Antipater
son of Doris

Aristobulus
son of
Mariamne 1

Herod Philip
son of
Mariamne 2
First husband
of Herodias

Mark 6:17

Herod Antipas
son of Malthace
Tetrarch of
Galilee
4 BC – AD 39
Matt. 14:1–10;
Mark 6:14–28;
Luke 3:1; 13:31ff;
23:7–12

Archelaus
son of Malthace
Ethnarch of
Judea
4 BC – AD 6

Matt. 2:22

Herod Philip
son of Cleopatra
Tetrarch of Iturea
and Trachonitis
4 BC – AD 34

Matt. 14:3–11
Luke 3:19;

Herod of Chalcis

Herod Agrippa I
King of Judea
AD 37–44

Acts 12:1–24

Herodias
Consort of
Herod Antipas

Matt. 14:3–11;
Mark 6:17–28

Bernice
became consort
of brother
Herod Agrippa 2

Acts 25:13–27

Herod Agrippa II
Tetrarch of
Chalcis
and
northern territory
AD 48–70

Acts 25:13–
26:32

Drusilla
married Felix
procurator of
Judea
AD ?52 – ?59

Acts 24:24

Salome

Matt. 14:6–11

The Citadel, Jerusalem, site of Herod's palace.

Government of Palestine

Herod the Great (40 – 4BC)

Idumea/Judaea/Samaria	Galilee/Peraea	Ituraea Trachonitis
Archelaus (4BC – AD6)	Herod Antipas (4BC – AD39)	Herod Philip (4BC – AD34)

Procurators

Coponius (6–9)

Ambibulus (9–12)

Annius Rufus (12–15)

Valerius Gratus (15–26)

Pontius Pilate (26–36)

Marcellus (36–38)

Maryllus (38–44)

Procurator (34)

Herod Agrippa I,
King of Judaea 37–44

Procurators

Cuspius Fadus (44–46)

Tiberius Alexander (46–48)

Ventidius Cumanus (48–52)

Antonius Felix (52–59)

Porcius Festus (59–61)

Herod Agrippa II,
Tetrarch of Chalcis
and northern territory 48–70

There were also peaceful provinces within the Empire. These were ruled by two magistrates with the rank of proconsul from the main centre in the province. They were responsible directly to the Senate. The proconsuls in Philippi wanted to get Paul and Silas out of the city when they discovered that Paul as a Roman citizen had been badly treated (Acts 16:35). The clerk at Ephesus was concerned lest the unrest in the city in reaction to Paul should cause trouble, and he therefore encouraged Demetrius and the silversmiths to take legal action before the proconsuls (Acts 19:38), who were the magistrates.

Athens. The rocky outcrop in the foreground was known in Paul's time as the "Areopagus".

Some cities of great importance, such as Athens, were allowed to govern themselves and to be tax free, so long as the peace was kept. In Athens, there was an "education committee" as part of the organization of the city. Paul had to explain his teachings to this "Areopagus" as it was called (Acts 17:19). When it was wise, for religious reasons, to grant some form of self-government, the Romans allowed this. Even in Judea, where trouble was always likely, the Jews were allowed to have a ruling council of the Sanhedrin, which dealt with religious matters (Matthew 27:1; Acts 4:5–21; 5:21–41).

Although the Roman government could be oppressive, it brought benefits as well. Law and order were enforced, soldiers acting as a police force in time of peace (Matthew 27:65). It was true that they could be used to put down riots and punish the local population (Pilate was recalled to Rome because he used troops to massacre a religious gathering in Samaria), but the troops made travel much safer by clearing the countryside of bandits and the sea of pirates.

The Roman roads, which have been described earlier in the book, made travel much quicker and easier. Many people appreciated the buildings, entertainment, and water supply. Roman citizenship itself conferred many advantages, one of which was that one could not be punished without trial (see Acts 16:38). People born in Rome were originally

Palestine in the time of Christ

Damascus •

SYRIA

• Tyre

• Caesarea Philippi

ITURAEA

TRACHONITIS

MEDITERRANEAN SEA

• Ptolemais

• Capernaum

GALILEE

Sea of Galilee

• Sepphoris

• Nazareth

DECAPOLIS

• Caesarea Maritima

• Scythopolis

SAMARIA

• Samaria

R. Jordan

PERAEA

• Joppa

• Jericho

JUDAEA

• Jerusalem

• Qumran

Bethlehem •

• Hebron

Dead Sea

IDUMAEA

Masada •

NABATAEA

The Forum, Rome. The Colisseum can be seen in the background.

the only citizens, but citizenship was extended to include those who had done great service to the Empire, and they were able to pass on the privileges to their children. In time, when the Empire was short of money, citizenship could be sold to those who were willing to pay the price.

Now look at your Bible

A law for society

Leviticus 4:22–31; 19:10; 23:22.
Leviticus 4 is an example of a law that was not immediately applicable to contemporary society because in the clan life of people involved in the Exodus there were no such distinctions in society. Leviticus 19 and 23 were written before the Jews had fields and vineyards. It is common to read in many books about the text of the Old Testament that such laws really belonged to a later period of Israel's history and were "written back" into this period. I prefer to believe that God prepared for the development of society by giving laws in advance.

It is interesting to compare laws in Exodus 20 with those in Deuteronomy and then those in Leviticus because they correspond to three successive periods of development in Jewish history. The laws of liberty for a slave are interesting in this respect. In Deuteronomy 15:12–18, slaves were to be released after seven years, and when King Zedekiah did not release slaves, Jeremiah referred him to this seven-year law (Jeremiah 34:8–14). The law in Leviticus 25:40 seems to be for a later period, because the short terms for slavery did not work. Jeremiah did not quote it as appropriate for his time.

Was David Elhanan?

2 Samuel 21:19. Elhanan the son of a Bethlehemite killed Goliath the Gittite, the shaft of whose spear was like a weaver's rod. This is so similar to David son of an Ephrathite of Bethlehem who killed Goliath of Gath, whose spear was like a weaver's rod (1 Samuel 17:7), that some people wonder if David was the coronation name and Elhanan the original name.

Opening and shutting

Isaiah 22:22. This verse describes the authority of the master of the palace. Eliakim was to have the key of the house of David, and what Eliakim would open no one else could shut, and what he shut no one else could open. These words are used of Christ in Revelation 3:7, because Christ has such authority in the kingdom of heaven. This is quite distinct from what Jesus tells Peter in Matthew 16:9. The binding and loosing Peter was given was also given to the other disciples (Matthew 18:18). When a person acts in accordance with God's Word, it can be declared that he is bound or free by someone who knows that Word.

Rights of citizenship

Acts 22:25–29. When Paul was bound, and an attempt was made to scourge him, there was consternation when it was realized that he was a Roman citizen, because such treatment of a citizen was contrary to the law. The tribune, who was the officer commanding the unit in Jerusalem, had apparently purchased his own citizenship at a time when it was put up for sale. If Paul was free born and came from Tarsus in Cilicia, his father probably had performed some service for the republic (not the Empire) for which citizenship had been conferred on himself and his family.

Warfare

Warfare is an expensive undertaking. When troops are away from their own country, there is a loss of manpower. The weapons, clothing, food and other supplies for an army all have to be paid for. It is not possible to engage in extensive warfare or for a king to have a large army until there are funds to finance it. The finance was available for the Jewish people in the time of Solomon, and it was only during this period that the nation had a standing army, which included chariots and perhaps cavalry. At other times other means had to be found for warfare. If the Jewish people could not do so they were subject to more powerful nations who had the resources to maintain a large army — and by paying "tribute" money themselves, they actually helped to provide the resources of those nations.

Before the monarchy
Before the days of the monarchy, it was a case of every available man's being ready to take up arms. This was true in Abraham's time. When his nephew, Lot, had been taken prisoner, Abraham took 318 fighting men from his family and by means of surprise and night attack was able to rescue Lot and to capture a great deal of material goods (Genesis 14:14–16).

The same process worked in the time of the Judges, but at this time the "judge" was able to call upon all the able-bodied men over twenty to join him in the operation. When Deborah and Barak resisted the Canaanites, they called upon people from the tribes of Ephraim, Benjamin, Zebulun, Issachar, Reuben, Dan, Asher and Naphtali (Judges 5:14–18), and only the men from Meroz did not respond (Judges 5:23). The tribes of Simeon and Judah were not called on this occasion.

On the other hand, Saul called the armies from all

Jericho, lush green against the dusty brown of the surrounding desert.

the tribes together by cutting two oxen into twelve pieces (1 Samuel 11:7). On this occasion they rallied to the relief of Jabesh Gilead (1 Samuel 11:1–2). To fight was a religious duty. During this period there was no regular army, and there was only negligible training and very few weapons. It is clear that the Jews believed that God was on their side. He was the Lord Almighty (1 Samuel 15:2), the God of the armies of Israel (1 Samuel 17:26), but he did not effect victories through large, well-equipped armies.

Spies were sent to Jericho, and an ally found in Rahab (Joshua 2:1–7). The city was captured after a ritual dedication of the city to God, which had reduced the inhabitants to fear (Joshua 6:1–5). The walls themselves may have been brought down by a God-timed earthquake. Ai could not be taken by a full frontal attack, but was taken by drawing the defenders out of the city to battle so that the city could then be put to flames by men in an ambush (Joshua 8). The Canaanites were thrown into panic by a surprise attack and were demoralized through a severe hailstorm (Joshua 10:9–11). At a time when the Jewish army had no chariots to meet the Canaanites, the Canaanite chariots were disabled by their wheels becoming bogged down in thick mud when the river Kishon burst its banks (Judges 5:21). Gideon defeated the demoralized Midianites (Judges 7:21) by a surprise attack of dedicated men in the middle of the night (Judges 7:19–20). Such tactics were typical of the Israelite militia when there was no standing army.

Saul's and David's army

The development of the army took place between the times of Saul and Solomon. Saul collected valiant men around him as a personal bodyguard (1 Samuel 14:17), and this was the beginning of a group of professional retainers. It was on this basis that David himself first joined Saul (1 Samuel 18:2), and, after the slaughter of Goliath, David's prowess prompted Saul to inquire whether there were any others in his family who had similar ability (1 Samuel 17:57–58). There were no proper supplies for the army at that time. Either they were provided by the families of the soldiers (1 Samuel 17:17–18) or by living off the land (1 Samuel 25:18–19).

David's bodyguard was larger in size and therefore more developed. While he was on the run from King Saul, a sizeable group of several hundred joined him and proved to be a private army. There were six hundred in the group, and thirty of them became an inner core of officers (see 2 Samuel 23:8–39). Abishai was chief of staff (v. 18), Joab was army commander (2 Samuel 20:23), and Benaiah was commander of the bodyguard (2 Samuel 23:23; cf. 20:23). As a private army they terrorized the country when David was in exile in Ziklag (1 Samuel 27:8–12) and became the basis for a regular standing army when David became king (see 1 Chronicles 27:1–15, and compare the names with 2 Samuel 23:24–39).

Along with the experts in the standing army, numbers were supplemented by a "territorial army," which was recruited from the tribes on a rotation basis. Even though he had the services of experts (1 Chronicles 12:2, 8, 32–33) and though he began to use his troops in head-on confrontations with the enemy (2 Samuel 8; 10:9–19), there was no tremendous strength. He found it necessary only to retain a hundred horses, when opportunity arose, as a basis for a chariot force (2 Samuel 8:4). By use of his army he was able to extend his kingdom considerably, and as a result was able to incorporate foreign mercenaries into his personal bodyguard. The Cherethites and Pelethites were from the Philistines. It was probably the desire to see how strong he really was that led David to want to hold a census, which had such disastrous consequences (2 Samuel 24; especially v. 2).

Solomon's army

It was Solomon who built up a professional army, for through taxation and trading he was able to accumulate sufficient wealth to pay for it (1 Kings 10:25–27). In times of national emergency the regular army was supplemented by conscripts. Recruiting officers went through the tribes on such occasions and were still in use at a much later date (2 Kings 25:18; 2 Chronicles 11:1). Solomon also built up the fortified cities to protect the major highways into and through his kingdom and provided chariot units to defend the cities (2 Chronicles 1:14).

Several rules for conscription were set out in

The citadel at Arad has been partially reconstructed. Solomon fortified it as one of his strongholds.

Deuteronomy 20:5−9. People who had built a house but had not yet undertaken the religious ceremony of dedication; people who had not yet had the first crop from a newly planted vineyard; people who were betrothed but were not yet married; and people who had lost their enthusiasm for war (the elderly?) were exempted. This was not simply humane treatment, but followed a religious conviction at the time which held that all undertakings had to be completed.

As the wealth of the kingdom declined after Solomon it became increasingly difficult to put a professional army into the field. Towards the end of the monarchy and during the times of the Maccabees, the Jewish army reverted to a militia, and in New Testament times there was no army at all. The Jews were successful in the hills where surprise tactics and hand-to-hand fighting were in order, but they were much weaker on the plains where their enemies could muster chariot units. The God of Israel was therefore (incorrectly) reckoned to be a God of the hills rather than a God of the plains (1 Kings 20:23).

The foot-soldier

During the rise and fall of the Jewish army, the infantry was the core and the basis. The infantryman's weapons were therefore the key ones. In the Bible we have the Hebrew names for the weapons, and it is not easy to identify them.

Protective armour was available. The Assyrians had high pointed helmets, which covered the ears. Coats of mail consisted of metal scales sewn onto a tunic. Saul's helmet and armour were probably almost unique in Israel at the time, available to him because he was king. It was not at all unusual for a soldier to be armed with only a weapon such as a sling. Saul was anxious to protect David with the armour because it was a custom that champions should decide the outcome of slavery rather than a general battle in which the majority of the opposition would be maimed or killed. Saul wanted to take no chances (1 Samuel 17:38−40).

Shields were round, each formed of leather stretched over a wooden framework about a handle. It was necessary to oil the leather to prevent its

Various metal weapons dating from the Bronze Age, including a short sword, spear heads, and an axe blade.

cracking (2 Samuel 1:21). For weapons, the infantryman carried a short sword (practically a dagger), which was sheathed on the lefthand side, and a throwing spear (1 Samuel 18:10–11). A pike was also often in use. It seems to have been a short, pointed weapon for hand-to-hand fighting (Numbers 25:7–8; 2 Chronicles 11:12).

There were specialist soldiers who could use slings. Slings were powerful weapons when the stones, like small oranges, were hurled with devastating accuracy and force (Judges 20:16; 2 Kings 3:25). The archers were also specialists. Metal heads, flat, or with three or four vanes, sometimes barbed so that they could not be pulled out of a wound, were fixed to wooden shafts. The early bows were little more than pieces of springy wood, the two ends sprung together with a strip of dried sheep's gut; but by the time the Assyrians were in power, their bows were made of a laminated wood and horn construction, which gave the arrows great power and penetration. These bows were too expensive for many nations, and this led to the superiority of the Assyrian army.

Chariots

The chariot was developed primarily as transport for the archer so that he could move about freely. It was a light wooden vehicle with a rope floor, having pouches for arrows attached to the inside of the framework. Horses were yoked to the chariot, and a third (spare) horse ran free beside the chariot (see 1 Kings 22:34). The bow became a key weapon of defense on the ramparts of a city (see 2 Samuel 11:20), and as a consequence the Assyrians developed enormous wooden shields for the protection of their own archers. The "engines to shoot arrows and stones" from the walls of Jerusalem made by King Uzziah were similar shields that protected the archers on the ramparts (2 Chronicles 26:14–15).

Weapons were also developed during this period for warfare at sea, although this did not involve the Jewish people. Warships were built by the Egyptians, Philistines, Phoenicians, Greeks, and by the Romans.

Cities were built so as to resist sieges, and this has been described on page 187. As cities became

The Assyrians battle with Arab warriors. An Assyrian relief from *c.* 645 B.C.

The Assyrians capture a city, using siege engines, storming ladders, and archers; Assyrian relief c. 730 B.C.

stronger, armies developed engineering units so that tunnels could be made under the walls to weaken the foundations, gates could be set on fire, and limestone walls reduced to powder by the application of great heat through fires lit up against them. Battering rams were built to break the masonry down. A heavy ram was suspended within a wooden frame and was pulled backwards and upwards so that when it was released its metal head would strike the wall with great force.

In the meantime, the defenders used every means they could to deter the engineers, pouring down heavy rocks, boiling liquids, and firebrands. If the wall was breached, the infantry poured into the city; if the archers on the walls could be picked off one by one until there were none left, the walls were scaled with ladders. During a siege there was a signaling unit in operation. There are records of such signals during the Assyrian siege of Israel (Jeremiah 6:1 may refer to this). Ezekiel was familiar with siege warfare (Ezekiel 4:1–3; 26:9–10).

Campaigning

When warfare took place it was normally at a time when food was available to live off the land and when weather conditions made war feasible (2 Samuel 11:1). So far as the Jewish army was concerned, the central "administration" unit (Numbers 2:17) was surrounded by four divisions (Numbers 2) and was preceded by an advance guard.

There was no "declaration of war." War started as soon as one army entered another's territory. Then there was a parley. The invader offered the defenders their lives in return for their service, and sometimes there were other conditions as well. If the defenders gave in they were either enslaved or forced to pay protection money. If the defending army refused their opponent's terms, the attack on the city would begin. The city's water supplies were cut off if this was possible, and its food supplies were blocked off by completely surrounding the city, sometimes with siege walls. The surrounding army might have to withdraw if sallies from the city were successful (Judges 20:31–32), because of illness and death (caused by God) in the camp (2 Kings 19:35–36), or because there was relief on its way from another quarter (2 Kings 24:7). The weather might also become so bad that the attacking army would be forced to retire until a later date.

If the siege war was successful, the women and children were enslaved, all the men were killed, booty was taken to give the soldiers their pay, and the city was then burned to the ground. The Assyrians were particularly cruel in this respect. The chief men of the defeated city were brought to the gates to be tortured, blinded, and burned alive. Scribes counted the number of dead from the severed heads brought to them as tallies.

War and religion

It was not possible to separate warfare from religion. The connection of the two was evident in many aspects of military practice. To the Jews, God was the Lord of Hosts who went before them into battle (Exodus 15:3; Judges 4:14; 1 Samuel 17:45; Isaiah 42:13). There was a sacred "Book of the Wars of the Lord" (Numbers 21:14). Before going to war, the men had to keep themselves ritually clean, not even engaging in sexual relationships (2 Samuel 11:11). Health laws were involved in the commandments concerning ceremonial uncleanliness, but there were other laws in operation as well as those

(Deuteronomy 13:13–14).

A military campaign commenced with an act of worship (1 Kings 8:44) and a response from members of the armed forces (Psalm 20). Prophets told the army commander exactly what he was to do (see 1 Kings 20:13–30) and the outcome of the battle (Judges 20:27 28), and they gave advice when it was needed (2 Kings 6:8–10). The war cry was a spiritual one (Judges 7:18).

Victory was understood as being God's, and everything taken in battle belonged to God. It was given to God by burning or by death, as cities were put "under the curse" or "under the ban," terms indicating a ritual giving to God. Any person breaking the curse became cursed (Joshua 7). God did not always take everything; there were occasions when he allowed the sharing of booty (Joshua 8:27); neither did he always seek the death of a population. His decree concerning a people depended upon the degree of their wickedness (Genesis 15:16). The holiness of the campaign was such that if the Jews turned against God, then God would use others to put the Jews themselves "under the ban" (Isaiah 10:5–6; Habakkuk 1:5–11) and would even fight against his own people (Jeremiah 21:5–7).

The Roman army

The Roman army is also of great importance in the Bible, for it was this army that finally overcame the Jewish people, eventually scattering them so that they could not return to their land for two thousand years. The people of New Testament times were so familiar with the Roman soldier that illustrations and metaphors from military life were frequently used. Ephesians 6:13–17 uses the parts of the Roman soldier's armour to show how a Christian should defend himself. Colossians 2:15 sees Jesus leading a "triumph" through the streets so as to show his victory over the powers of evil. 2 Timothy 2:3–4 reminds the young minister that he must not mix his calling with "civilian pursuits."

Caesarea was the principal base for the Roman army in Judaea. The city had been built by Herod the Great for the Romans, as there was a natural harbour south of Mount Carmel. Detachments of soldiers from Caesarea were normally on duty in Jerusalem, stationed at Castle Antonia. Nationals

Replicas of a Roman siege engine and catapult, near Masada.

would often be incorporated into the army, but because military service involved religious worship and obligation (Augustus was recognized as a god after his death, but Caligula believed himself to be a deity while he was still alive) and because weapons had to be carried at all times (including the Sabbath), Jews were exempted. The army in Judaea therefore consisted of Italian and Syrian troops, commanded by Roman officers.

There was no difficulty in recruitment, for wages, raised by local taxation, were reasonable — one denarius a day — food was reasonable — two pounds weight per day — and on retirement each soldier received an allotment of land, often near the borders of the Empire, where their experience would be of supreme value in case of invasion.

The legions numbered about six thousand men, under a legate (ex-senator) in New Testament times. There were ten divisions (cohorts) of about six hundred men under military tribunes (see Acts 22:24–29). Each division was divided into three maniples (or units), which were themselves divided into two centuries, each under command of a

A Roman centurion (foreground) and legionary soldier. Notice the legionary's two swords and javelin, and his large shield.

centurion. Four legions (the third, sixth, tenth, and twelfth) were based in this area. The centurions were always chosen from among Romans who were stable and reliable and who had demonstrated their courage and maturity. There were fifty-nine centurions to a legion and they seem to have been respected by New Testament writers (see Matthew 8:8–9; Acts 10:1; 27:43).

In addition to the infantry units, specialist troops were appointed to each legion: engineers, bowmen, cavalry, medical officers. Each century had its own trumpeter, orderly, and standard bearer. The standards often bore heathen symbols, and, as a consequence, agreement had been reached between the Jews and the Romans that the standards should not be taken out of Caesarea. On one occasion Pilate had them brought into the Temple, and in the ensuing riot there was a collapse of a tower and a number of people were killed (see Luke 13:4). The standard bearer was considered to be a special person among the officers.

In battle the maniple was recognized as the fighting unit and was used flexibly according to the

The torso of a man wearing Roman protective armour.

demands of the particular battlefield. In addition to the protective armour listed in Ephesians 6, the soldier had a dagger about 9 inches (23 centimetres) long, which did service as a tool when required; a larger, double-edged sword about 23 inches (60 centimetres) long and held in a sheath that hung from the waist; and a javelin a little over 6½ feet (2 metres) long. It had an iron head with a sharp point to pierce shields and a barb to prevent its removal. It was thrown before hand-to-hand contact.

The Romans also built formidable siege weapons. The catapult shot javelins or spears over the wall and into the city. The ballista could sling heavy stones for about 2,300 feet (700 metres) and the Onager, light stones for about 1,300 feet (400 metres).

In addition to the regular army, there were praetorian guards, originally commanded by the praetors, magistrates at one level below the consuls (see Philippians 1:13). They had been reconstituted as the emperor's bodyguard. They had special standards of their own and were paid at double the rate of the ordinary soldier.

Now look at your Bible

Great military losses

Amos 5:3. Although there was a regular army in Amos's time, recruiting officers still went about in times of national emergency and conscripted ninety percent of the able-bodied men. The point about this passage is that the armies are to be so totally destroyed that there will be none who return.

Numbers

There are problems of understanding numbers in connection with groups of people in the Bible. Judges 20:17 says that 400,000 men marched against Benjamin, but Judges 5:8 says that 40,000 was the greatest number that could be raised from all the tribes put together. The lower number fits with the number who went into battle at Jericho (Joshua 4:13). When David took his military census (2 Samuel 24:1–9), 800,000 men were available in Israel and 500,000 in Judah, but many years later there were only 60,000 heads of families prosperous enough to pay tax (2 Kings 15:19–20), which would give a total population of about 800,000.

The disparity in the numbers may be due to the fact that we still do not understand the system of numbering. It sometimes happens that a particular word can represent a number or can have an entirely different meaning. A "score" means "twenty," but it also means a "tally." (If a newspaper reporter records that Liverpool made a score against Everton in a British football [soccer] match, it does not mean that they put the ball twenty times into the Everton net, although someone reading the account many years later might *mis*understand it that way.) It may be that "fifties," "hundreds," and "thousands" refer to units within an organization and not to actual numbers. We will have to wait for full understanding.

Leisure

There was little time for leisure in ancient days, but the wealthy had some time and money to follow leisure pursuits. The children, as always, made up games to play and amused themselves with simple toys. There was also an element of leisure in the religion of the Jewish people. The Sabbaths were for relaxation and rest and the religious festivals were times of excitement and stimulation. Yet the religion held back any pursuit of leisure for its own sake. Games and leisure activities were looked upon as a means of shaping bodies and minds.

Games
Children normally played in the open because it was dark inside the houses. Even though outdoor games and toys predominated, there were many indoor games as well. The outdoor games included "hop scotch," running, use of bow and arrow for target

Two Roman soldiers play at dice.

and distance shooting (1 Samuel 20:20–21; Lamentations 3:12), aiming stones into a pit, marbles aimed through three arches, and games with balls (throwing and catching, juggling).

Young children seem to have played with rattles. They were pottery boxes containing pieces of broken pot, and they had perforations to let out the sound when shaken. Other rattles were made in the shape of dolls and birds. They were rather heavy, and some people therefore believe that they were normally used in music or in worship.

There were many board games in use too. One of the oldest games known is the so-called Royal Game of Ur, which was in use about 1800 BC. Another board has been found with three rows of four squares top and bottom and twelve squares in the middle. Another board with fifty-eight holes arranged around a shape like a violin was found in Megiddo. Every fifth hole was special, surrounded by a medallion of gold. Other boards indicate that something like chess or draughts (checkers) was played, and "Mancala" was common. Most of the board games seem to have been played with dice — either a two-sided die in the form of a disc or a four-sided die in the shape of a pyramid.

Although dice were in use, no form of gambling was allowed among the Jewish people. This may have resulted from the feeling that dice were sacred

Dice from Dan, in northern Israel.

in some way. The high priest used two discs, black on one side and white on the other, shaken from the pouch or breastplate to discern the will of God (Exodus 28:30; 1 Samuel 28:6). It was used to find out a guilty party (Joshua 7:16–21), and in New Testament times the person who replaced Judas Iscariot as one of the Twelve was chosen by lot (Acts 1:26). It may, however, simply have been that there was an inbuilt reaction against the covetousness that is part of gambling. No gambler was allowed to give evidence in court; it was assumed that he could not be trusted. Gambling games were played by others. The soldiers gambled for the seamless robe of Jesus while he was on the cross (John 19:24).

More significant was a game called "Basileus," or "King." A wooden skittle (bowling pin) was moved about markings on the ground according to the throw of dice. When the skittle had moved to the appropriate places for robing, crowning, and being given a sceptre, the person who made the last throw called, "King!" and collected the stakes laid out by his companions. In view of Matthew 27:27–31, it is clear that soldiers at Castle Antonia played "King" with Jesus, substituting him for the wooden skittle and using a soldier's cloak, reed, and crown of thorns in their mockery. (Markings for this game can be seen on the paving stones at Gabbatha in Jerusalem to this day.)

Outside the Jewish community, girls played with dolls. Bodies were sometimes made of pottery, and hair was made of beads and mud. Some dolls that have been found have holes at key points on the limbs, which makes it appear they were used as puppets. Pottery furniture, dolls'-house-size, has been found too.

Wooden, pull-along toys have been found in Egypt. These toys were not found in the Jewish community because it was believed they infringed the commandment that there should be no graven image or any likeness. "Imitation" games were often played, however. Jesus described the children of his day playing at weddings and funerals in the marketplace (Luke 7:32).

Gardens

Parents seem to have appreciated more gentle pursuits. Jewish people appreciated gardens, but they were possessed by only the very rich. Gardens, when they existed in the villages, had to provide food and drink for the owner (Song of Songs 4:13; 6:11). The wealthy were able to have courtyard gardens within the city; failing that they provided themselves with gardens outside the city walls where they were able to go in the cool of the evening.

There was not merely one garden of Gethsemane, but a large number of them where the wealthy citizens of Jerusalem used to go in the evening on the lower slopes of the Mount of Olives. The garden featured in the last hours of Jesus' life may well have belonged to Joseph of Arimathea, who also provided a tomb in a garden (John 19:38–41).

Royalty was able to afford magnificent pleasure gardens. Gardens were also a feature of Babylon (Esther 7:8) and of Rome. There was lavish use of water to provide ornamental ponds and fountains; Herod built himself such a garden at Jericho.

Literature and painting

Literature seems to have been for the most part religious. Most of the literature of the Jewish people has been incorporated into the Bible, but Numbers

The garden of Gethsemane.

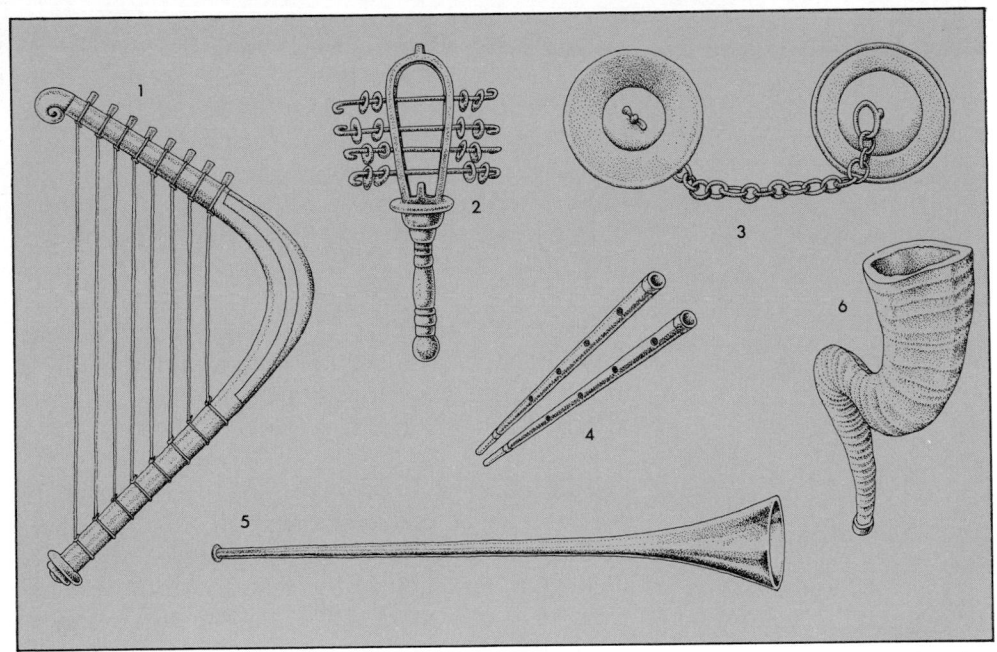

**Musical instruments of
Bible times.**
1. Kinnor
2. Menanaim
3. Meziltaim
4. Halil
5. Hazora
6. Shophar

21:14 and Joshua 10:12–13 mention other books that were in use at the time. Books were kept in preservative libraries and in private collections and were not lent out on a public basis until the arrival of Greek culture in 300 BC.

There was little painting because of the prohibition in Deuteronomy 5:8, "You shall not make for yourself an idol in the form of anything in heaven above or in the earth beneath or in the waters below." The urge for creativity found expression in architecture and design (Exodus 31:2–6) and in building — although in these areas, there was need for outside help (1 Kings 5:6; 7:13–15). Gem cutting and interior and exterior decoration seem to have been the Jews' particular forte.

Musical instruments
Music was very much a part of religious life, and musicians had always been important. They were classed along with smiths and those who possessed flocks and herds. Jubal was recognized as the father of all who played the pipe (Genesis 4:20–21). We therefore find many examples of music in Bible times. The instruments that were played are not always easy to identify from their Hebrew names, but the following instruments (arranged alphabetically) are the most important ones used:

The *halil* (1 Kings 1:40; Isaiah 5:12) was a pipe bored out of wood or bone. It took its name from the verb *halil*, which means "to bore." The sound was produced by a reed, and the reeds were carried around in a pouch. It had a light sound, but it could be used to express the sadness of grief (Jeremiah 48:36). It was always used by ordinary people and never for worship.

The *hazora* (Numbers 10:5) was a metal trumpet. Those mentioned in the Bible were made of silver, but many have been found made of bronze. It gave a sharp sound (see 1 Corinthians 14:8).

The *kinnor* (1 Chronicles 15:16; 2 Chronicles 5:12) was a stringed instrument shaped like a harp (the Sea of Galilee has a similar shape and is often called Kinneret). The strings were made of stretched sheepgut. It was used in the Temple and festivities (Isaiah 5:12), to accompany prophecies (1 Chronicles 25:1), and to change moods (1 Samuel 16:23). We do not know the number of strings or whether a plectrum (pick) was used.

Replica of a kinnor from Megiddo dating from c. 1200 B.C.

A musician playing the nebel. Notice the soundbox at one end of the instrument.

Replica of a nebel, or lyre.

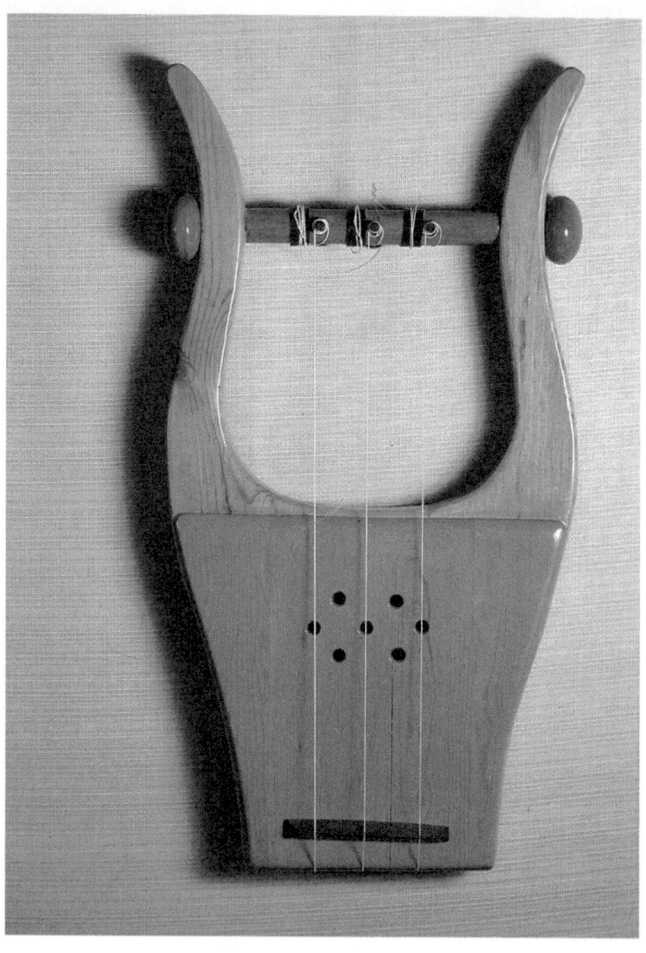

The *menanaim* was a percussion instrument made of metal plates that produced a sound when moved. The plates were probably pierced by metal rods held in a wooden frame that looked something like a hand mirror. The Egyptian sistra was probably very similar.

The *meziltaim* were cymbals made of copper. They were banged together in the Temple (1 Chronicles 15:10) to mark the beginnings, pauses, and endings of the chapters that were sung.

The *nebel* was another stringed instrument (Psalm 71:22) with up to ten strings. The word *nebel* was normally used for a skin bottle or jar, and the instrument may have got its name from a swollen soundbox shaped like a skin bottle.

The *qeren* was a wind instrument made from an animal horn. If the horn was a ram's horn, it was called a *shophar*, which had an important place in worship (Psalm 98:6; Psalm 150:3).

The *tof* was a percussion instrument with a membrane (Isaiah 5:12). The drums varied in size and were played either with bare hands or with sticks. Two people played a large one (Exodus 15:20).

Hebrew music

The interesting thing in Hebrew music was its accent on rhythm rather than on melody. There were very few melodies. There were popular melodies like folk songs, and these were in fact used in the singing of a number of psalms. Psalm 22 was set to the tune "Aijeleth hash-Shohar" ("The hind of the morning"), Psalm 56 to "Jonath elim riholaim" ("The silent dove of them which are afar off"), and Psalm 60 was set to "Shushan Eduth" ("The lily of testimony").

Singing was antiphonal, one group following another. First Samuel 18:6 says they sang "to one another." The repetitive nature of the psalms was so that two groups of people could sing in this way.

Jewish coins with depictions of hazora, or metal trumpets (left) and a nebel, or lyre (right).

David was particularly important in the compilation of the psalm book that became the Temple hymnbook. He incorporated some of his compositions (Psalms 18, 23, 51, 57) but collected many others as well. He appointed people to look after the music in the Temple (1 Chronicles 16:42; 25:6–7).

The accent on rhythm indicates that dance was as important as music, and this is an emphasis we find as we note the references to music in the Old Testament. Laban protested that there should have been a celebration before Jacob left with Leah and Rachel (Genesis 31:27), and Miriam led a celebration in song and dance when the Red Sea had been safely crossed (Exodus 15:21). David danced before the Ark as it was brought back to Jerusalem (2 Samuel

The shophar, or ramshorn trumpet, is still used in Jewish worship.

Philistine figurine of a musician playing the meziltaim, or cymbals.

6:14–15). Trumpets were used to rouse people in the mornings (Numbers 10:12), to call people to war (Numbers 10:9), and to announce Jubilee (Leviticus 25:8–9).

Music was always part of the celebration of victory (1 Samuel 18:6) and the coronation of the king (2 Chronicles 23:13). It was used to create the right mood for ecstatic prophecy (1 Samuel 10:5; 2 Kings 3:15), as well as for lifting moods (1 Samuel 16:16) and for sheer enjoyment (Isaiah 5:12). It was this joy that went out of the music while the Jews were in captivity (Psalm 137:1–5; Isaiah 24:8).

Music also seems to have been associated with mood in Jesus' time (Matthew 9:23). When Jesus referred to children playing funeral, he was actually referring to their singing funeral dirges. Some translators therefore refer this to the songs of weddings, too (Luke 7:32). The prodigal son was given a party in which music was involved (Luke 15:25). Hymns were sung, and the Jews always sang Psalms 115–118 at Passover. James said that the singing of psalms expresses our happiness (James 5:13), and music is still there in the book of Revelation (Revelation 5:9–10; 14:2–3).

Some of the hymns of the early church have been recorded in the New Testament. Philippians 2:5–11 and Ephesians 1:3–14 are believed to be hymns. Christians took the words of Mary (Luke 1:46–55) and Zacharias (Luke 1:67–79) and used them in worship at an early date.

Athletic sports

Entertainment and spectator/participatory sports did not develop until Greek and Roman times. Races had been run in Israel (Jeremiah 12:5), but they were not for entertainment. It was the promotion of sport in the Greek fashion in 170 BC that led to the division among Jews between Sadducees and Hasidim (see p. 254).

The Greeks believed that it was as important to be healthy as it was to be educated. In Greece there were four celebrations of games: the Isthmian, Nemean, Pythian, and Olympian, the last by far the

Model of the hippodrome, Jerusalem, as it may have been in the time of Christ.

Roman sculpture of a discus thrower.

most important and held every four years. The Olympian games were in honour of the god Zeus, and because the games began with offerings to gods and to heroes, they were actually religious occasions. Short races were followed by long ones, and then the pentathlon of jumping, running, discus, javelin, and wrestling. There was also chariot racing, boxing, running in armour, and contests between heralds and trumpeters.

Contestants trained under rigid rules, and thirty days before the games commenced they came together under close supervision. They had to exercise regularly, avoid luxuries, and obey certain rules (1 Corinthians 9:25; 2 Timothy 2:5). When an event was over, a herald proclaimed the name of the winner and his city, and the winner was presented with a palm branch, which later became a wreath made from the leaves of a sacred olive tree (1 Peter 5:4).

The Olympian games were one of the topics of conversation in New Testament times and frequently provided illustration and metaphor (Romans 15:30; Philippians 1:27; 3:14; 2 Timothy 4:7; Hebrews 12:1; Jude 3). Two of the events need special mention in view of such references. In wrestling, the opponent had to be held down and thrown down. The victor then put his foot on his opponent's neck. Such wrestling had an honourable history. Jacob wrestled at Peniel, and Genesis 32:24–25 indicates that he was not able to overcome his opponent within the rules. Judges 15:8 also uses a wrestling term. In boxing, there was a difference between the early and later rounds. In the early rounds, arms were bound with soft leather, and the winner was the first person to knock the opponent down. If the spectators became bored because the contest was too even, the arms were bound with studded leather to bring the contest to a bloody climax.

The Colisseum, Rome. In theatres such as this the Romans staged games and contests as popular entertainment.

Spectator sports

Spectator sports and entertainment were fully developed by the Romans so as to satisfy the common people's lust for excitement and blood. Even the rush for seats was an excitement in itself; there were no reserved seats until the time of Augustus. In the arena, condemned criminals fought against wild animals — lions, bears, elephants, and hyenas — and the crowd would urge on the contest. Paul says that he fought against wild beasts at Ephesus (1 Corinthians 15:32), but he may have been referring to the experiences recorded in Acts 19 in a metaphorical way (see also Hebrews 10:33).

In order to maintain the crowd's excitement, the early contestants wore armour, but by midday they were led naked into the arena. When Paul wrote, "For it seems to me that God has put us apostles on display at the end of the procession, like men condemned to die in the arena. We have been made a spectacle" (1 Corinthians 4:9), he may have been referring to this practice.

Other spectator contests to the death involved the gladiators. They were specially trained slaves. The use of gladiators originated in connection with funerals as a means of dispatching slaves to go with their master while at the same time providing entertainment for the funeral guests. Then contests between gladiators became a state entertainment.

Gladiators were trained in the use of different techniques and weapons. Some fought with swords and shields. A wounded gladiator had to lay down his arms. If the spectators gave the "thumbs up" signal, his opponent was being given permission to kill him; the thumbs down meant that his life was spared. Others used a net and a trident to try to beat an opponent with sword and shield. Most spectacular was the mass battle, eighty-five men on each side. The last one remaining alive received a crown.

Another popular sport was chariot racing, which took place in the hippodrome. Charioteers were the sports heroes of the day. They raced seven laps (six miles) of the stadium, protected with crash helmets and lashed to their chariots. If there was a crash, the charioteer had to cut himself free. It was also big business. Wealthy patrons had slaves trained to race the chariots and to buy the equipment, and much money was placed in bets on the result of races.

The theatre

The theatre was an important building for public meetings as well as for drama (see Acts 19:29). The Jews watched very little drama and acted very little. This may have been because the part of the dramatist was taken by the storyteller, who kept alive the history of Israel. It may also have been because the Greeks turned the theatre into a religious occasion.

Theatres appeared throughout the Greco-Roman world. The Romans built them wherever a natural site made it convenient to provide a tiered auditorium, without having to make a free-standing building. The auditorium was semicircular, around a stage and its buildings. The seating was arranged in an upper and lower tier and was graded according to rank. Special accommodation was reserved for distinguished guests. Access was gained through vaulted passageways, interconnected with vaulted corridors; the passageways divided up the tiers into blocks of seats. Theatre was quite popular; there were three theatres in the city of Gerasa.

The Roman theatre at the Decapolis town of Scythopolis, biblical Beth Shan.

Leisure for Tourists in Israel Today

We have already looked at what awaits the visitor to Jerusalem (see p. 216). A visit to Israel has become a means of leisure and holiday for many. The following suggestions are made so that people can enjoy a stay in the country and at the same time see their Bibles come to life.

Near the Dead Sea
You can visit places near the Dead Sea. Transport from Jerusalem will take you to Jericho, stopping at the Inn of the Good Samaritan on the way. It is in

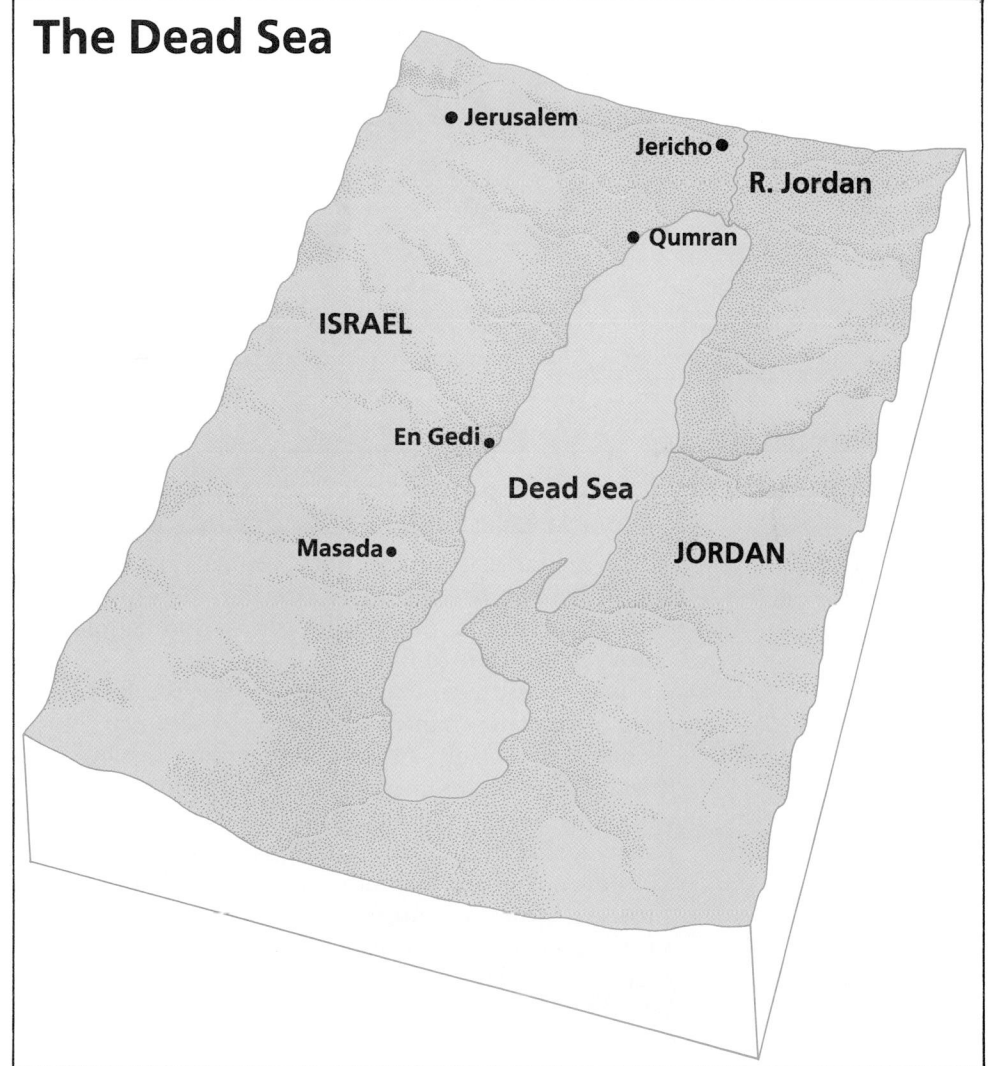

The Dead Sea

The monastery of St. George of Koziba in Wadi Qilt.

fact a Turkish khan, but because you can see Jerusalem in the distance, after having gone down from Jerusalem to Jericho, the Good Samaritan story is brought to life.

It is possible to travel through the Wadi Qilt on the ancient Roman road, and to experience the silence of the desert. At the end you find the New Testament site of Jericho, which is some distance from the Old Testament site. The Old Testament site is spectacular in revealing a Canaanite town that was built long before Joshua's time. (There is nothing of Joshua's time remaining.)

Farther south, Qumran, where the Essene monastery was situated, can be visited, and a distant view of the caves of the Dead Sea Scrolls can be had. Farther south again is En Gedi, and a (hot) climb takes you up to the area where David hid from Saul. Most spectacular of all is Masada, the Herodian fortress where the Zealots made their last stand. There are a number of places along the Dead Sea where bathing can take place, and some places where there are thermal springs as well.

Hebron and Beer Sheba

You can travel south of Jerusalem beyond Bethlehem to explore Hebron and Beer Sheba. Hebron was the burial place of Abraham and Sarah, and their graves are still there under a building that has been converted into a mosque, part of which was built originally in Herodian times (the Cave of Machpelah). Beer Sheba is a modern city of concrete set in an area of green fields. It is a superb illustration of the fulfilment of the promise that the desert will blossom like the rose, because the agricultural development has taken place only recently.

Farther south into the desert are the ancient Nabataean cities of Avdat and Shivta. In Shivta, you can wander through ancient streets, tread old winepresses, and find the ruins of dams that once preserved water in the wadis. Ein Avdat is a natural

Herodian walls surround the Cave of Machpelah, Hebron.

St. Peter's Church, Jaffa, biblical Joppa.

beauty spot where you can climb down and walk through the gorge. On the return journey near Bethlehem it is possible to stop at "Philip's Well," where, it is believed, Philip baptized the Ethiopian. You can also visit Solomon's pools near Bethlehem, which provided much of the ancient water supply of Jerusalem.

The Mediterranean coast

On the western coast, there are a number of interesting places to visit. If the approach is made through Kiriath Jearim, you can see where the Ark rested on its way to Jerusalem and one of the possible sites of Emmaus. It is then possible to go through the Valley of Elah, where David fought with Goliath, and pick up stones from the stream bed. The most ancient ruins in Ashkelon, on the coast, are Roman, but it recalls the stories of the Philistines. Farther north, Joppa (Jaffa) has an atmosphere all of its own with a church that commemorates the story of Cornelius.

Tel Aviv has no ancient biblical interest, but the visitor who believes that the resurgence of Israel is foretold in the Bible will delight in a modern, attractive city. The only biblical interest in Haifa is that it

Modern Israel

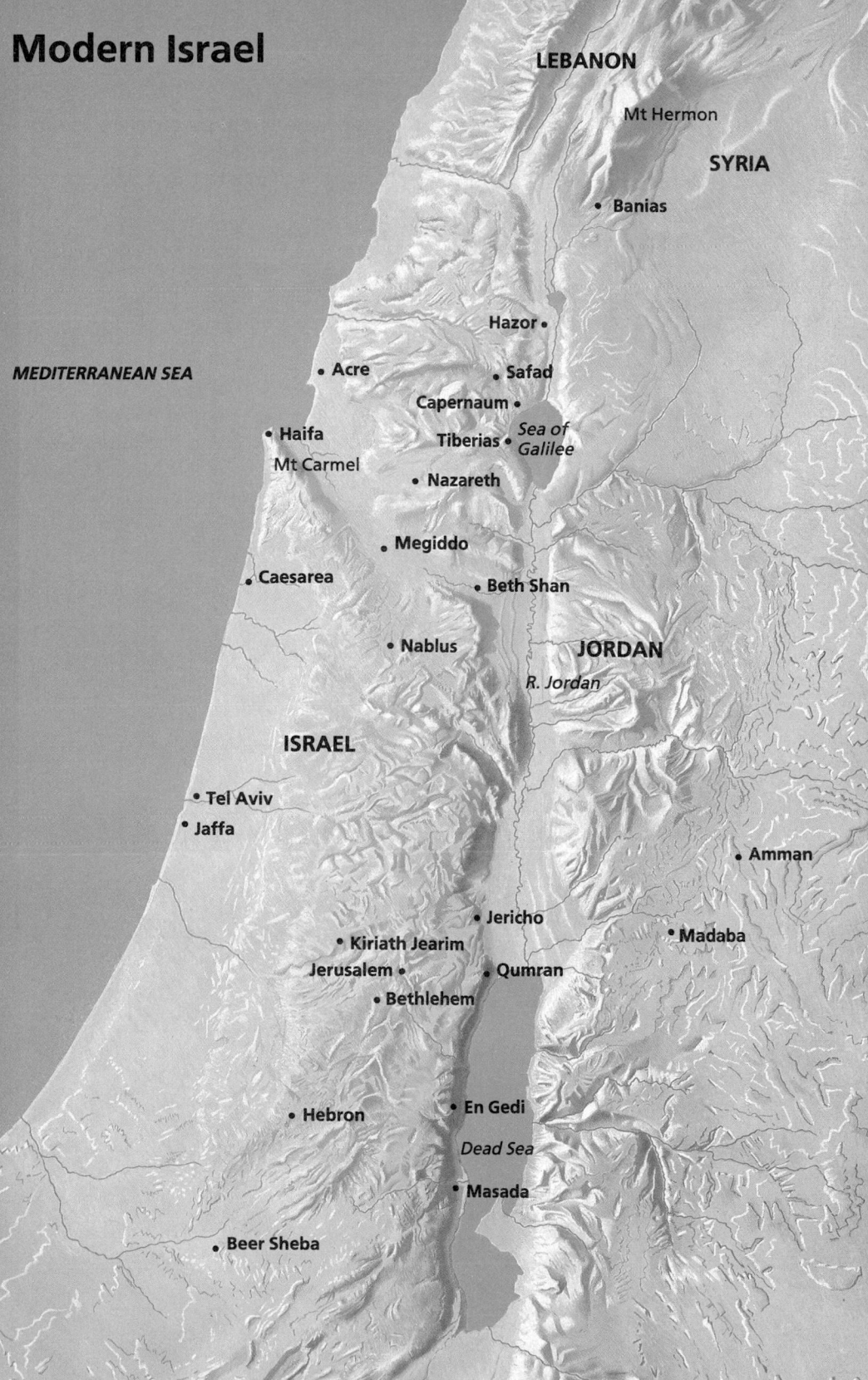

LEBANON

Mt Hermon

SYRIA

• Banias

Hazor •

MEDITERRANEAN SEA

• Acre

• Safad

Capernaum •

• Haifa

Tiberias • *Sea of Galilee*

Mt Carmel

• Nazareth

• Megiddo

• Caesarea

• Beth Shan

• Nablus

JORDAN

R. Jordan

ISRAEL

• Tel Aviv

• Jaffa

• Amman

• Jericho

• Kiriath Jearim

• Madaba

Jerusalem •

• Qumran

• Bethlehem

• Hebron

• En Gedi

Dead Sea

• Masada

• Beer Sheba

is built on Elijah's Mount Carmel, but it too is an attractive city.

The place of supreme interest on the coast is Caesarea. The site is dominated by the ruins of the Crusader city, but there are many Roman remains (the aqueduct and the theatre, for example), and the seashore is where Paul came on his last journey to Jerusalem.

The West Bank

North of Jerusalem you can follow the route through Samaria to Galilee. Bethel can be visited, although there is little to see. In Nablus (Shechem) the "Well of Jacob" is still to be seen in the crypt of a Russian Orthodox church, and the water can be drunk. The church itself was never finished, because it was being built at the time of the 1917 revolution in Russia. From the garden outside you can look up to Mount Gerizim and Mount Ebal and recall the ancient covenant between God and Israel and the story of Jesus at the well with the Samaritan woman.

Farther on is Samaria — the ruins of the Roman city — with an excellent forum and theatre. Some of the walls from King Ahab's time are still to be seen.

The site of biblical Shechem, modern Nablus.

The Roman forum, Samaria.

As you enter the southern area of Galilee there are many sites to visit from the time of the Judges, the time of Saul, and the time of David. Ein Harod is where Gideon stopped before the battle with the Midianites. The water is full of leeches, so, like Gideon, you have to be careful how the water is drunk. Mount Gilboa, behind, is where Saul and Jonathan fought their final battle, and Beth Shan (which again has a spectacular Roman theatre as well as the ancient tell) was where the bodies of Saul and Jonathan were taken.

The Sea of Galilee

The Sea of Galilee itself is set in open countryside in a way that is quite different from New Testament times. Then there were many cities around the lake, and the hills were wooded. Today a boat can be taken from Tiberias to the other side of the lake to a spot below ancient Hippos, where there is a kibbutz restaurant selling St. Peter's fish. Traveling north on the western shore of the lake, you pass Magdala (Mary's home). After crossing the little plain of Genesaret you can ascend the hill where the Beatitudes were given.

Above: Detail of birds found on the Sea of Galilee from the mosaic floor in the Church of the Multiplication of the Loaves and Fishes, Tabgha.

Opposite: The Church of the Beatitudes, near Capernaum.

Most places in the area are commemorated by churches, all of which are simple, beautiful, and distinctive. The Church of the Beatitudes, set in fields above the lake, is a good example. On the lakeside itself are two churches of Tabgha. One commemorates the feeding of the five thousand and has lovely mosaics of the bird life of New Testament times; the other commemorates the postresurrection appearance of Jesus when he made breakfast for the disciples.

Farther on is "Sower's Bay," where Jesus taught from Peter's boat, and the ruins of Capernaum. The most interesting feature of this site is the synagogue — not the one from the time of Jesus, but the one that succeeded it. Nevertheless, a guide will point out many remains of the site that go back to the time when it was "his own city."

Nazareth

West of Galilee is Cana (where a church reminds visitors of the story of the water turned to wine) and Nazareth. Nazareth is a busy, sprawling, dusty place with lots of noise. It is dominated by the Basilica of the Annunciation. Some people think it is one of the most beautiful churches in the world; others do not like it. Either way it cannot be forgotten. The church

Above: Mount Tabor rises spectacularly from the Valley of Esdraelon.

Opposite: The Church of the Annunciation, Nazareth.

is built over what is believed to have been the cave below the home of Joseph and Mary.

An ancient synagogue and water cisterns can also be seen, and the fountain along the main street reminds visitors of Mary's collection of water for daily needs, even if the real source is in a church some distance away.

Near to Nazareth is Mount Tabor. A visit to the mountain demonstrates why it was used as a rallying point for Deborah and Barak. Because it is "a mountain apart," Mount Tabor convinces others that it was the place of the transfiguration. The church at the summit has a glorious mosaic in gold, which is illuminated by the sun's rays through the western window at the end of the day and reminds viewers of the transfiguration itself.

Megiddo and Acre

Farther to the west is Megiddo. Visitors can walk through Solomon's gateway, see his stables and buildings, look at the high place of Canaanite religion, and walk through an underground tunnel to the source of water for the town. Below the site of the city is the valley of Armageddon. It is a spectacular site, well-presented.

Nearby is Bet She'arim — a Jewish shrine. It was to this place the Sanhedrin was banished after the final destruction of Jerusalem, and the catacombs of the centre can be explored. It is a beautiful site, with a garden that contains an ancient olive press and synagogue.

On the coast again is Acre (Akko). Although the interest here is Crusader rather than biblical, a visit to what has become the subterranean city of the Crusaders is unforgettable. It must not be forgotten that the Crusaders were an important element in the history of the Holy Land, and spectacular remains are to be seen throughout the country. Belvoir Castle, above the Jordan valley just south of the Sea of Galilee, and Nimrod Castle, near Mount Hermon, give a good impression of the Crusaders' engineering and building skills.

Entrance to one of the rock-cut catacombs at Bet She'arim.

These rock-cut niches at Banias, biblical Caesarea Philippi, once held statues of Pan.

North of Galilee

North of Galilee there are several places worth visiting. Safad (Zefat) is the place where the Jews first began to return to the Holy Land during Jewish persecution in Europe. Ancient synagogues can be visited and at the same time tourists enjoy visiting the artists' studios in the quarter they have made their home. Safad is beautifully placed among the mountains. It is an example of the "city set on a hill which cannot be hid."

Farther north is Hazor, the largest city of Canaanite times, and now probably archaeologically the best laid out site in Israel, with an excellent museum that shows many aspects of Canaanite religion; Banias (Caesarea Philippi), one of the sources of the Jordan, where Peter made his great confession of faith; Tell Dan, a delightful nature reserve and the site of the ancient sanctuary that was set up in opposition to the Jerusalem Temple; and Mount Hermon, which some people believe to be the site of the transfiguration. It is a beautiful area, with skiing in winter and a beautiful circular lake (Birket Ram) that fills the cone of an ancient volcano.

East of Jordan

We live in an age in which leisure pursuits include travel to most places of the world. Israel probably has more history, beauty, and significance within its small area than most places. A visit to Israel not only illustrates much of the Bible, but it makes it come alive in the sense that reading a story in the Bible about a place has a personal significance when one has visited it, which a mere reader never experiences. It must, however, never be forgotten that the Holy Land does not stop at the river Jordan.

East of the river Jordan is the Kingdom of Jordan, always ready and willing to welcome visitors. There are not many sites, but what is there is more than worth the time spent. The capital, Amman, is itself the ancient city of Ammon of the Ammonites. It was known as Philadelphia in New Testament times — a Roman city of the Decapolis. The Ammonite citadel and the Roman theatre can be visited.

South of Amman is Madaba (with a church containing a wonderful mosaic map of Jerusalem and of the Holy Land in the third century AD) and the King's Highway through the desert, which passes the Crusader fortress of Kerak to reach the Nabataean city of Petra. Petra is probably one of the most wonderful places in the world — a city cut off by time in a rose-red, secluded valley. Near Madaba is the spot on Mount Nebo where Moses died after he had looked across into the Promised Land. North of Amman is Jerash, another city of the Decapolis that is almost as well preserved as Pompei and is reached by crossing the river Jabbok where Jacob wrestled.

It is hoped that this brief travelogue will encourage people to go to the land of the Bible and will give them some idea of what to look for when they are examining tour brochures. It takes a steady three weeks to see things adequately and to absorb all that there is to see and experience.

Religion

The first four stories of the Bible spell out why it was that God needed to act to save humankind. The story of creation (Genesis 1) tells us that we live in God's world, where his rule and laws operate. When the rules are broken, as in the second story of Adam and Eve, there is separation from God. The results of the sin and separation become clear in the other stories. Sin brings the judgment of God (Genesis 6–8; see especially 6:5) and social chaos (Genesis 11:1–9), as human beings become separated from each other.

These stories give the reason for all that follows. In his love for humankind, God as Creator wanted to restore humanity to all that he intended it to be. To do this it was necessary for God to deal with human sin. We know, from the New Testament, how this was done. God entered this world as a human being in the person of Jesus. Having entered the world he showed us how to live. Jesus said, "I have set you an example that you should do as I have done for you" (John 13:15). He allowed himself to be put to death, although he was innocent, so that as God he could take upon himself the punishment for the sins of the whole world. Peter put it, "He himself bore our sins in his body on the tree" (1 Peter 2:24), and Paul wrote, "Having canceled the written code, with its regulations, that was against us and stood opposed to us; he took it away, nailing it to the cross" (Colossians 2:14).

Jesus died and rose so it would be possible for him to indwell us by his spirit and overcome death for us. But also Jesus helps those who believe in him to overcome the bias toward sin that is at the heart of every human being: "If we have been united with him in his death, we will certainly also be united with him in his resurrection" (Romans 6:5). The problem was how to get from man's need at the beginning of time to the point where, in Jesus, those needs could be met.

A covenant relationship

In Old Testament times God chose to enter into a close relationship first with an individual, then with his immediate family, and finally with his descendants so that they would gradually be prepared for his personal coming and for a deeper relationship than had hitherto been possible. Abraham was the individual (Genesis 12:1–2), and the covenant relationship entered into with Abraham and his family (Genesis 15:9–18) was renewed with his grandson Jacob (Genesis 28:13–15) and with Moses (Exodus 3:6; 24:3–8).

It is fairly common to hear Christians say that Christianity is not so much a religion as a relationship; it is not often realized that exactly the same was true for the Jewish people. God did not found a Jewish religion but entered into a covenant relationship with his people. It would seem that during Moses' time when religion was important in neighboring nations, God gave the Jews a carefully circumscribed religion that would help sustain the covenant relationship. Consequently the religion of the Jewish people was quite different from that of their contemporaries.

Because God used the Jews' religion to prepare the way for Jesus, Judaism did not stand still but developed. The Jews came into contact with contemporary religions, and therefore their religion developed by reaction to and interaction with them. Holy places, holy days, holy persons, and holy events therefore became part of the Jewish faith, but all was not what God had hoped it would be. Like the commandment allowing divorce, the Jewish cult seems to have been an accommodation to human weakness (Matthew 19:8). God wanted a broken and a contrite spirit rather than sacrifices (Psalm 51:17), justice rather than festival days (Amos 5:21–24), and instead of offerings of rams and oil he wanted people who were just, loved kindness, and walked humbly with their God (cf. Micah 6:8).

The law that provided for the trappings of a religious system was never intended to be an end in itself but was intended to reveal the extent of human need (Romans 3:19; 7:5, 7–9) so that we would be led to Christ (Galatians 3:24–25). It was intended to be a means of showing the kind of life God wanted us to live through the power of his Spirit (Romans 8:4).

And herein lay the conflict between Jesus and the Jewish religious leaders at that time. The religion of the Jews therefore had an important place in God's plan, but it was never intended to be an end in itself. It was a means of sustaining the covenant relationship until God himself should come.

Assyrian religion

There was little or no connection between the religion of Israel and the ancient religions of the Assyrians (where Abraham first experienced religion) or the Egyptians. It is true that perhaps in the hope they might bring some kind of protection, Rachel stole the household gods from her father (Genesis 31:19). However, even though Jacob later buried the offending articles, such idols turned up on a number of occasions in subsequent history (Genesis 35:4; Judges 17:5; 1 Samuel 19:13; 2 Kings 23:24; Zechariah 10:2).

The references in Zechariah 10:2 and Ezekiel 21:21 indicate household gods were used in divination, always a feature of Assyrian religion; and the fact that they could be hidden in the camel's saddlery (Genesis 31:34) indicates that they were small. However nothing has so far been found to indicate exactly what the idols were like. Suggestions have therefore been made that they would rot, or that they would be identified as something else. Some scholars have even suggested that they were rag dolls or mummified infants' heads.

In ancient Mesopotamia, people believed in families of gods. Anu was the king of heaven and was very remote. His son, Enlil, ruled over the earth's surface and was treated as king of the gods. Ishtar was Anu's wife and was in charge of war and love. Each god had a main temple where people went at festival times.

The gods themselves and the fantastic mythology that was used to describe events such as the creation, were quite different from the religion of the Jews. In the Babylonian creation story, for instance, Tiamat, the primeval ocean, gave birth to dry land (Ki) and heaven (Anu), and all the gods descended from Ki and Anu. The ocean decided to destroy them all but was, in the end, conquered by the young god Marduk. Marduk made the earth from half of Tiamat's body and the sky from the other. In the battle,

Tiamat's helper, Kingu, was destroyed, and mankind was made from Kingu's blood mixed with clay.

Egyptian religion

One might have expected some kind of influence from Egyptian religion, particularly as Joseph married Asenath, who was a priest's daughter (Genesis 41:50), and because the Jewish people had been in Egypt for so long a period (Exodus 12:40–41). It appears, though, that the Jews kept their religion and their lives quite separate from the Egyptians. Jacob accepted Joseph's two sons into the family (Genesis 48:5–6), and Joseph's descendants identified the God they worshiped with Jacob (Israel) and not Egypt (Exodus 5:1). There is therefore no sign of Egyptian polytheism, which included Re (the sun), Yeb (the earth), Thoth (the moon), Hapi (the Nile), and Amon (the god of hidden powers). There is no mention of the animals that were linked with the gods and whose form often replaced them in contemporary art (Thoth and the ibis, Hapi and bulls, Horus and falcons).

The gods of Egypt were believed to be like human beings, and in their huge temples, which were barred to ordinary people, priests fed them, washed and clothed them, and took them out on festival days. Nothing could be more different from the God of Israel. Although the Jews believed in some kind of life after death (they were "gathered" to their "people," Genesis 49:29, 33, and Joseph's body was mummified, Genesis 50:26), there seems to have been little in common between Egyptian belief in life after death and that of the Jews. Egyptians believed that the soul went through the halls of the dead and needed subsistence for the journey until it arrived at the halls of judgment.

Canaanite religion

It therefore seems strange that the Canaanite religion was so great an attraction for the Jewish people and led to the spiritual chaos that brought about the judgment of God. Canaanite religion was an elaborate system that resulted from the need to ensure regular crops in an uncertain climate. Although the pantheon of gods was presided over by El, the key god was Baal, who was god of the storm, springs, and water. (There are references to Baal in Judges

2:13; 1 Kings 16:31; Jeremiah 19:5, and many other places.)

The rainfall of winter and the drought of summer were believed to indicate that Baal had died and that there was a need for him to be brought to life again by magic rites. (Weeping for Tammuz, who was a Babylonian deity, was similar. It was believed that human tears could help the god bring back the rains; Ezekiel 8:14.)

Similarly, the Canaanites believed that the gods could be helped to bring about fertility of the soil if the people fertilized one another in the places of worship. Therefore, there was a crude sexuality in the name of religion. Every Canaanite sanctuary had its own prostitutes for that purpose. Each sanctuary was dominated by a wooden pole, or asherah, which symbolized the female sex principle in the name of the goddess Asherah, and by an erect stone, or mazzebah, which symbolized male sexuality.

The Canaanites believed that the gods could be persuaded, even coerced, by magic ritual. This led to the extreme of child sacrifice. Sanctuaries to the gods were made on artificial mounds, or "high places," often placed on hilltops in the belief that they brought the worshipers physically closer to the gods. Assimilation of the Canaanite religion was a steady process, and in Elijah's time the prophet believed that true worshipers of the God of Israel were a very small minority (1 Kings 19:10).

The reason the Canaanite religion had such an attraction was probably that when the Jews arrived in Canaan they found that they had a relatively inferior form of culture. They did not know how to build, to perform arts, or even to farm adequately because they came from a seminomadic background. The Canaanites were sophisticated and successful by comparison, and seemed to know what should be done to ensure good crops. When such feelings of inferiority were aided and abetted by excuses for sexual license, it is not difficult to understand why the Canaanite religion had so great an influence.

Holy laws
Against the background discussed above, the Jewish religion developed with its own holy law, holy

The Judean wilderness. The patriarchs often encountered God in lonely and unpromising places.

places, holy occasions, holy objects, and holy ritual. The law (Torah) has already been discussed (p. 82), and it was a key point of Jewish religion. It was a guide to good relationships with God and with other people. Torah means "guidance" and "instruction." The law was not always perfect. Jesus, for example, said that the divorce laws had been put in because "your hearts were hard" (Matthew 19:8). At the same time the Torah revealed the character of God: his holiness, justice, and goodness. It was possible to see what God was like from the standards he required.

Holy places

In patriarchal times, holy places were places where it had proved possible to meet with God, and such places were marked with an altar and sacrifice. When Abraham left Haran for Canaan and stopped

at Shechem, God appeared to him and said that the land was promised to his descendants. Genesis 12:7 then records that Abraham "built an altar there to the Lord, who had appeared to him." Altars were also built at Bethel (Genesis 12:8) and Hebron (Genesis 13:18), and Jacob renewed the altar at Bethel (Genesis 35:1).

Such places became holy places for the family. Jacob buried under a tree in Shechem the household gods he had brought from Laban's family (Genesis 35:4), and Hebron became the burial place for members of the family (Genesis 23:19; 25:9; 49:29–31). Joseph was buried at Shechem (Joshua 24:32). The same principle was followed until the time of the Temple at Jerusalem (Exodus 20:24), so that Gideon in effect made a sacrifice on an altar when the angel of the Lord appeared to him (Judges 6:19–21), and so did Manoah (Judges 13:19–20).

The Tabernacle. Notice the altar for sacrifice, the bronze laver, and the curtained entrance to the Tabernacle itself.

The Tabernacle

Alongside the sacred spots where God had revealed himself, a central place for worship was brought into being. During the period of the Exodus it could best be described as a tent-temple, which was the most useful structure for people who were either traveling or in camp in the Kadesh Barnea area (Numbers 13:26—14:38). The tent-temple was known as the Tabernacle.

The central shrine was made up of upright wooden planks, gilded and supported by a system of beams, tenons and heavy silver sockets that stood on the ground. This created a three-sided structure thirty cubits (forty-five feet, fifteen metres) long and fifteen cubits (twenty-two feet, seven metres) wide, open to the sky and at its narrow east end. A roof was provided by curtains of white linen, embroidered with figures of cherubim, which were protected by successive layers of sackcloth, red ramskins, and goatskins (Exodus 26:1–30).

The Tabernacle. Notice the altar for sacrifice, the bronze laver, and the curtained entrance to the Tabernacle itself.

Inside, the thirty-cubit-long room was divided in two by a curtain hung on gilded pillars to create a "Most Holy Place" (ten cubits by ten cubits by ten cubits) and a long "Holy Place." A curtain of similar material was hung over the entrance to prevent the eyes of the curious from seeing inside (Exodus 26:31–36). The Ark of the Covenant (Exodus 25:10–22) was placed in the Most Holy Place, and the table of showbread (25:23–30), golden lampstand (25:31–40), and altar of incense (30:1–10) in the Holy Place. Outside the curtained entrance was an altar for sacrifice (27:1–8) and a large bronze laver or washing place for ceremonial cleansing (30:17–21).

Plan of the Tabernacle and its courtyard.

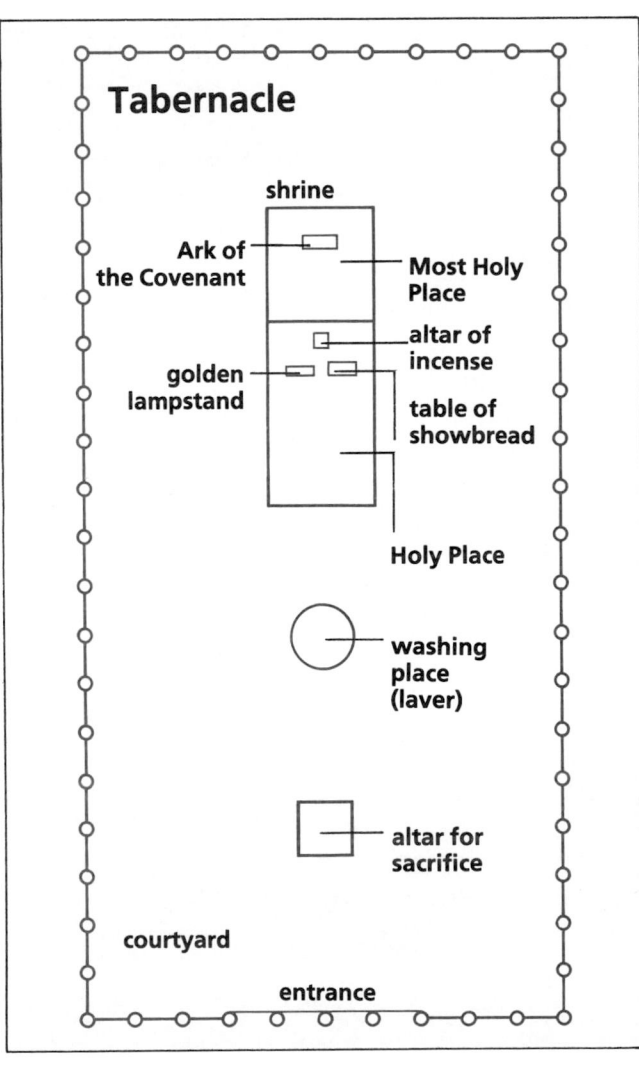

The Sinai Desert.

It was a characteristic of religion in the area at the time that the space around the central shrine or altar was holy, as well as the shrine itself. Moses was reminded that the ground around the burning bush was holy (Exodus 3:5). The shrine was therefore separated from the outside world by a large courtyard. The courtyard of the Tabernacle was a hundred cubits long and fifty cubits wide, formed by the erection of a linen wall five cubits high, suspended between gilded poles. The poles themselves were supported by guylines and tent pegs, their bases held in heavy bronze sockets. Entry into the courtyard was through embroidered hangings set in the narrow, eastern end (Exodus 27:9–19).

The Temple

When the Jews settled in Canaanite territory the Tabernacle was made more permanent in form at Shiloh (Joshua 18:1; Judges 18:31). It was permanent enough to be called a temple, for Samuel and Eli to have rooms there, and for entrance doors to be opened and closed (1 Samuel 3:2, 15). Even after the Philistines destroyed Shiloh, captured the Ark of the Covenant, and returned it to the Jews via Beth Shemesh (1 Samuel 6:1–10) and Kiriath Jearim (1 Samuel 7:2), it was still in some kind of tent-temple (2 Samuel 6:17; 7:2) and stayed there until Solomon built a permanent temple.

Solomon's Temple. Notice
the huge laver supported
on the backs of twelve
bronze bulls, and the
pillars, named Jachin and
Boaz.

Solomon's Temple

Solomon's Temple followed the same general principle as the Tabernacle. It was a building in two main sections to house the Ark of the Covenant and the other holy objects — table, lampstand, and altar of incense. But there were differences. The whole structure was made of stone overlaid with timber and precious metals, and it was set upon a raised platform that was approached by steps. An entry porch was built onto the front of the building, and the building itself was flanked with three tiers of small rooms that could be used for storage, offices, and for personal accommodation. The Temple was twice as large as the Tabernacle, but it was not greatly impressive, being in plain stone and about one hundred feet (thirty five metres) long. More impressive were the holy objects immediately in front of the porch.

Solomon's Temple. Notice the huge laver supported on the backs of twelve bronze bulls, and the pillars, named Jachin and Boaz.

Plan of Solomon's Temple.

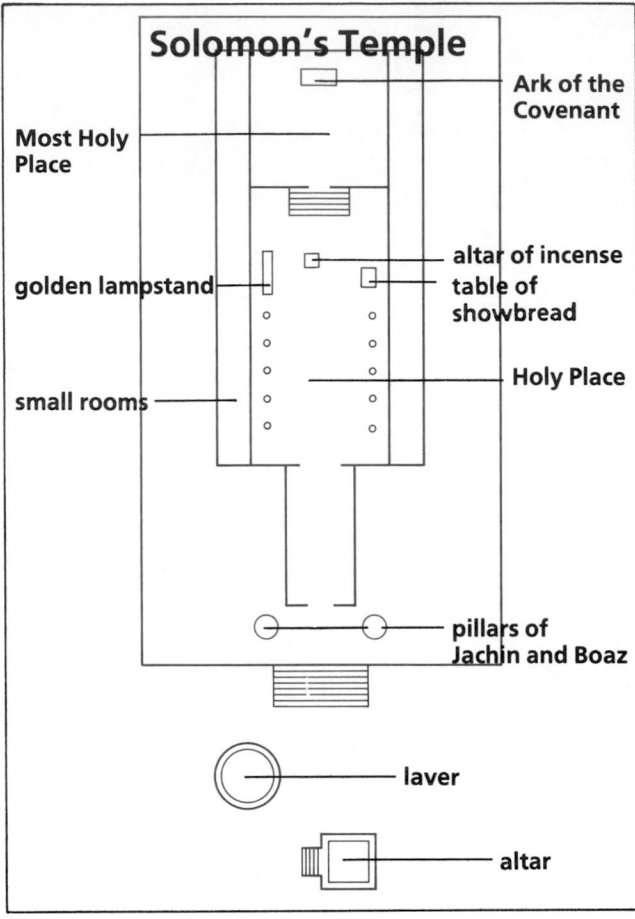

Solomon's Temple

- Ark of the Covenant
- Most Holy Place
- altar of incense
- golden lampstand
- table of showbread
- Holy Place
- small rooms
- pillars of Jachin and Boaz
- laver
- altar

The porch itself was entered between two free-standing pillars that were given the names Jachin and Boaz. In front of the porch was a huge laver supported on the backs of twelve bronze bulls and holding ten thousand gallons of water. Also in front of the porch was a great three-tiered altar that acted as an incinerator for sacrifices. It was about fifteen feet (five metres) high (1 Kings 6; 7:15–51). This temple, too, was placed in a large courtyard.

Other shrines

It was intended that the Temple should be the one shrine for the whole Jewish people (Deuteronomy 12:11; 1 Kings 8:29), but there were other centres of worship as well. Jeroboam, king of the northern kingdom of Israel, set up sanctuaries based on bull-shaped thrones for God, at the northern and southern extremities to his kingdom (see 1 Kings 12:25–30).

Beside those illegitimate holy places there were many others. Some were associated with the revelation of God, such as Shechem, which Jeroboam made into the capital of his kingdom (1 Kings 12:25), but others seem to have been set up at the whim of the people. The Jews had entered a country where Canaanite gods were worshipped at high places, and it was easy for the Jews to take over those places for the worship of God. In some cases, as with Gideon's father, they did not even bother to worship Israel's God (Judges 6:25–32).

Other shrines were set up to worship Israel's God, but they were set up in a highly irregular way (Judges 17:3). Judges 17 describes a shrine with a graven image where a Levite acted as priest and tells how the Levite was kidnapped and the contents of the shrine stolen by members of a tribal raiding party who wanted to set up their own shrine. Hezekiah and Josiah (2 Chronicles 31:1; 34:1) were involved in thoroughgoing reforms that involved the removal of such illicit places of worship with the object of centralizing worship in Jerusalem (2 Kings 18:22; 2 Chronicles 34:3–7). But there was no real reformation without purification, and this was brought about through the experiences of the Exile.

Rebuilding the Temple

When the Exile was ended and the Jews were given permission to return to their country and rebuild their Temple under the patronage of the Persian emperor (Ezra 1:3), they rallied under Zerubbabel. After considerable opposition and disappointment, the Temple was rebuilt. Although it did not have the same glory as Solomon's Temple (Ezra 3:12–13; Haggai 2–3), it seems to have been very similar. It was built much like Solomon's Temple (Ezra 5:8; 6:4; cf. 1 Kings 6:36; 7:12), and there were rooms about the structure where things could be stored (Ezra 8:29) and where people had quarters (Nehemiah 13:4–9).

It lasted half a millennium until the time of Herod the Great. During this period it was described by a number of people who actually saw it. It seems that the main courtyard of the Temple was now divided by a "wall of the inner court of the sanctuary" beyond which only Jews might go.

The synagogue

When Solomon's Temple had been destroyed and the Jews were in exile, they survived by gathering together on the Sabbath to learn about their law and traditions. This practice was found to be so useful that when they returned they wanted to continue it and began to build places where they could "gather together." Those places, known as *synagogues* (which literally means "gathering-together-places," began to be built wherever there were at least ten adult males in the community. By the time of Jesus they were familiar sights throughout the country. They were always easy to find because if not built in the actual community centre, they were built on the highest ground, or were made the highest building by some architectural feature, such as a dome or augmented base.

All synagogues were built to a common pattern so that the Jew could feel "at home" wherever he worshiped. Only the men entered the main door of the building; women entered through a separate door and sat in a gallery at the rear. At the end of the building, opposite the entrance, was a curtained alcove where the cupboard (or ark) containing the synagogue scrolls was kept. In the centre of the building was a raised bema or pulpit, and on the bema, a lectern where the prescribed portions of the law and the prophets were read and the sermon was preached. Those called to read ascended by the stairs nearest to them and descended by another set of stairs. "Moses Seats" faced the congregation from the end of the synagogue by the ark, and they were occupied by the more important scribes and Pharisees (Matthew 23:2).

In the normal service, psalms were sung, the Scriptures were read, and the sermon was preached (Luke 4:16–21). A time of questions and discussion followed. This seems to have been utilized by Stephen to ask questions that would lead to the proclamation of the Christian gospel (Acts 6:9–10).

A number of elders arranged the details of the service and all other aspects of life at the synagogue; the senior elder, or chief ruler (Luke 8:41), took charge of the service. He could invite a preacher, and it is clear that Paul received invitations this way (Acts 13:5; 14:1). In effect, the synagogue replaced the illegitimate places of worship, but without providing a place for sacrifices.

Herod's Temple. See how the Castle Antonia (right) overlooks the Temple. The large gate in front of the Temple is the Nicanor Gate.

Herod's Temple

Herod's Temple was built to ingratiate the Jews and was much more elaborate than the previous structures. The Temple buildings themselves were increased to twice the height of those of Solomon and Zerubbabel. The courtyard was extended southward to include the site of the old palace buildings and was surrounded by massive, pillared porches. The courtyards were paved with marble and parts of the building were overlaid with gold. The Temple reflected the development of divisions in the faith, for not only was there a Court of the Gentiles where only Gentiles could go, but there was a Court of the Women, a Men's Court, and a Court of the Priests, which indicated the limits to which people might go in their progress toward the central shrine.

The main platform of the Temple was bounded by walls that provided the rear walls for the four porches. The eastern porch, or colonnade, was known as Solomon's Porch. It was pierced by the Golden Gate, which was an exit from the city to the

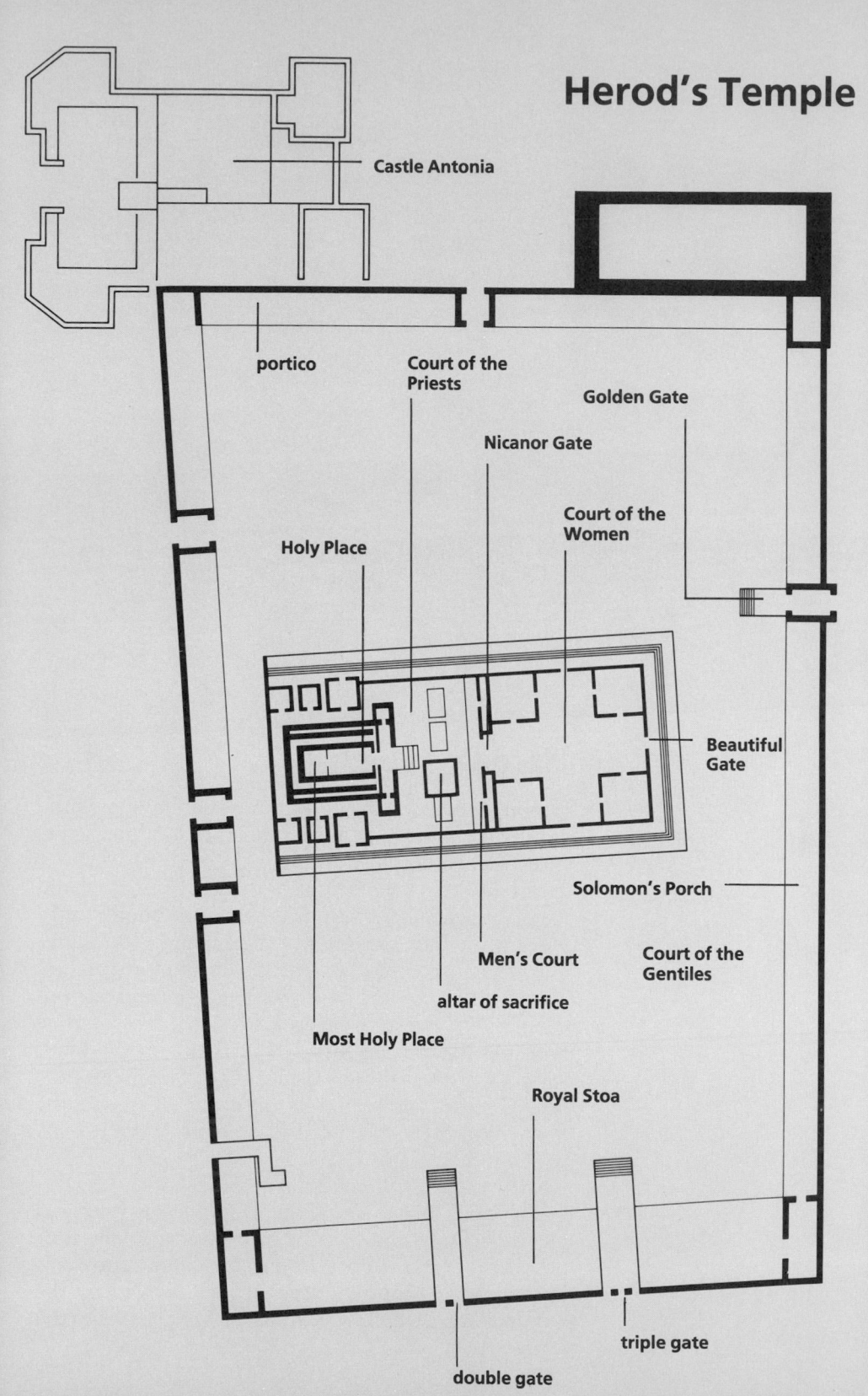

Herod's Temple

Castle Antonia

portico

Court of the Priests

Golden Gate

Nicanor Gate

Court of the Women

Holy Place

Beautiful Gate

Solomon's Porch

Men's Court

Court of the Gentiles

altar of sacrifice

Most Holy Place

Royal Stoa

triple gate

double gate

Scale replica of Herod's Temple and the Castle Antonia, Jerusalem.

Mount of Olives. The porch itself provided the Pinnacle (Matthew 4:5) with a drop of more than four hundred feet (one hundred and thirty metres) into the valley below. The Court of the Gentiles was at once a thoroughfare, a marketplace, and a place for exchange of money to purchase sacrificial animals (Matthew 21:12–13).

Herod entered the Temple from a viaduct that was built across the city, and soldiers from Castle Antonia had access from a flight of steps. The inner boundary of the Court of the Gentiles was marked by a low wall, or *chel*, which had gaps at intervals so that Jews could pass through. Notices said that a Gentile went through at the risk of his life (see Ephesians 2:14; Acts 21:28). The main gate to the Court of the Women was the Beautiful Gate, facing the east (Acts 3:2).

Inside the courtyard were four rooms: one for wood for sacrifice, one where those performing vows could stay for quietness and separation (see Acts 21:26), one where instruction could be received and questions asked — perhaps the place where Mary and Joseph found the twelve-year-old Jesus (Luke 2:46), and one where salt was stored to spread on the slippery marble courtyards during wet weather (see Matthew 5:13). Also in the courtyard were to be found thirteen chests for monetary offerings, each topped with a trumpet-shaped receptacle (see Matthew 6:2). It was here that Jesus saw the widow who had put her all in the Temple treasury (Luke 21:1–3).

Men could ascend steps through the Nicanor Gate (so named after the Syrian general whose head was displayed in the Temple in Maccabaean times) to a narrow courtyard where they could look over a low wall into the Court of the Priests. There the priests performed at the altar of sacrifice, which, with the laver, was placed before the Temple porchway. It was possible to see through the porchway to the darkened interior that was lit by the lampstand and the altar of incense (Luke 1:9), which, like the

Stone steps leading to the entrance to Herod's Temple.

Part of the Herodian stonework at the Temple Mount. The curved stonework jutting from the wall originally carried a bridge leading from the Temple area.

table of showbread (Matthew 12:4), was there as it had been in earlier times.

The thick veil that separated the Holy Place from the Most Holy Place was rent in two as the building rocked in the earthquake accompanying the death of Jesus (Matthew 27:51). Beyond it was an empty space. The Ark of the Covenant had never been renewed, and the only feature was the rock of Moriah, which pierced the floor.

There were many other rooms in the Temple precincts. The Sanhedrin met in the Hall of Hewn Stones. There was a room where the priests who were on duty met to see who would be chosen by lot to enter the Holy Place for the day (see Luke 1:8–9), and there were places for storage and places to stay. It was a magnificent building — one of the wonders of the ancient world — and it seemed incredible to those who knew it that Jesus said it would be completely destroyed (Matthew 24:1–2).

Holy occasions

Sabbath

At a time when a person could hardly escape from the tyranny of work, the *Sabbath,* or "rest," was a physical relief and a spiritual blessing (Isaiah 56:2, 4–7; 58:13–14). It was too valuable an occasion to allow it to be eroded by working and trading. In Nehemiah's day, the gates of Jerusalem were shut against traders, and he drove them away from outside the walls (Nehemiah 13:15–22).

Although the Sabbath became law at the time of the Exodus (Exodus 20:8–11), and the Jews had got used to the idea on the way to Mount Sinai (Exodus 16:4–5, 22–27), the idea of a twenty-eight-day month was already in existence, involving a seven-day cycle. Noah had sent out the dove at seven-day intervals (Genesis 8:10), and Jacob had to wait seven days before he could marry Rachel (Genesis 29:27–28). The idea of a *sabbata* probably had its origin in Babylon, but they were days of fear when people kept indoors because of terror of the gods, and there was actually no regular cessation of work.

The character of the Jewish Sabbath was completely different. Even so a Sabbath-breaker was put to death after God had revealed himself (Numbers 15:32–36), and the Jewish people may have been motivated to keep the Sabbath because of fear rather than enjoyment. In Amos' time their only thought was when it would be over so that they could make money (Amos 8:5; cf. Jeremiah 17:18–27), and for this attitude they were condemned.

By the time of Jesus, the Sabbath had become a burden. It was still a time for the wearing of one's best clothes and for going to synagogue in the evening to return to the best meal of the week, but there were detailed laws in operation that legislated for every aspect of the day. They determined how far a person could walk (a "Sabbath day's journey" was 2,000 paces) and what a person could do. If a house fell on someone, for example, the unfortunate person could be left inside if he could live through the ordeal until the next day; a scribe could not carry his pen in his belt.

Jesus perceived that the whole purpose of the Sabbath, which should be a joy for man, had been changed (Matthew 12:1–4; Mark 2:23–26; Luke 6:1–11). Jesus taught that he was Lord of the Sabbath (Mark 2:28), and because his resurrection took place on the first day of the week, Christians began to keep this day as a day of rest rather than the seventh day (Acts 20:7).

Other festivals

In addition to the sabbaths, there were a number of festivals that were originally kept in the dry part of the year because the males were expected to travel to the central shrine to celebrate together. God promised that when they did this, he would ensure that their lands were never attacked by an enemy (Exodus 34:23). The three "pilgrimage feasts" were all harvest festivals for thanksgiving, for the barley harvest, the wheat harvest, and the grape harvest that concluded the agricultural year. They were not, however, to be mere harvest festivals that would have been celebrated by the Canaanites, too.

God deliberately linked the harvest festivals with religious events so that the Jews would remember his mighty acts on their behalf. The festival of Unleavened Bread was joined with the Passover, and people remembered the departure from Egypt; the giving of the law on Mount Sinai was linked to the wheat harvest at the festival of Weeks; and the forty years of living in tents was commemorated during the grape harvest.

Such festivals were no burden. At a time when people were isolated by geography and the intensity of their work, the festivals gave an opportunity not only to cease from work but to be able to meet one's friends in God's presence. The men discovered that such times were so good that they took their wives with them (1 Samuel 1:9, 21), and the festivals became major family occasions (Luke 2:41–44). At Passover contemporary writers estimated that some two-and-one-half million people moved toward Jerusalem in the days of the New Testament.

The festivals of Passover and Unleavened Bread (14th–21st Nisan)

(Notes about the Jewish calendar will be found in the "Now Look at Your Bible" section at the end of this chapter.) Religiously, the Passover was a remembrance of the time God released the Jews from

The Jewish Calendar

Month	Day	Festivals	Meaning of word	Our equivalent months
1. Abib or Nisan	14th	Passover	Sprouting	March/April
	15th – 21st	Unleavened Bread		
2. Iyyar or Ziv			Flowering	April/May
3. Sivan	6th	Weeks or Pentecost		May/June
4. Tammuz				June/July
5. Ab				July/August
6. Elul				August/September
7. Tishri or Ethanim	1st	Trumpets	Flowing rivers	September/October
	10th	Day of Atonement		
	15th–21st	Tabernacles		
8. Marchesvan			Rain	October/November
9. Chislev	25th	Lights or Dedication		November/December
10. Tebeth				December/January
11. Shebat				January/February
12. Adar	13th–15th	Purim		February/March

Egypt. A lamb had been killed for each Jewish family, resulting in the angel of death's "passing over" their homes (see Hebrews 11:28). Unleavened Bread was a reminder of the same time, when there had been no time to leaven the dough because of the haste (Exodus 12:7; 13:3–10). It was also a harvest festival when the firstfruits of the barley were offered (Leviticus 23:11).

By New Testament times these festivals had become a major spring festival time. Before the festival itself, roads were repaired and tombs whitened so that people might avoid accidental defilement that occurred when a place of the dead was touched (Matthew 23:27). In homes, too, there was busy preparation. All cooking utensils had to be thoroughly cleansed or new ones purchased.

On the 13th Nisan, the house was searched by the father of the household to ensure that there was no leavened bread in it. Homes in Jerusalem were prepared for visitors, because each household was expected to take in guests. Lambs or goats were purchased on the 14th and taken to the Temple for sacrifice, about one animal for every ten to twelve people. The fat was burned and the blood offered on the altar before the carcasses were hung up for collection, at which time they would be taken home and roasted on a spit of pomegranate wood. People wore their best clothes, but they were ready as if to depart on a journey. However, they reclined, on couches if possible, because God had given them rest.

Led by the father of the family, a standard ritual was followed in which everyone remembered the events of the departure from Egypt, prompted by the youngest member of the family, who asked the leading set of questions. The unleavened bread, bitter herbs, and savoury chutney (*charoseth*), which symbolized the haste, the bitterness, and the work (the *charoseth* was like mortar) their ancestors had done, all reminded them of the past. Thanksgiving was made to God with cups of red wine. The four cups that were used had to be purchased even if it meant pawning one's possessions. Only unleavened bread could then be eaten for the week that followed, and, during the period, public offerings and additional sacrifices were made.

The festival of Weeks, or Pentecost

This was a one-day festival held on the 6th Sivan in the middle of the wheat harvest and the end of the barley harvest to give thanks. Only one day could be spared for the festival at a time when the wheat harvest was in full swing. The thanksgiving centred upon two loaves. A small field was reaped, and the grain separated and ground. The flour was then made into two huge loaves, and when baked they were waved to the sky in thanksgiving to the God who was watching over all (Leviticus 23:15–21). Freewill offerings were brought, and the Temple treasury was opened.

At the same time the giving of the law on Mount Sinai was central to people's thinking (Deuteronomy 16:12). The festival was to be held a week of weeks (seven weeks, or fifty days) after the festival of unleavened bread (Leviticus 23:16), hence the name. This was approximately the same length of time it took the Jews to reach Mount Sinai after their departure from Egypt (Exodus 19:1), and in the Hasmonean period, the remembrance of the giving of the law assumed great importance (Jubilees 1:1; 6:17). The Greek translation of the Bible in the time of the New Testament translated the "fifty days" of Leviticus 23:16 as *pentekosta hemeras* and so gave rise to the name *Pentecost*, which is the term used in the New Testament (Acts 2:1; 20:16; 1 Corinthians 16:8).

The festival of Tabernacles or Ingathering
(Exodus 23:16; 34:22)
This was another week-long festival from the 15th to 21st Tishri, which marked the completion of the whole harvest by the ingathering of the grapes. Because this was the time when everyone went out into the vineyards for their "communal working holiday" (see p. 106) and lived in tents, it was an excellent time to remember the religious lessons of the forty years when the whole nation had been living in tents between Egypt and Canaan (Leviticus 23:34–36; 39–44; Deuteronomy 16:13–15). At the end of the agricultural year in the land to which God had brought them, thanksgiving was appropriate.

By New Testament times there was a spectacular ritual. Tents made of palm leaves were placed on rooftops, in courtyards, and in gardens, and people lived in them for the week unless there was exceptionally heavy rain (a rarity) or there was a case of severe illness. Two priestly processions left the Temple each morning; one went to collect leafy boughs, and the other went to the Pool of Siloam. When the priests returned there was a procession round the altar (once around for the first six days of the festival and seven times on the last day — a reminder of the ritual at Jericho, Joshua 6:3–4) — and a tabernacle, or booth, was made for the altar itself. The water was poured out on the Temple steps so that it would flow down and out through the Temple to the world outside, and so indicate the way that the Jewish faith would satisfy the world.

During the festival four large candelabra were set up in the Court of the Women, their large bowls full of oil, and their wicks made of garments the priests had been wearing during the preceding year. Everyone in Jerusalem could see the light, and there was music and dancing beneath with flaming torches.

The light symbolized the revelation and truth of the Jewish faith.

The festival of Trumpets

In addition to the three pilgrimage festivals, two other special days were kept during the month of Tishri. On the first day of the month, a festival that became known as the festival of Trumpets was held. Trumpets were blown at the beginning of every month (Numbers 10:10), but Tishri was a special occasion because the month came to be the beginning of the civil new year, and therefore special ceremonies were held.

Ram's horn trumpets were blown throughout the day, no work was to be done, and additional sacrifices were offered. Sometimes the festival was held for two days in case there was some mistake about the arrival of the new moon. It was a day of self-examination in asking how God saw each person, and it was for this that the trumpets were blown — to cause God to hear and to remember his covenant, to frighten away Satan the accuser, and to awaken sin-sleepy Israelites to repentance.

The Day of Atonement

Tishri 10th marked the Day of Atonement (Leviticus 16). In many ways the day was a climax to the Jewish religious year. All year the priests had been offering sacrifices to God to make the people acceptable to him; but the priests and their equipment became ceremonially affected by sin, and the Day of Atonement was instituted to bring about a "spiritual spring cleaning" so that, for another year, the way of approaching God through sacrifice would remain open. The high priest was the only person who could be involved, and in New Testament times, so that there could be no mistake, he was carefully groomed by the elders and practised the ritual daily during the preceding week.

On the Day of Atonement the high priest was kept awake through the hours of darkness, and when morning came he was dressed in simple white robes to begin the ceremonies. He first confessed the sins of the people with his hand resting on the neck of a sacrificial bull that was killed and the blood collected. Two goats then stood before him, and lots were cast to see which goat should be God's and which should be the people's. God's goat was killed and its blood mixed with that of the bull. Then, quite alone, the high priest went with incense and coals from the altar into the Most Holy Place. The incense was burned, and when it filled the place it was believed that the high priest was acceptable to God.

In Old Testament times this was followed by the sprinkling of the mercy seat — the top of the box of the Ark of the Covenant — with the recovered blood; in New Testament times there was no Ark, so the Holy Place and everyone and everything connected with sacrifice was sprinkled with blood. Consciences were cleared by the remaining goat, which received the sins of the people by the laying on of hands. It was taken to the desert where it was released to symbolize the taking away of sin. This goat was known as the scapegoat. The carcasses of the sacrificial animals were then burned, away from the area. The writer to the Hebrews saw the ceremony as an imperfect picture of what Jesus did for us (Hebrews 9:7–14; 10:19–22; 13:11–12).

Purim
Two other festivals were added at later times to celebrate national victories that the Jews had gained over their enemies. *Purim* was celebrated during the 13th–15th of Adar to commemorate the time when Esther had been used to save her people from genocide during the reign of a Persian king called Ahasuerus. During the festival the book of Esther, which tells the whole story, was read. When the name of Haman, the villain, occurred, it would be drowned by shouts and boos; when the name of Mordecai, the hero, was read, it was greeted with cheers.

The 13th was a day of fasting, but the 14th and 15th were occasions for merrymaking. Second Maccabees 15:36 mentions the festival in connection with another. A decree was made after the defeat of a Syrian general named Nicanor that his defeat was to be celebrated on the 13th of Adar, the "day before Mordecai's Day." This day would have been kept in New Testament times, but is no longer remembered.

The festival of Lights
The festival of Dedication, or Lights, celebrated

another victory from Maccabaean times — when Judas Maccabaeus entered the Temple in Jerusalem after the Syrians had been driven out in 164 BC and the Temple purified. Palm branches were carried, and the Temple was illuminated. In many ways Lights was similar to the festival of Tabernacles (see 2 Maccabees 10:6). Every household had its own candle to bring to remembrance the legend that when the Temple was entered there was only one day's supply of oil for the golden lampstand, but the oil lasted for eight days. The festival began on the 25th of Chislev, and because that month corresponds to December, there is some link between the festival and the celebration of Jesus' "official birthday" in the West. The festival coincided with a number of winter festivals, which relieved the darker times of the season.

Holy ritual

The ritual of Jewish religion involved sacrifice (in common with that of other religions founded in the same area and time). It was used at all the major festivals, in private use as well as for public usage, and was of many different kinds; indeed there is no proper, general word for *sacrifice* in the Old Testament. *Corban* (see Mark 7:11) is used as often as not. Details of the whole sacrificial system will be given in a larger work of reference (see the select bibliography), but it is useful and interesting to understand the *types* of sacrifice as they are laid down in the opening chapters of Leviticus.

The *Olah*, or burnt offering, seems to have been a means of consecration and dedication of the worshiper to God. Such consecration cannot take place without a recognition that the worshiper is imperfect for such dedication. Therefore confession must be made and removal of sin must take place by the laying on of hands in identification with a sacrificial animal. The animal's blood was sprinkled on the altar. Large animal offerings were cut up, and everything was burned on the altar. In human terms, God took pleasure in such acts of sacrifice (Leviticus 1:3–17; 6:9–13).

The *Minha*, the meal or cereal offering, was a voluntary offering made from grain or flour and was normally accompanied by other forms of sacrifice (see Numbers 15:1–16). Part of the sacrifice was sprinkled with frankincense and burned upon the altar, but the remainder was given to the priests for food. It seems to have been a gift to God, but a gift made in order to maintain God's favour (Leviticus 2:1–16; 6:14–18).

The *Selamim*, or peace offering, was a fellowship meal in which the worshiper and his friends sat down to a meal with God in peace. After confession and sacrifice, God's portion of the meal — the fat — was burned upon the altar. The remainder was eaten by the worshiper, his family, and friends (Leviticus 3; 7:11–21, 28, 34). This offering could be used to express thanks, to accompany a vow, or to be a freewill offering.

The *Assam* (guilt offering) and *Hattath* (sin offering) were offerings that had to be made when a person had upset God or someone else. They were made when a person had become ceremonially defiled (Leviticus 5:2–3), such as through childbirth or leprosy (Leviticus 12; 14:1–32; Mark 1:44; Luke 2:22), when a civil offense had been committed against a neighbor (Leviticus 6:1–7), offenses committed when a person was overwrought through emotion (Leviticus 19:20–22), or perhaps through error (Leviticus 4:1).

The scale of sacrifice was related to rank, and after the blood had been poured out at the altar and the fat burned, the rest of the carcass was taken away and burned. If the offense involved damage to a neighbour then restitution had to be made, too (Leviticus 6:4). (See also Leviticus 6:25—7:10.) It is important to remember that there was no sacrifice that dealt with deliberate sin and defiance of God's laws.

The sacrificial system

When human beings enter into a covenant relationship with God and keep their side of the bargain by avoiding all known sin, there is a desire to enter into a deeper relationship with God — to give themselves to his service, to express thanksgiving, to support his servants, to have fellowship, and to say "sorry" for wrong accidentally done. The sacrificial system demonstrated that a deeper relationship with God was possible, but that in order for it to take place there was a need for continual cleansing from sin.

At the same time the system demonstrated its own

inadequacies and so pointed to the need for another means to be found not only to establish a deeper relationship with God, but to deal with the whole problem of deliberate sin. This other means was all made possible through Jesus (Hebrews 10:1–8).

Holy People

The Levites

Levi, one of the twelve sons of Jacob, had three sons: Gershon, Kohath, and Merari (Genesis 46:8, 11). When the family grew during the stay in Egypt, the family of Levi grew into a tribe, and the families of the three sons into tribal divisions. Aaron, Miriam, and Moses were born into the Kohathite division of the tribe (Exodus 2:4; 6:16–20; 15:20). When the Jews worshiped the golden calf at the foot of Mount Sinai, it was the Levites who stood with Moses against the idolatry and in consecrating themselves to God. In so doing they destroyed many of the idolators (Exodus 32:26–29).

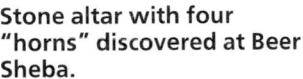

Stone altar with four "horns" discovered at Beer Sheba.

Their consecration resulted in involvement in the building of the Tabernacle (Exodus 28:1–30) and in

caring for it. When the Tabernacle was moved the Kohathites carried the furniture (Numbers 3:30–32), the Gershonites carried the curtains and hangings (Numbers 3:24–26), and the Merari-ites carried and set up the Tabernacle itself (Numbers 3:35–37; 4:29–33). According to Numbers 3:40–51 the Levites acted as substitutes for the firstborn of every Jewish household.

Because God had saved the lives of the Jewish firstborn at the time of the first Passover (Exodus 11:5; 12:12–13), the firstborn technically belonged to God, but the Levites were to act in the service of God instead (Numbers 3:12–13, 40–51). As those set apart to the service of God, they were not expected to go to war (Numbers 1:3; cf. v. 49) or to have to grow their own food within a tribal area. They were to be scattered throughout the Promised Land to live among the people (Numbers 35:1–8), and they were to be supported by the people's tithes (Numbers 18:21).

The high priest

Within the division of the Kohathites, Amram's own family became priests. On the one hand this put them in charge of the Levites. Ithamar supervised the Gershonites (Numbers 4:28) and the Merari-ites (v. 33); Eleazar supervised the Kohathites (v. 16.) On the other hand the priests were distinct from the Levites because the priests alone were able to touch the holy things — anything to do with the actual altar, the lamp, or the table of showbread (Numbers 4:5–15).

The priest did not always make the actual sacrifice, but he did take the blood to the altar (e.g., Leviticus 3:2). Aaron himself became the high priest (sometimes called the chief priest). He wore special clothes (Exodus 28), and he alone went in to the Most Holy Place on the Day of Atonement (Leviticus 16:2). Aaron interpreted the fall of the sacred lots that were held within his breastplate.

Aaron had four sons: Nadab, Abihu, Eleazar, and Ithamar. Nadab and Abihu died because they committed sacrilege in their religious duties as priests (Leviticus 10:1–3), and the high priesthood then passed over to Eleazar and was held within his family (Numbers 20:25–29). Eli was a priest of Eleazar's family. The high priesthood seems to have been lost from Eleazar's family to that of Ithamar (see 1 Kings 2:27; cf. 1 Chronicles 24:3).

It was Solomon who put the line back to Eleazar's family by placing Zadok in the high priestly position, and this position was held in the family until his descendant was deposed by Antiochus Epiphanes in the time of the Maccabees. Not only were high priests appointed by the ruling power in this later period (Annas was deposed by the Romans and replaced by Caiaphas — see Luke 3:2; John 18:13–24), but when they became strong enough to resist the rulers, they adopted their own style of kingship.

The dearth of priests

When the Jews entered Canaan and a central sanctuary was set up, there was no work for the Levites as porters, and because of the deaths of Nadab and Abihu, there were very few priests. The Jews were entering a country where worship was enacted at local shrines, and the demand for priests was greater than the supply, while there was at the same time a surplus of Levites.

The story of Judges 17–18 indicates the way that the institution of Levites and priests broke down. Micah, a Levite who had settled in Judah, became a priest, first to his family (17:10–12) and then to a group of Danites (18:19). He was not only involved in the priestly work of giving oracles (18:5) but was breaking the basic commandments (18:18).

The monarchy itself seems to have caused further deterioration in God's intention. The king often virtually replaced the high priest, and the Temple became a royal shrine. Very little is heard about the high priest throughout the period of the monarchy. During this period the Levites were involved in the music of the Temple (1 Chronicles 15:16), and they began to work before some of the holy furniture, which was forbidden in the days of the Tabernacle (1 Chronicles 9:26–29; 23:28–32). When the Jews were exiled to Babylon, and there was no temple or sacrifice, the distinction between priests and Levites was reduced still further.

It was Ezekiel, in looking forward to a restored Israel, who demanded a sharp distinction between priests and Levites again (Ezekiel 40:46; 43:19). He said that the priests had been faithful to God through the period of the monarchy (Ezekiel 44:15–16; he called them "descendants of Zadok") in comparison with the Levites (48:11). This demand for separation may have been the reason many Levites appeared to be anxious to return to Jerusalem after the Exile (Ezra 2:36–40; 8:15–20). Once they were back, they became involved in the teaching of the law (Nehemiah 8:7–9) and in normal religious duties (Nehemiah 11:3; 12:27–31).

Priests and Levites

The priests and Levites were about their work in New Testament times. They are familiar in the story of the Good Samaritan (Luke 10:31). Zacharias, father of John the Baptist, was the priest on duty in the Holy Place when he was told about the forthcoming birth of John (Luke 1:8–9). Jesus told the leper who had been healed to go and show himself to the priest (Matthew 8:4; see Leviticus 14:2). In New Testament times, the members of the high priestly families were all called high priests or chief priests and were constantly in conflict with Jesus and the early Christians.

As the Jewish people became familiar with the work of the high priest, priests, and Levites, they would have grasped the idea that lay behind it all — *representation*. On the one hand the priests and Levites represented the people before God as they led in worship and at the altar, and, on the other, they represented God before the people as they taught and explained his laws.

The prophets

Alongside the priests and Levites was another group called to a representative work. The prophets, like the priests, represented people before God. Samuel prayed for the people at Mizpah (1 Samuel 7:5); Elisha prayed that his servant would see God's protecting armies (2 Kings 6:17); Jeremiah was told that he should not pray for the people since God would not hear him because their sins were too great (Jeremiah 7:16).

The prophets' real importance however was that they represented God and spoke for him to the people. Abraham (Genesis 20:7) and Moses were both regarded as prophets (Deuteronomy 18:15–19). In the Deuteronomy passage it is clear that a prophet is always called by God (v. 18), has God's authority (v. 19), and what he says will be proved true (v. 22). The prophet therefore was known as God's servant (2 Kings 17:13, 23; Ezra 9:11; Jeremiah 7:25). The prophet always stood for God's standards and called people to him (Deuteronomy 13, esp. v. 4), and it was this that distinguished a true prophet from a false prophet (for example, 1 Kings 13:18–22; 22; Jeremiah 28).

Prophets were not simply people who were politically or socially aware. They were people who by revelation from God had been made aware of the significance of historical events and of the needs of common people. There were two elements to their work, which may be described as *foretelling* and *forthtelling*. They spoke about future events so as to warn about the consequences of present action (e.g., Amos 1:2), and they often spoke out against the society in which they lived.

In the early period of Israel's history there seem to have been two distinct kinds of prophet. One was known as a *roeh* or see-er (seer); he was a solitary, impressive person who is typified by Samuel (1 Samuel 9:11, 18–19; 1 Chronicles 9:22). The other was known as a *nabi*, who was a member of a group who prophesied ecstatically (1 Samuel 10:5–6, 10–13; 19:20–24). At a later period the words became interchangeable with another general word, *hozeh*. Different characteristics could be seen in different prophets. Some prophets therefore spoke through divination (Zechariah 10:2), analysis of political events (Isaiah 5:12), assessment of character (1 Samuel 16:1), visions (Isaiah 6:5), telepathy (2 Kings 6:12), and the ability to see details in the future (1 Kings 13:2; Isaiah 44:28).

A person became a prophet by becoming aware that God was speaking to him and having to transmit the message. The consciousness came in different ways and was then transmitted through the prophet's own unique personality. Jeremiah says simply that the hand of the Lord touched him and words were put into his mouth (Jeremiah 1:9). Other prophets had visions and dreams (1 Samuel 28:6, 15; Zechariah 1:8). Sometimes the prophetic message was given by recounting the vision (Isaiah 6), at other times by telling parables or stories (Isaiah 5:1–7), by acting an oracle (2 Kings 13:14–19;

Jeremiah 19; Ezekiel 4:1–3), or by writing (Isaiah 30:8).

Some of the prophets had groups of followers or disciples who were known as "sons of prophets" (2 Kings 4:38). They would repeat the prophet's message and sometimes write it down. There were many more prophets than just the ones we know of through their recorded prophecies or through historical events. Groups of prophets worked at centres of worship (1 Samuel 10:5) and were therefore associated with priests and Levites (2 Kings 23:2; Isaiah 28:7). Because they were therefore aware of the abuses of the sacrificial system and realized that the moral lives of the worshipers did not square with their ceremonial, the prophets tended to attack the ceremonial. They did what Jesus did centuries later with the woman of Samaria when he pointed out that true worship acceptable to God is in "spirit and in truth" (John 4:24).

Holy objects

In the Jewish religion there were special objects that were holy in the sense that they belonged to God and must not be touched by ordinary people. When Uzzah touched the Ark of the Covenant, he died (2 Samuel 6:7), and when Nadab and Abihu offered "unauthorized fire" or improper incense, they too were struck down (Leviticus 10:1–2). There were several objects that had this kind of sacredness. They were involved in the Holy Place and the Most Holy Place in the central place of worship.

The **Ark of the Covenant** was, in many respects, the most important object of all. It is described in Exodus 25:10–22. It consisted of a box surmounted by two figures of cherubim. Provision was made for staves to be inserted through rings so that it could be carried. The box measured about four feet by two feet by two feet (120 centimetres by 60 centimetres by 60 centimetres) and contained the two stone tablets of the Ten Commandments (Exodus 25:16; Deuteronomy 10:1–5), a pot of manna, and Aaron's rod (Hebrews 9:4–5). The Ark was a throne for the invisible God who was seated on the wings of the cherubim and whose voice came from above it (Exodus 25:22). The golden calf that Aaron made was probably intended as a throne, and the two bull calves that Jeroboam made at Bethel and

Dan would have served the same purpose.

In the Holy Place were three objects: a **table**, a **lampstand**, and an **altar**. The table was known as the **table of showbread** and was of standard form with a top of about three feet by one foot six inches (90 centimetres by 45 centimetres). It is described in Exodus 25:23–30. Twelve baked cakes were placed on the table in two rows of six.

Showbread was actually called "bread of the presence," because it was in the presence of God (1 Samuel 21:6). It was renewed every Sabbath by one of the priests, and the old showbread was then removed to be eaten by the priests (Leviticus 24:5–9; 1 Samuel 21:6).

The Holy Place was illuminated by a **golden lampstand**. Three branches ending in flower-shaped holders projected from each side of a main stem, which also supported a lampholder (Exodus 25:31–36).

In between the table of showbread and the lampstand was an **altar** on which incense was to be burned. It was only three feet (90 centimetres) high, with a top one foot six inches (45 centimetres) square, made of acacia wood, and overlaid with gold (Exodus 30:1–10). The **incense** itself was also sacred and could not be made for any other purpose than for worship. It consisted of frankincense, the resin from beneath the bark of boswellia trees; galbanum, which was probably the gum of a Persian plant; and two ingredients that are as yet unknown, stacte and onycha (Exodus 30:34–38).

The Jews were also familiar with the sacred lots, known as the Urim and Thummim, by which the will of God was sometimes divined by the high priest. The high priest wore a canvas bag on his chest. On the outside was a golden breastplate, studded with precious stones. Inside were the two lots. They were probably discs, coloured black on one side and white on the other. When the stones were cast from the bag, two whites meant Yes; two blacks meant No; and a black and a white meant Wait (see Exodus 28:30; Leviticus 8:8; Numbers 27:21; 1 Samuel 28:6; Ezra 2:63).

There were other sacred objects that were special to the ordinary people. In Detueronomy 6 is the basic creed of Israelite religion: "Hear O Israel: The Lord our God, the Lord is one. Love the Lord your

God with all your heart and with all your soul and with all your strength" (vv. 4–5). It goes on to say that the Jews were to bind these instructions as a sign on their hands and between their eyes, and that they should be written upon the doorposts of the house (vv. 8–9).

Many Jews took the commandments quite literally and placed the creed in small boxes. Those tied to the wrist and forehead were known as *tcphillim* (*phylacteries* in the New Testament), and the box fixed to the doorpost was called a *mezuzah*. The present form of phylactery was not made final until after the time of Christ, although they were worn by the Pharisees of his day (Matthew 23:5). They were hollow boxes about one and one-half inches

A Jewish boy celebrating his bar mitzvah at the Western Wall, Jerusalem. Notice the tephillim (phylacteries) on the wrist and forehead of both man and boy.

A Jew at prayer, with
tephillim bound to his
wrist and forehead.

(38 millimetres) square, made of the skin of ritually
clean animals. Inside were the words of Exodus
13:1–10; 13:11–16; Deuteronomy 6:4–9; and
Deuteronomy 11:13–21, written by hand on parch-
ment. They were fastened to the wrist or to the
forehead by long leather thongs. The mezuzah did
not come into existence before the times of the
Hasidim (see p. 254). The mezuzah seems to have
been used to try to make the Jews more thoughtful
about their own faith at the time of competing
Greek thought.

Greek and Roman religion
As a result of their experiences throughout their
long history, most Jews were unaffected by Greek
and Roman religion. Those affected by Greek religion were known as the Sadducees (see p. 255).
Those most affected by Roman religion were those
who were prepared to make some kind of political
affinity with the ruling power.

The old Minoan Greeks had followed a fertility
religion not unlike that of the Canaanites, but by the
time of the New Testament this had developed into
a sophisticated polytheism. It was believed that the
gods were just like human beings (although they
were more powerful) and lived on Mount Olympus.

The Romans largely took over the Greek religion
so that Zeus (Greek) is the same as Jupiter (Roman),
and similarly Poseidon is the same as Neptune,
Hermes as Mercury. Religion was largely bound up
with culture; games, meals, arts, and all forms of
celebration were always in honour of the gods.

But there were many people who were dissatisfied
with this form of religion. Emperor worship developed at Rome, philosophy took its place
alongside religion in Greece so that a form of
atheism developed, and in Athens people were beginning to consider the possibility of an unknown
god (Acts 17:23). Mystery religions began to develop in which people were admitted to successive
degrees of understanding as they undertook rites
that brought them into closer communion with the
god or gods.

Now look at your Bible

The Jewish Calendar
Exodus 12:2. The Jewish calendar is a lunar calendar of twenty-eight days, resulting in a shorter year than that in the West. When the calender became a month out of gear, an additional month called *Adar Adar* was inserted. Months always began with the new moon. Easter always follows Passover, which is at full moon in Abib. The Easter festival varies with the moon, and a change is made from late April to late March when the additional Jewish month is inserted.

The prohibition against likenesses
Exodus 20:4. The commandment against idols ("graven images," KJV) and likenesses (forms) seems to have been made against the possible incursions of Canaanite religion. This has a spiritual importance, namely that no material representation can be made of a spiritual God, which is covered by the prohibition against idols. The warning against forms ("likeness," KJV), however, is something different. The likeness was a mask worn over the face and used in Canaanite religious ritual. Examples of likenesses have been discovered at Hazor.

When does Sabbath begin?
Exodus 20:8. Jewish days began not at midnight but at six o'clock in the evening. Monday afternoon, for example, was followed by Tuesday evening. (This is why in Genesis 1 the days of creation are described as an evening and a morning, and why it was necessary for the high priest to be kept awake through the hours of darkness on the Day of Atonement.) The service at the synagogue that welcomed the Sabbath was therefore followed by a night's sleep before teaching was continued the following morning. At six o'clock on the Saturday evening, the Sabbath was over and people were free to go about their normal tasks.

Living water
John 7. It was on the last day of the festival of Tabernacles (v. 2) that Jesus proclaimed as he stood in the Temple (vv. 14, 37) that if anyone thirsted he could go to him and drink and receive complete inner satisfaction (vv. 37–38). Jesus was obviously saying in a dramatic way that it was not the Jewish faith (symbolized by the pouring out of the water from the pool of Siloam) that would satisfy the world, but rather Jesus through the gift of the Holy Spirit. It was also on the last day that Jesus said he was the light of the world (John 8:12). Jesus is therefore clearly taking up the symbolism of the candelabra from the festival.

The Last Supper
John 13:1–2. The normal translation of these verses is, "It was just before the Passover Feast. Jesus knew that the time had come for him to leave this world and go to the Father. Having loved his own who were in the world, he now showed them the full extent of his love. The evening meal was being served..." This gives a picture of Jesus holding a *special* celebration with his disciples with a

simulated Passover in contrast to the accounts in the other gospels (e.g., Mark 14:12), which say it was actually the day the Passover lamb was killed that the Last Supper was held.

Critical scholars therefore teach that John deliberately manipulated the date so that he could represent Jesus as being crucified and hung on the cross at the same time as the Passover lambs were hung. This very nice representation from the critical point of view is based on what appears to be a contradiction. In fact, a contradiction does not necessarily arise. John 13:1 may be regarded as a separate statement in itself — that before Passover began, Jesus knew he was going to die and committed himself to his disciples to see the whole drama through. Then his commitment was fulfilled during the Passover meal.

Select Bibliography

Most readers of this book will find the following books of interest and of help in following things through. They come from three main countries — Israel, the United Kingdom, and the United States; all are obtainable through international book agencies. Some are very old; they are worth borrowing from a library or obtaining from a secondhand bookseller.

Alexander, D., and P. *The Lion Handbook to the Bible.* (*The Eerdmans Handbook to the Bible*) 2d ed. Lion, 1983. A well produced book providing a simple commentary on the whole Bible, together with background articles to aid the understanding.

Alexander, P. *The Lion Encyclopaedia of the Bible.*2d ed. Lion, 1986. Another well produced book in sections dealing with such aspects as home and family life, government and organization, and a useful Bible atlas.

Alon, A. *The Natural History of the Bible.* Israel: Steimatzky, 1969. This is a nontechnical book with the occasional beautiful photograph on certain aspects of natural history. It is not exhaustive.

Avi-Yonah, M. *Encyclopaedia of Archaeological Excavations in the Holy Land.* Oxford University Press; Englewood Cliffs, N.J.: Prentice-Hall. A four-volume issue dealing with every archeological site in the Holy Land. The best there is, superbly produced, but very expensive.

Bahat, D. *Historical Atlas of Jerusalem.* Jerusalem: Carta, 1973. A useful atlas of Jerusalem in black line drawings, particularly on the development of the city since AD 70.

Beitzel, B. *The Moody Atlas of Bible Lands.* Chicago: Moody Press, 1985. Excellent set of all new maps covering Old Testament and New Testament Bible lands. Helpful text commentary with almost every map. Useful for both laymen and scholars.

The Book of Bible Knowledge. Scripture Union, 1982. A nicely illustrated and well-produced book for young people interested in Bible background. Popular rather than scholarly.

Comay, J. *The Temple of Jerusalem.* London: Weidenfeld & Nicholson, 1975. A coffee table book written at popular level and surveying the history of the Jews through the Temple site.

De Vaux, R. *Ancient Israel — Its Institutions.* McGraw Hill; Darton, Longman & Todd, 1961. Written from the liberal Catholic tradition but superb scholarship and extremely useful.

Douglas, J.D. (ed.), *The Illustrated Bible Dictionary.* Carol Stream, Ill.: Tyndale. Probably the best Bible dictionary produced by conservative evangelical scholars, in three volumes. It is in full colour and deals with all the subjects mentioned in this book, and every aspect of Christian doctrine. Expensive but indispensible.

Edersheim, A. *The Life and Times of Jesus the Messiah.*
Sketches of Jewish Social Life in the Time of Christ.
The Temple, Its Ministry and Services. These books, written nearly a century ago by a converted Jewish scholar, reinterpret the Bible against its background. They are still superb and

have been recently republished by Eerdmans.

Haraveuni. *Tree and Shrub in Our Biblical Heritage.* Israel: Neot Kedumim. *Nature in Our Biblical Heritage.* Israel: Neot Kedumim. These books in full colour have been produced at a settlement in Israel where members are recreating vegetation from biblical days. It is one of the most definitive approaches to biblical natural history, and incorporates much Jewish material.

Heaton, E. W. *Life in Old Testament Times.* Batsford, 1956. Excellently written and a useful supplement to this book. It was later republished as a paperback by Carousel.

Hollis, C., and R. Brownrigg. *Holy Places.* New York: Praeger, 1969. Another coffee table book that looks at places in Israel sacred to Muslims, Christians, and Jews and deals with their background and history.

Israel Pocket Library. *Jerusalem.* Jerusalem: Keter. A small paperback packed with information on the history of Jerusalem.

Josephus, F. *The Jewish War.* Grand Rapids: Zondervan, 1982. This particular issue of Josephus's work, written at the time of Christ and giving Josephus's view of the history of the period, has an archaeological commentary and notes with the text. It is a beautifully produced book.

Kollek, T., and M. Perlman. *Jerusalem.* Jerusalem: Steimatzky, 1968. A well-produced and illustrated book that deals with the whole history of Jerusalem from the Jewish perspective.

Mazar, B. *The Mountain of the Lord.* New York: Doubleday, 1975. A nicely produced account of the excavation of the Temple area, by one of the archaeologists involved.

Negev, A. *Archaeological Encyclopaedia of the Holy Land.* New York: Putnams, 1972. Indispensable. It deals with all of the sites and background. Written by Israeli scholars.

Pfeiffer, C. and H. Vos. *The Wycliffe Historical Geography of Bible Lands.* Chicago: Moody Press, 1967. Examines and evaluates biblical, historical, and archaeological evidence about ten major countries and land areas of Bible times. Contains many informative black and white photographs. Needs some updating and revising.

Schurer, E. *The Life of the Jewish People in the Time of Jesus Christ.* Edinburgh: T. & T. Clark. This book is so basic to background historical scholarship that it has been recently updated and re-issued in three volumes. It takes a liberal-Protestant perspective.

Thompson, J. A. *Handbook of Life in Bible Times.* Madison: Intervarsity, 1986.

Unger, M. *The New Unger's Bible Handbook.* Revised by Gary N. Larson. Chicago: Moody Press, 1984. Published in the United Kingdom as *The Hodder Bible Handbook* by Hodder & Stoughton. A new edition of a standard reference tool on basic background to each Bible book. Color photographs, drawings, charts, and tables have been added to enhance the usefulness of this book.

———. *Unger's Bible Dictionary.* Chicago: Moody Press, 1966. A complete and reliable dictionary for studying Bible backgrounds. The work is being completely revised and updated. Nearly all new pictures to be included.

General Index

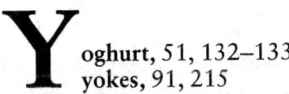

Scriptural Index

Photograph acknowledgments

British Museum: 73, 78, 108, 110, 122, 175, 227, 273, 292, 293
Tim Dowley: 22, 28, 32, 53, 72, 81, 95, 104, 112, 116, 121, 126, 135, 141, 142, 167, 168, 188, 189, 190, 197, 198, 199, 203, 204, 207, 218, 219, 223, 233, 263, 279, 282, 284, 287, 304, 314, 316, 318, 320, 323, 328, 352, 353
Sonia Halliday: 2/3, 87
F. Nigel Hepper: 103
Anne Holt: 96
Laura Lushington: 102, 106, 107
Zev Radovan: 15, 25, 33, 34, 44, 55, 80, 88, 94, 101, 109, 147, 157, 158, 159, 162, 166, 183, 291, 302, 309, 311, 363
Scripture Union: 19, 37, 40, 118, 151, 226, 253, 306, 308, 322, 341
Jamie Simson: 23, 36, 51, 100, 138, 156
Peter Wyart: 6, 19, 27, 45, 46, 47, 59, 71, 91, 98, 105, 111, 125, 127, 133, 134, 150, 160, 169, 187, 192, 196, 200, 201, 210, 212, 213, 214, 220, 221, 222, 224, 231, 235, 237, 239, 248, 259, 261, 267, 280, 289, 296, 298, 310, 312, 313, 319, 324, 325, 326, 327, 329, 336, 351, 371

THE BIBLICAL WORLD OF THE PATRIARCHS MAP 1

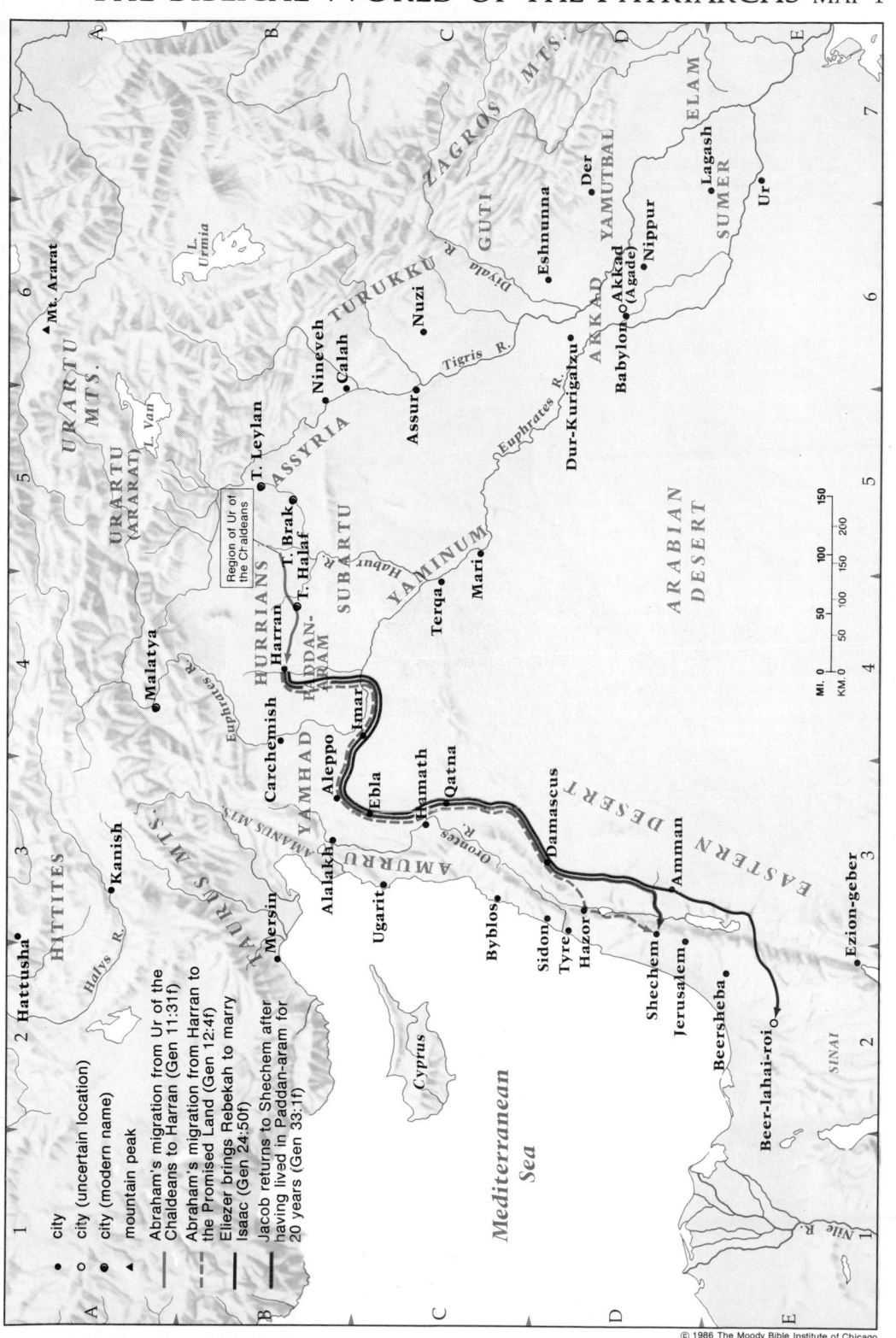

Legend:

- • city
- ○ city (uncertain location)
- ● city (modern name)
- ▲ mountain peak

— Abraham's migration from Ur of the Chaldeans to Harran (Gen 11:31f)

–– Abraham's migration from Harran to the Promised Land (Gen 12:4f) Eliezer brings Rebekah to marry Isaac (Gen 24:50f)

— Jacob returns to Shechem after having lived in Paddan-aram for 20 years (Gen 33:1f)

MAP 2   PALESTINE: POLITICAL REGIONS

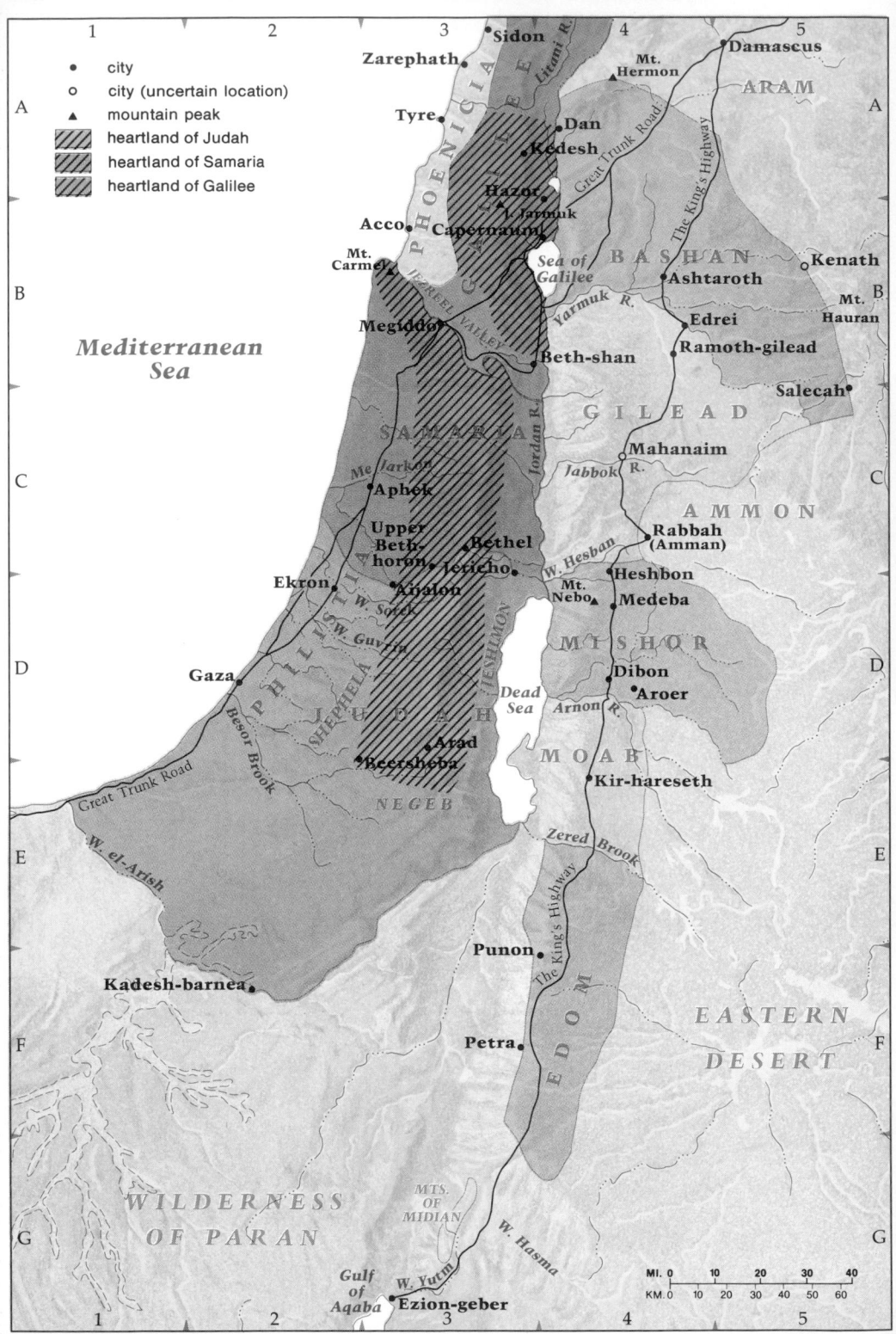

Legend:
- • city
- ○ city (uncertain location)
- ▲ mountain peak
- heartland of Judah
- heartland of Samaria
- heartland of Galilee

THE ROUTE OF THE EXODUS

MAP 3

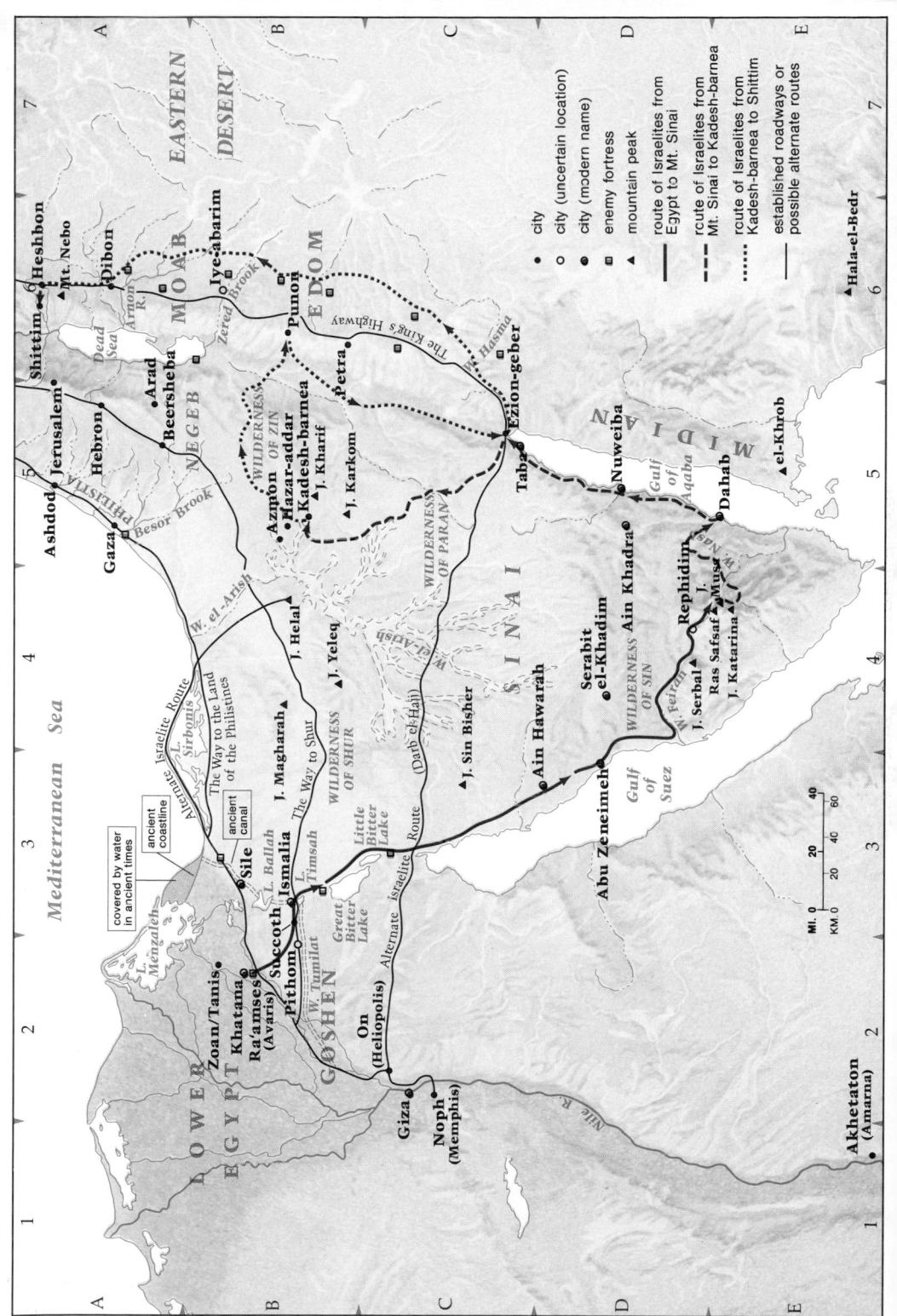

MAP 4

THE TWELVE TRIBES OF ISRAEL

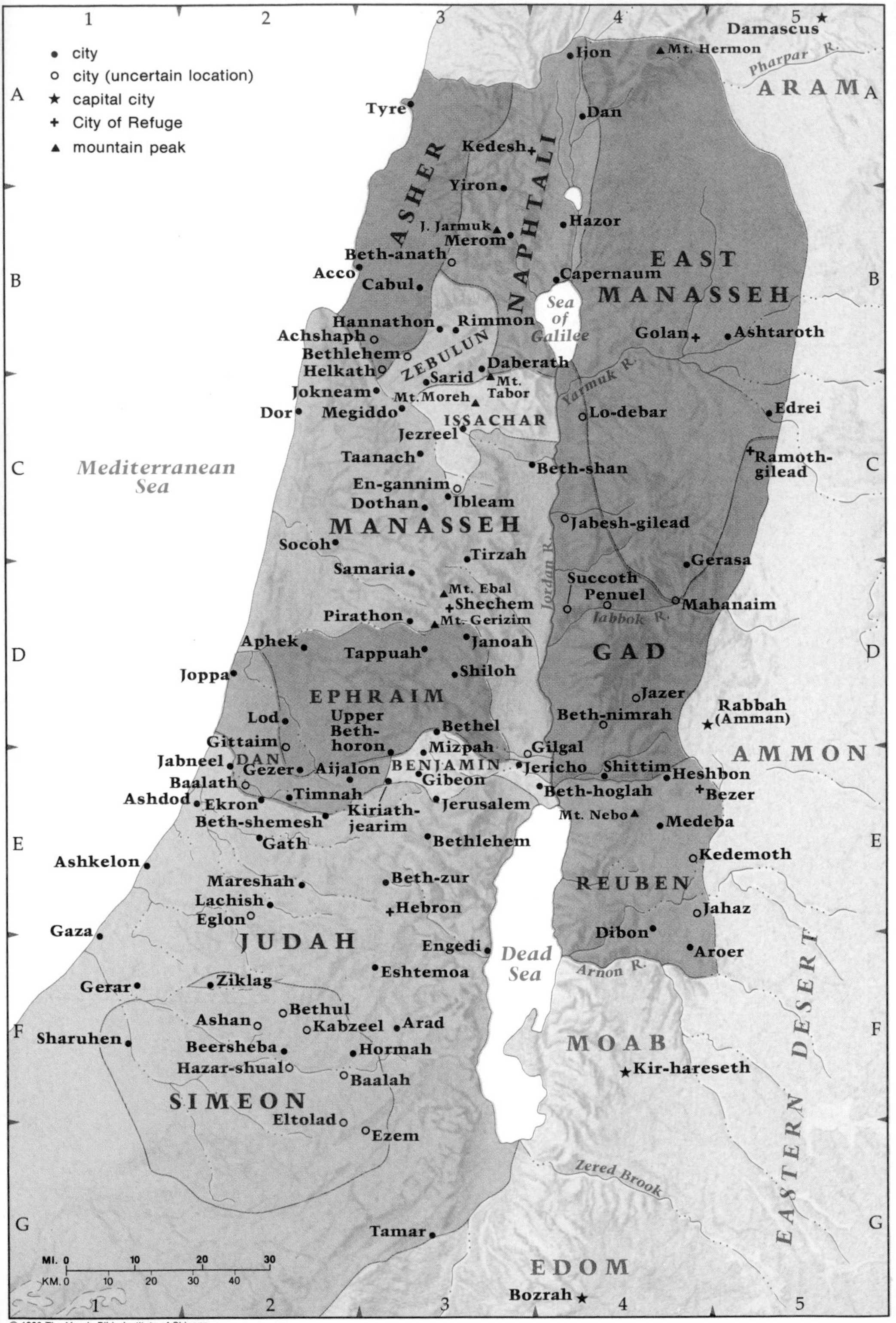

Legend:
- • city
- ○ city (uncertain location)
- ★ capital city
- + City of Refuge
- ▲ mountain peak

Grid columns: 1, 2, 3, 4, 5
Grid rows: A, B, C, D, E, F, G

Damascus ★

Ijon
Mt. Hermon ▲
Pharpar R.
ARAM

Tyre
Dan

ASHER
Kedesh +
Yiron
NAPHTALI

J. Jarmuk
Merom
Hazor

Beth-anath
Acco
Cabul
Capernaum
EAST MANASSEH
Sea of Galilee

Hannathon
Rimmon
Golan +
Ashtaroth
Achshaph
ZEBULUN
Bethlehem
Helkath
Daberath
Jokneam
Sarid
Mt. Tabor
Dor
Megiddo
Mt. Moreh
ISSACHAR
Lo-debar
Edrei
Jezreel
Taanach
Beth-shan
Ramoth-gilead
En-gannim
Dothan
Ibleam
Jabesh-gilead
MANASSEH
Socoh
Tirzah
Gerasa
Samaria
Mt. Ebal
Succoth
Penuel
Mahanaim
Pirathon
Shechem
Mt. Gerizim
Jabbok R.
Aphek
Janoah
GAD
Tappuah
Joppa
Shiloh

Mediterranean Sea

EPHRAIM
Jazer
Lod
Upper Beth-horon
Bethel
Beth-nimrah
Rabbah (Amman) ★
Gittaim
Mizpah
Gilgal
AMMON
Jabneel
DAN
Gezer
Aijalon
BENJAMIN
Jericho
Shittim
Heshbon
Baalath
Gibeon
Bezer +
Ashdod
Ekron
Timnah
Jerusalem
Beth-hoglah
Beth-shemesh
Kiriath-jearim
Mt. Nebo ▲
Medeba
Gath
Bethlehem
Kedemoth
Ashkelon
Mareshah
Beth-zur
REUBEN
Lachish
Hebron +
Jahaz
Gaza
Eglon
Dibon
Aroer
JUDAH
Engedi
Dead Sea
Arnon R.
Eshtemoa
Gerar
Ziklag
Ashan
Bethul
Kabzeel
Arad
MOAB
Sharuhen
Beersheba
Hormah
Hazar-shual
Baalah
Kir-hareseth ★
SIMEON
Eltolad
Ezem
EASTERN DESERT

Zered Brook

Tamar

MI. 0 10 20 30
KM. 0 10 20 30 40

EDOM

Bozrah ★

KINGDOMS OF SAUL, DAVID & SOLOMON MAP 5

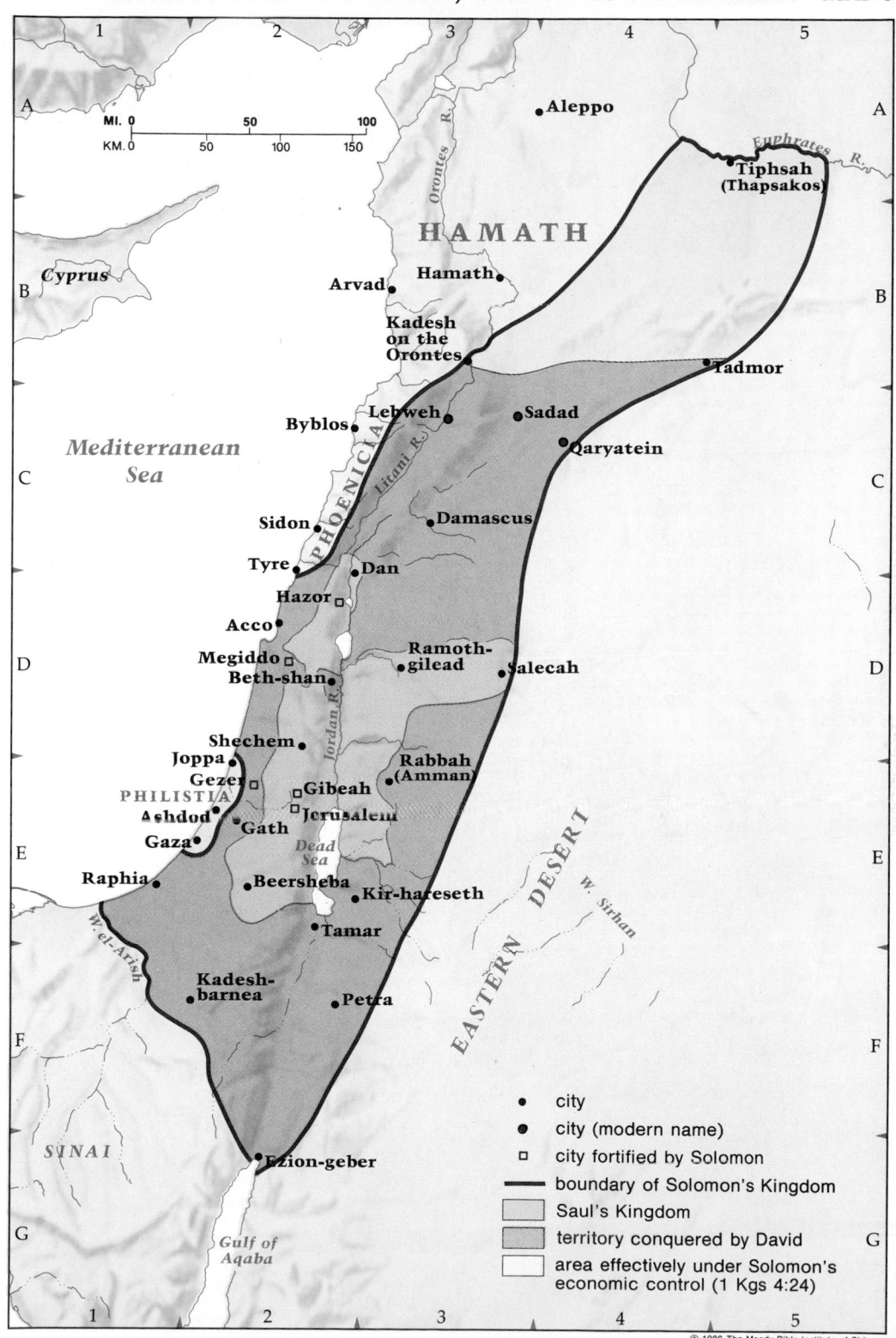

MI. 0   50   100
KM. 0   50   100   150

Cyprus

Mediterranean Sea

Aleppo

Orontes R.

Euphrates R.

Tiphsah (Thapsakos)

HAMATH

Arvad   Hamath

Kadesh on the Orontes

Tadmor

Byblos   Lebweh   Sadad

PHOENICIA

Litani R.

Qaryatein

Sidon   Damascus

Tyre   Dan

Hazor

Acco

Megiddo   Ramoth-gilead   Salecah

Beth-shan

Jordan R.

Shechem

Joppa   Rabbah (Amman)

Gezer

PHILISTIA   Gibeah

Ashdod   Jerusalem

Gaza   Gath

Dead Sea

Raphia   Beersheba   Kir-hareseth

Tamar

W. el-Arish

EASTERN DESERT

W. Sirhan

Kadesh-barnea   Petra

SINAI

Ezion-geber

Gulf of Aqaba

- •   city
- ●   city (modern name)
- ▫   city fortified by Solomon
- ——   boundary of Solomon's Kingdom
- Saul's Kingdom
- territory conquered by David
- area effectively under Solomon's economic control (1 Kgs 4:24)

MAP 6 · THE DIVIDED KINGDOM: ISRAEL & JUDAH

Legend:
- • city
- ○ city (uncertain location)
- ★ capital city
- + sanctuary city
- ▲ mountain peak

Byblos · Beirut · Sidon · Damascus · Mt. Hermon · Tyre · Dan · Kedesh · Hazor · Acco · Mt. Carmel · Mt. Tabor · Sea of Galilee · Ashtaroth · Edrei · Mt. Hauran · Megiddo · Taanach · Beth-shan · Mt. Gilboa · Ramoth-gilead · Ibleam · Jabesh-gilead · Tirzah · Succoth · Mahanaim · Samaria · Mt. Ebal · Shechem · Penuel · Mt. Gerizim · Aphek · Shiloh · Joppa · Rabbah (Amman) · Bethel · Jericho · AMMON · Gezer · Ashdod · Aijalon · Jerusalem · Heshbon · Gath · Mt. Nebo · Medeba · Bethlehem · Ashkelon · Mareshah · Gaza · Hebron · Dibon · Beersheba · MOAB · Kir-hareseth · Bozrah · EDOM · Kadesh-barnea · EASTERN DESERT · WILDERNESS

PHOENICIA · ARAM · Litani R. · Kishon R. · Yarmuk R. · Jordan R. · Jabbok R. · Mediterranean Sea · ISRAEL · PHILISTIA · JUDAH · Besor Brook · Dead Sea · Arnon R. · Zered Brook · W. el-Arish

MI. 0 10 20 30 40
KM. 0 10 20 30 40 50 60

THE ASSYRIAN EMPIRE

MAP 7

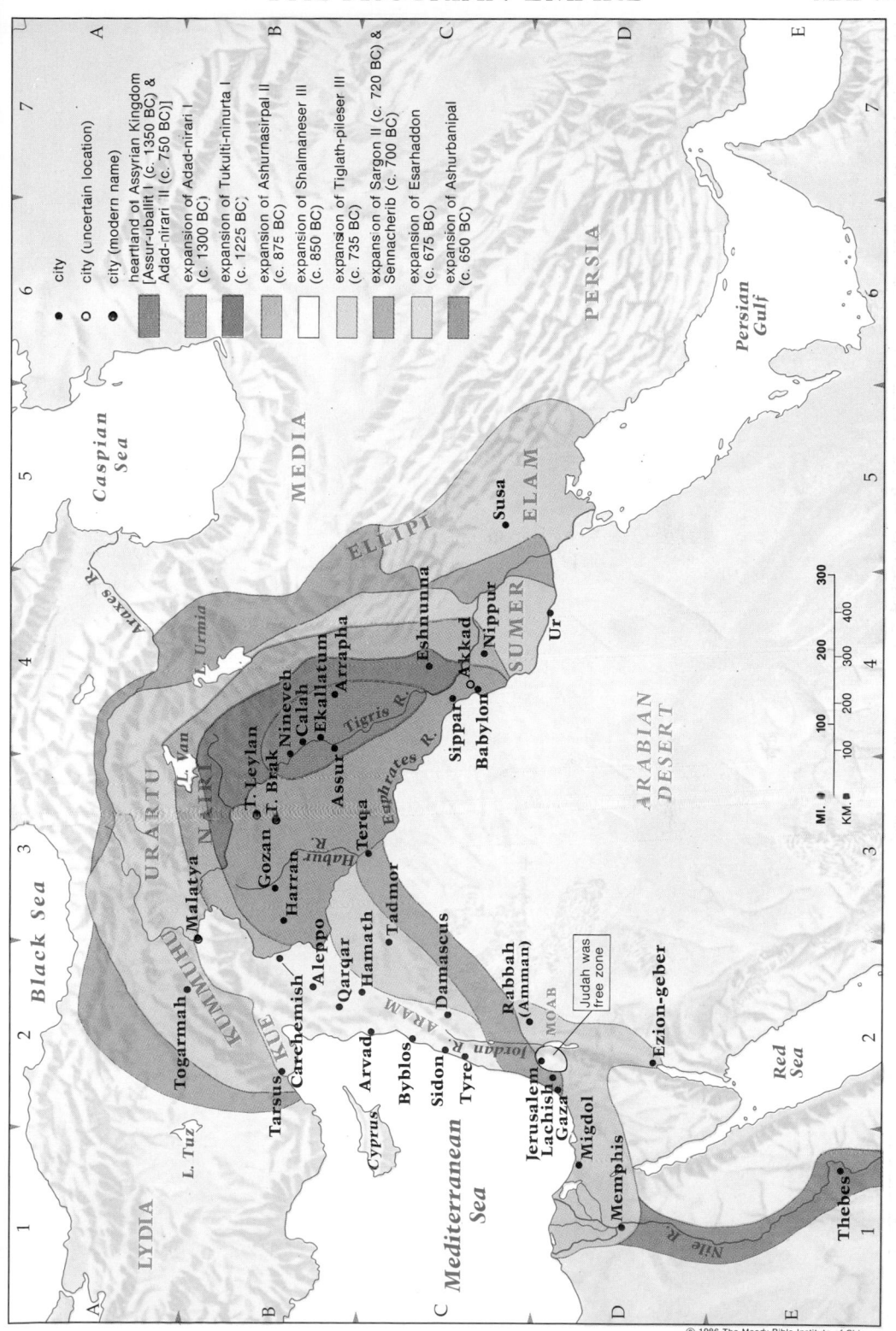

MAP 8

THE BABYLONIAN EMPIRE

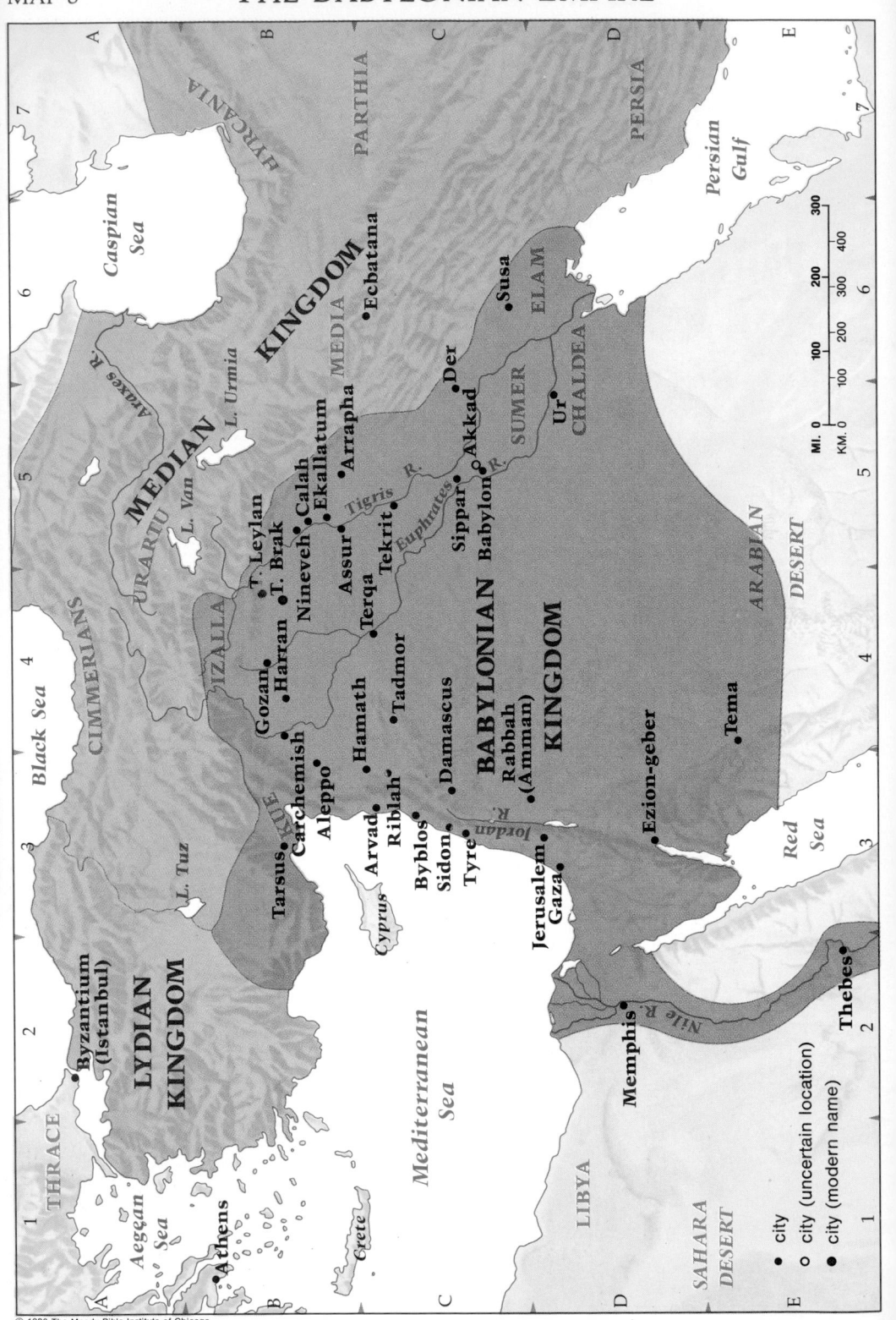

THE GREEK EMPIRE

MAP 9

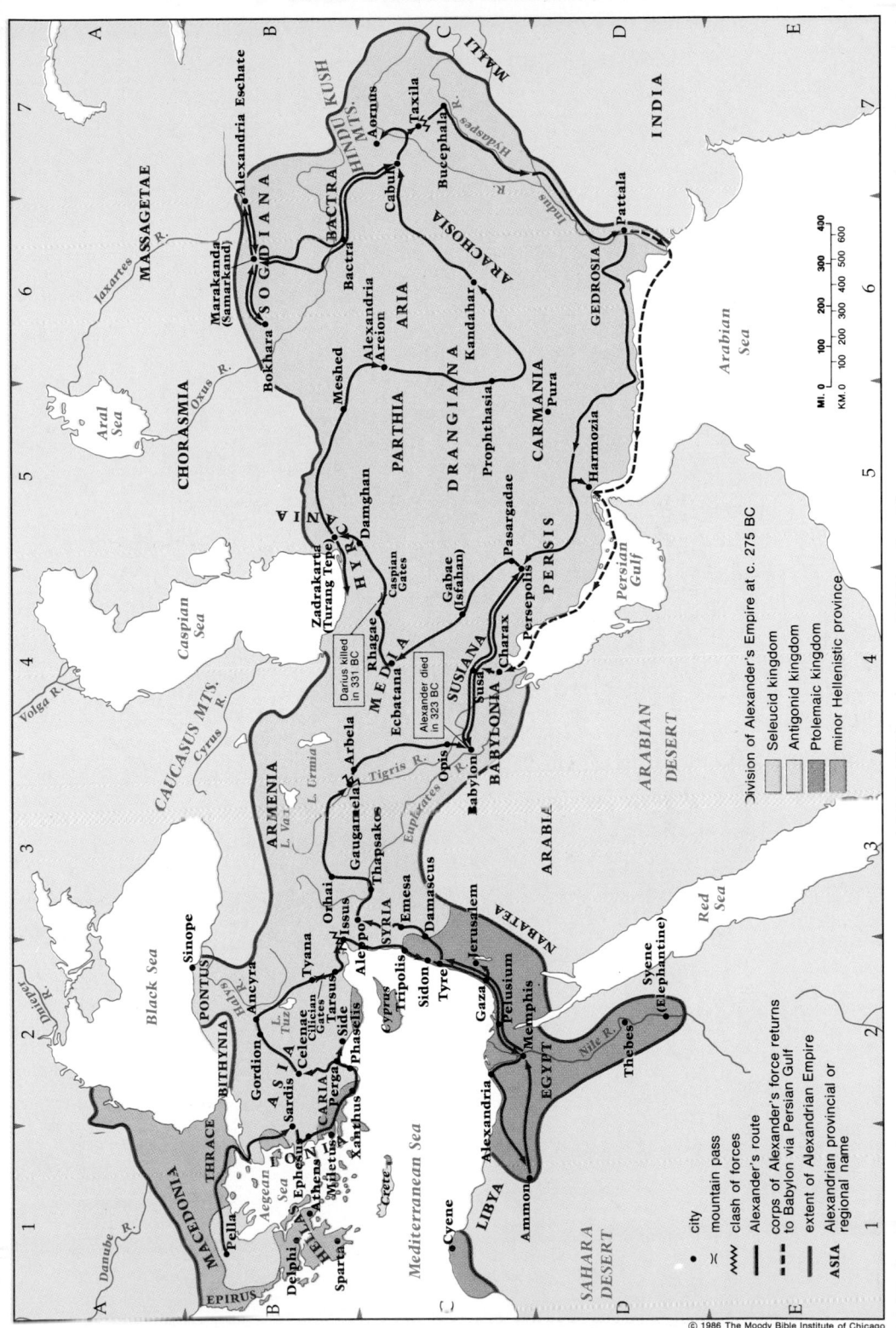

Legend:

- • city
-)(mountain pass
- ⋀⋀⋀ clash of forces
- ▬▬ Alexander's route
- ▬ ▬ corps of Alexander's force returns to Babylon via Persian Gulf
- ▬ ▬ ▬ extent of Alexandrian Empire
- ASIA Alexandrian provincial or regional name

Division of Alexander's Empire at c. 275 BC
- Seleucid kingdom
- Antigonid kingdom
- Ptolemaic kingdom
- minor Hellenistic province

Darius killed in 331 BC

Alexander died in 323 BC

MI. 0 100 200 300 400
KM. 0 100 200 300 400 500 600

MAP 10

OLD TESTAMENT JERUSALEM

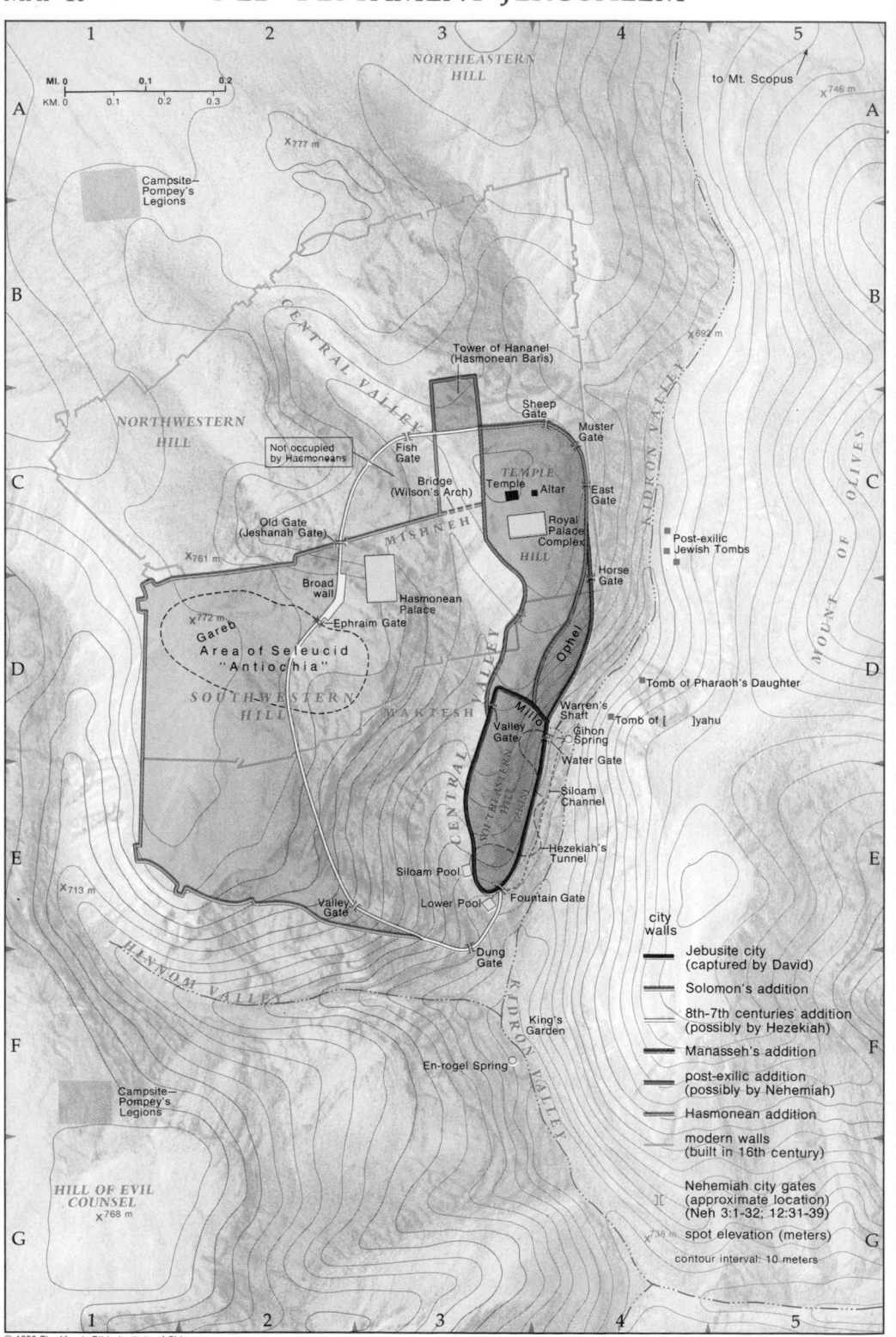

Legend:

- **Jebusite city** (captured by David)
- **Solomon's addition**
- **8th-7th centuries' addition** (possibly by Hezekiah)
- **Manasseh's addition**
- **post-exilic addition** (possibly by Nehemiah)
- **Hasmonean addition**
- **modern walls** (built in 16th century)
-][**Nehemiah city gates** (approximate location) (Neh 3:1-32; 12:31-39)
- X 738 m **spot elevation** (meters)

contour interval: 10 meters

NEW TESTAMENT JERUSALEM

MAP 11

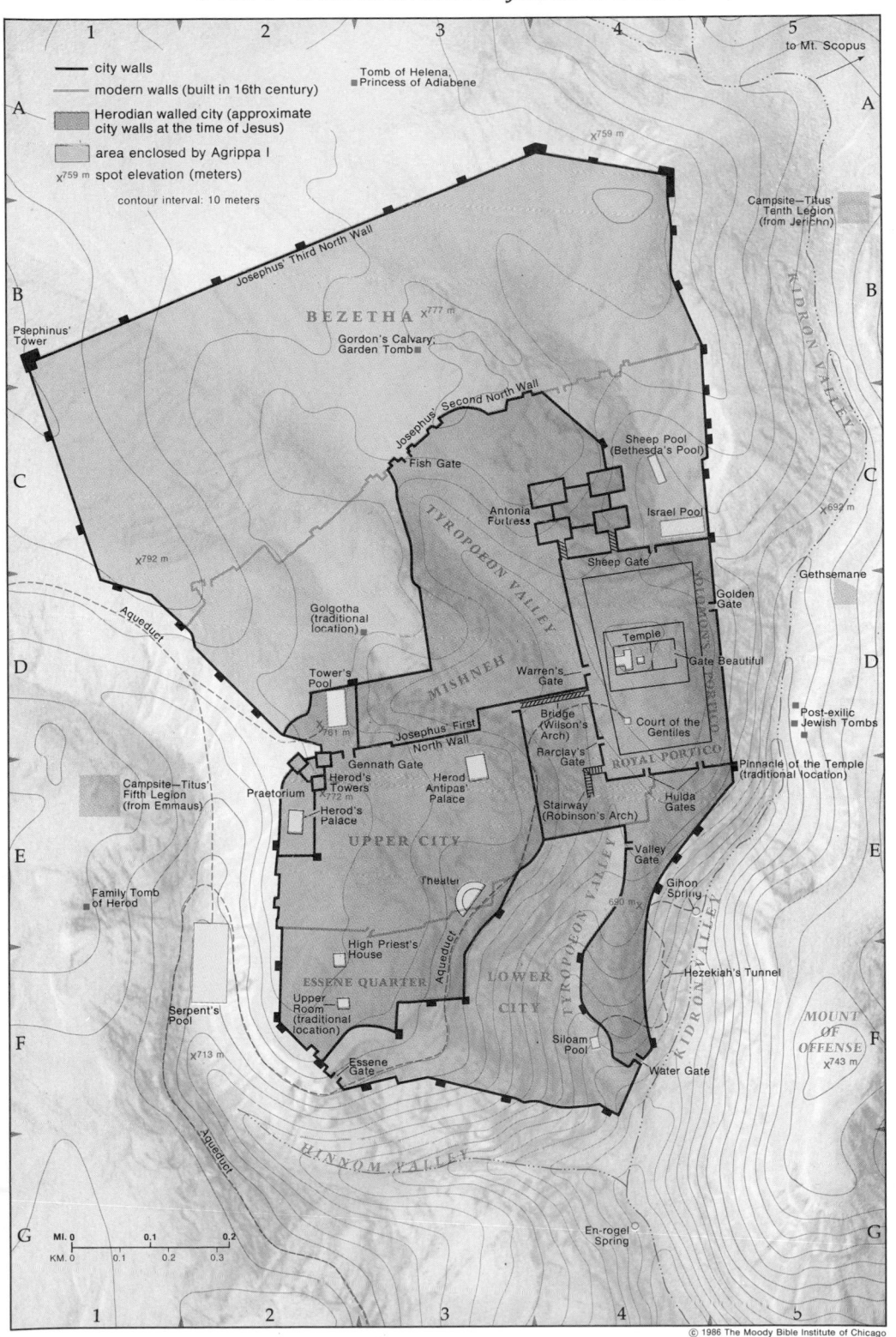

Legend:

- city walls
- modern walls (built in 16th century)
- Herodian walled city (approximate city walls at the time of Jesus)
- area enclosed by Agrippa I
- x759 m spot elevation (meters)
- contour interval: 10 meters

Labels:

to Mt. Scopus

Tomb of Helena, Princess of Adiabene

Campsite—Titus' Tenth Legion (from Jericho)

Josephus' Third North Wall

Psephinus' Tower

BEZETHA x777 m

KIDRON VALLEY

Gordon's Calvary; Garden Tomb

Josephus' Second North Wall

Sheep Pool (Bethesda's Pool)

Fish Gate

x692 m

Israel Pool

Antonia Fortress

Gethsemane

TYROPOEON VALLEY

Sheep Gate

x792 m

Golden Gate

Aqueduct

Golgotha (traditional location)

Temple

Gate Beautiful

MISHNEH

Tower's Pool

Warren's Gate

Court of the Gentiles

Post-exilic Jewish Tombs

x761 m

Josephus' First North Wall

Bridge (Wilson's Arch)

Barclay's Gate

ROYAL PORTICO

Pinnacle of the Temple (traditional location)

Gennath Gate

Campsite—Titus' Fifth Legion (from Emmaus)

Praetorium

Herod's Towers

Herod Antipas' Palace

Hulda Gates

x772 m

Herod's Palace

Stairway (Robinson's Arch)

Valley Gate

UPPER CITY

Family Tomb of Herod

Theater

Gihon Spring

690 m

Hezekiah's Tunnel

High Priest's House

KIDRON VALLEY

ESSENE QUARTER

Aqueduct

LOWER CITY

Serpent's Pool

Upper Room (traditional location)

TYROPOEON VALLEY

MOUNT OF OFFENSE x743 m

x713 m

Essene Gate

Siloam Pool

Water Gate

Aqueduct

HINNOM VALLEY

MI. 0   0.1   0.2

KM. 0   0.1   0.2   0.3

En-rogel Spring

MAP 12

THE MINISTRY OF JESUS

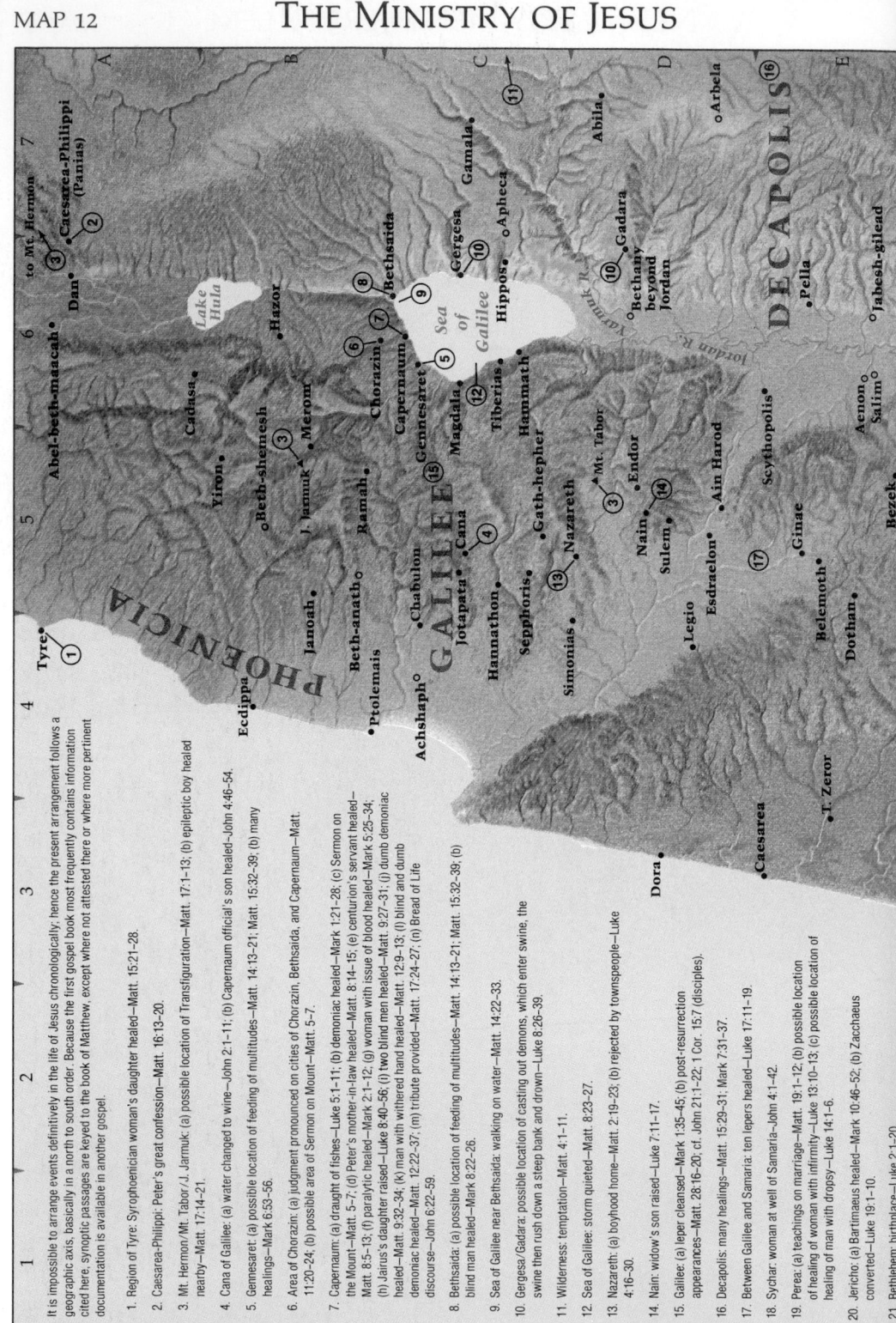

It is impossible to arrange events definitively in the life of Jesus chronologically; hence the present arrangement follows a geographic axis, basically in a north to south order. Because the first gospel book most frequently contains information cited here, synoptic passages are keyed to the book of Matthew, except where not attested there or where more pertinent documentation is available in another gospel.

1. Region of Tyre: Syrophoenician woman's daughter healed—Matt. 15:21–28.

2. Caesarea-Philippi: Peter's great confession—Matt. 16:13–20.

3. Mt. Hermon/Mt. Tabor/J. Jarmuk: (a) possible location of Transfiguration—Matt. 17:1–13; (b) epileptic boy healed nearby—Matt. 17:14–21.

4. Cana of Galilee: (a) water changed to wine—John 2:1–11; (b) Capernaum official's son healed—John 4:46–54.

5. Gennesaret: (a) possible location of feeding of multitudes—Matt. 14:13–21; Matt. 15:32–39; (b) many healings—Mark 6:53–56.

6. Area of Chorazin: (a) judgment pronounced on cities of Chorazin, Bethsaida, and Capernaum—Matt. 11:20–24; (b) possible area of Sermon on Mount—Matt. 5–7.

7. Capernaum: (a) draught of fishes—Luke 5:1–11; (b) demoniac healed—Mark 1:21–28; (c) Sermon on the Mount—Matt. 5–7; (d) Peter's mother-in-law healed—Matt. 8:14–15; (e) centurion's servant healed—Matt. 8:5–13; (f) paralytic healed—Mark 2:1–12; (g) woman with issue of blood healed—Mark 5:25–34; (h) Jairus's daughter raised—Luke 8:40–56; (i) two blind men healed—Matt. 9:27–31; (j) dumb demoniac healed—Matt. 9:32–34; (k) man with withered hand healed—Matt. 12:9–13; (l) blind and dumb demoniac healed—Matt. 12:22–37; (m) tribute provided—Matt. 17:24–27; (n) Bread of Life discourse—John 6:22–59.

8. Bethsaida: (a) possible location of feeding of multitudes—Matt. 14:13–21; Matt. 15:32–39; (b) blind man healed—Mark 8:22–26.

9. Sea of Galilee near Bethsaida: walking on water—Matt. 14:22–33.

10. Gergesa/Gadara: possible location of casting out demons, which enter swine, the swine then rush down a steep bank and drown—Luke 8:26–39.

11. Wilderness: temptation—Matt. 4:1–11.

12. Sea of Galilee: storm quieted—Matt. 8:23–27.

13. Nazareth: (a) boyhood home—Matt. 2:19–23; (b) rejected by townspeople—Luke 4:16–30.

14. Nain: widow's son raised—Luke 7:11–17.

15. Galilee: (a) leper cleansed—Mark 1:35–45; (b) post-resurrection appearances—Matt. 28:16–20; cf. John 21:1–22; 1 Cor. 15:7 (disciples).

16. Decapolis: many healings—Matt. 15:29–31; Mark 7:31–37.

17. Between Galilee and Samaria: ten lepers healed—Luke 17:11–19.

18. Sychar: woman at well of Samaria—John 4:1–42.

19. Perea: (a) teachings on marriage—Matt. 19:1–12; (b) possible location of healing of woman with infirmity—Luke 13:10–13; (c) possible location of healing of man with dropsy—Luke 14:1–6.

20. Jericho: (a) Bartimaeus healed—Mark 10:46–52; (b) Zacchaeus converted—Luke 19:1–10.

21. Bethlehem: birthplace—Luke 2:1–20.

MAP 12

24. Jerusalem: (a) discourse with Nicodemus—John 3:1–21; (b) Pool of Bethesda healing—John 5:2–9; (c) woman caught in adultery—John 8:2–11; (d) attempted stoning—John 8:12–59; (e) man blind from birth healed—John 9:1–12; (f) passion week, including crucifixion and resurrection; (g) post-resurrection appearances—John 20:1–18 (Mary Magdalene), 20:19–31 (with and without Thomas).

25. Mt. of Olives: (a) Olivet discourse—Matt. 24:3–25:46; (b) ascension—Acts 1:6–12.

- • city
- ○ city (uncertain location)
- ▲ mountain peak

Mediterranean Sea

PEREA

JUDEA

Dead Sea

Jordan R.

Jabbok R.

Mi. 0
KM. 0

Philadelphia
Jazer
Jogbehah
Mizpah
Mahanaim
Penuel
Taralah
Asophon
Bethennabris
Bethennabris
Shittim
Baal-peor
Besimoth
Nebo
Esbus
Bezer
Medeba
Kedemoth
Almon-diblathaim
Dibon
Aroer
Aroer

Adam
Sychar
Shechem
Mt. Ebal
Mt. Gerizim
Lebonah
Shiloh
Ephraim
Ai
Bethel
Mizpah
Michmash
Geba
Ramah
Gibeah
Upper Beth-horon
Beeroth
Gilgal
Jericho
Qumran
Engedi

Gophna
Thamna
Arimathea
Antipatris
Ono
Beth-dagon
Gath-rimmon
Joppa
Lod
Modin
Lower Beth-horon
Selebi
Gittaim
Gazara
Emmaus
Kiriath-jearim
Eshtaol
Zorah
Emmaus
Jerusalem
Mt. of Olives
Bethany
Bethlehem
Tekoa
Beth-zur
Ziph
Hebron
Charmela
Esthemoa

Jamnia
Gibbethon
Timnah
Bethannes
Gath
Azekah
Jarmuth
Socoh
Keilah
Lachish
Agla
Azotus
Ascalon
Gaza
Gerara

18
19
20
21
22
23
24
25

© 1986 The Moody Bible Institute of Chicago

MAP 13   THE MISSIONARY JOURNEYS OF PAUL

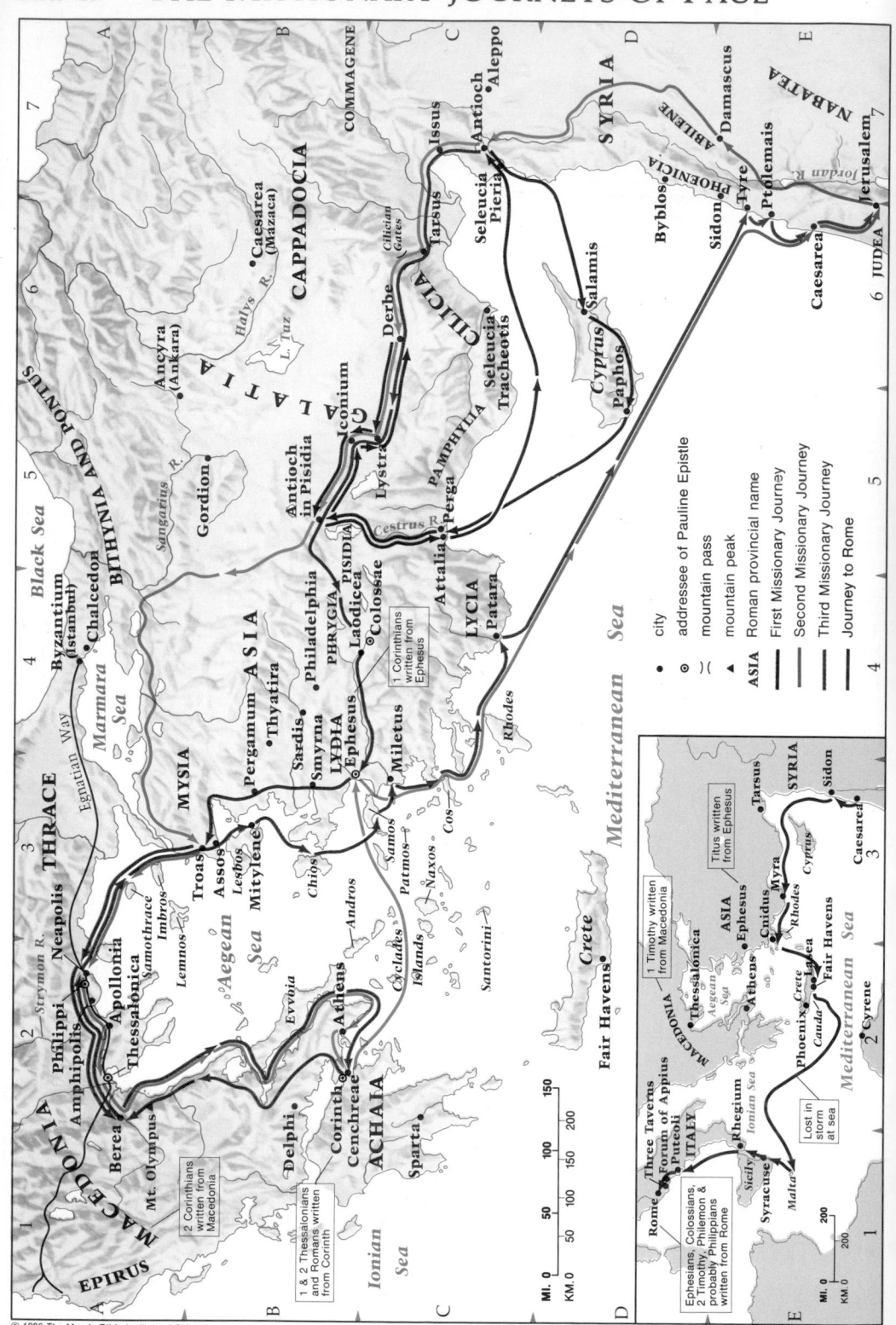

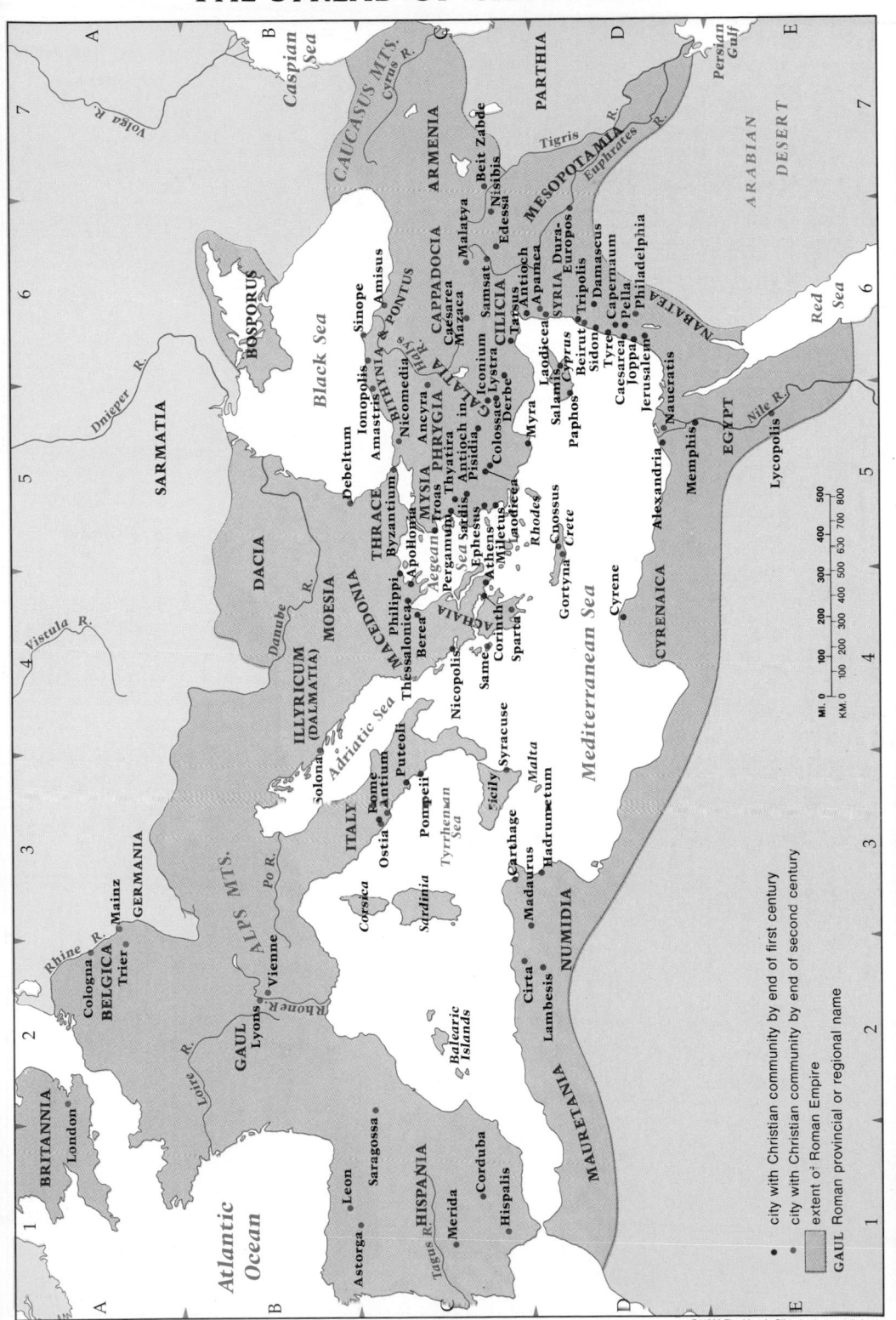

MAP 15

MODERN ISRAEL

- • city
- ● city (modern name)
- —— international boundary
- -- - 1949 Armistice boundary
- ···· disputed boundary
- —— international zone as designated by the United Nations Partition Accords—November, 1947
- territory allocated to Israel by the United Nations Partition Accords—November, 1947
- territory gained by Israel as a result of the 1948 War and 1949 Agreements (Jerusalem is a divided city)
- territory occupied by Israel after the 6-Day War— June, 1967 (not fundamentally altered after Separation of Forces Agreement following Yom Kippur War—October, 1973)
- territory occupied by Israel after the 6-Day War—June, 1967; returned to Egypt under terms of the Camp David Accord—September, 1978 (return completed— April, 1982)
- Lebanese territory temporarily occupied by Israel—March, 1978 to June, 1978

Sidon
Damascus
LEBANON
Litani R.
Mt. Hermon
Pharpar R.
Kiryat Shmona
SYRIA
Nahariya
GOLAN HEIGHTS
Acco
Safed
Sea of Galilee
Haifa
Tiberias
Nazareth
Yarmuk R.
Megiddo
Afula
Beth-shan
Jenin
Hadera
Jabbok R.
Netanya
Nablus
Shechem
Tel Aviv
WEST BANK
Amman
Ramallah
Rehovot
Jericho

Mediterranean
Sea

Jerusalem
Hebron
Gaza
Engedi
GAZA STRIP
Dead Sea
Arnon R.
Beersheba
JORDAN
El-Arish
Dimona
W. el-Arish
Zered Brook

EGYPT

Mitzpeh Ramon

Petra

Israeli tourist resort on narrow Egyptian coastal strip; under negotiation

Eilat
Taba
Gulf of Aqaba

MI. 0   10   20   30   40
KM. 0 10 20 30 40 50 60

© 1986 The Moody Bible Institute of Chicago